CONVIVIUMPRESS

Sergio Bastianel

Morality in social life

Translated by Liam Kelly

CONVIVIUMPRESS

SERIES EPISTEME

2010

Morality in social life

http://www.conviviumpress.com
sales@conviviumpress.com
ventas@conviviumpress.com
convivium@conviviumpress.com

7661 NW 68th St, Suite 108,
Miami, Florida 33166. USA.
Phone: +1 (786) 8669718
Teléfono: +1 (786) 8798452

Edited *by* Rafael Luciani
Translated *by Liam Kelly*
Revised *by* Doris Strieter *and* Tom Strieter
Designed *by* Eduardo Chumaceiro d'E
Series: *Episteme*

ISBN: 978-1-934996-14-0

Printed in Colombia
Impreso en Colombia
D'VINNI, S.A.

Convivium Press
Miami, 2010

Morality in social life

Contents

Introduction PAGE 16

PART ONE

Believers present in the life of society PAGE 19

1

The earth and the human person PAGE 21

1. *Morality, social interaction, politics* PAGE 25
   1.1. AN INTERSUBJECTIVE EXPERIENCE PAGE 27
   1.2. POLITICAL LIFE PAGE 29
   1.3. WHAT IMAGE OF CONSCIENCE? PAGE 32
   1.4. WHAT IMAGE OF GOD? PAGE 33
2. *Communion with God and interhuman communion* PAGE 34
   2.1. TO INHABIT THE «EARTH»: GIFT AND QUEST PAGE 35
   2.2. THE LOST «LAND» PAGE 38
   2.3. THE KINGDOM OF GOD ON THIS EARTH PAGE 42

2

Responsibility for the other person PAGE 47

1. *Genesis 2:4B-3:24: sin enters into the world* PAGE 50
2. *The gift of fraternity* PAGE 52
3. *The risk of fraternity (failure)* PAGE 56
4. *From ostensible to creative fraternity* PAGE 60

3

The ethics of the beatitudes PAGE 61

1. *Jesus and the contemporary way of thinking* PAGE 65
2. *The experience of the disciples* PAGE 68
3. *The new covenant in Jesus* PAGE 71
4. *«Blessed are you»* PAGE 75
5. *The privilege of the weak* PAGE 79
6. *An ethical culture* PAGE 83

4

The church's social doctrine as moral theology PAGE 89

1. *Moral theology and scientific expertise* PAGE 92
    - 1.1. MORAL THEOLOGY PAGE 93
    - 1.2. THE AUTONOMY OF DIFFERENT FIELDS PAGE 93
    - 1.3. INTERPRETIVE CORRELATION PAGE 95
2. *The contribution of Christian faith* PAGE 96
    - 2.1. THE GIFT OF THE COVENANT PAGE 97
    - 2.2. THE INSTITUTIONS: THE MONARCHY IN ISRAEL PAGE 99
    - 2.3. SLAVERY IN THE LETTER TO PHILEMON PAGE 101
3. *Theology and social morality* PAGE 102
    - 3.1. HELP IN TODAY'S STORY PAGE 103

PART TWO

Morality and social life PAGE 105

5

The relationship between charity and politics PAGE 107

1. *Christian charity* PAGE 110
2. *The common good* PAGE 112
   - 2.1. POLITICAL LIFE PAGE 112
   - 2.2. PLURALISM PAGE 113
   - 2.3. COMMUNION (THE COMMON GOOD) AS GOAL PAGE 115
3. *Dialogue as a Christian virtue* PAGE 117
   - 3.1. MISUNDERSTANDINGS PAGE 117
   - 3.2. DIALOGICAL RELATIONS PAGE 118
   - 3.3. TEMPTATIONS PAGE 120
4. *The witness of charity* PAGE 122
   - 4.1. THE CRISIS OF DEMOCRACIES PAGE 122
   - 4.2. SERVICE AND GRATUITOUSNESS PAGE 123
   - 4.3. THE WORKS OF CHARITY PAGE 124
   - 4.4. CHRISTIAN COMMUNITY AND POLITICAL COMMUNITY PAGE 126

6

Human values, moral values and economic structures PAGE 129

1. *An ethics of the economy?* PAGE 131
   - 1.1. ECONOMY AND MORALS PAGE 131
   - 1.2. A PERSONAL AND CULTURAL PROBLEM PAGE 132
2. *Personal morality* PAGE 133
   - 2.1. HUMAN VALUES PAGE 133
   - 2.2. MORALITY PAGE 134
   - 2.3. CHRISTIAN INTERPRETATION PAGE 136

3. *Structured moral and social life* PAGE 138

3.1. MORALITY AND SOCIAL INTERACTION PAGE 138

3.2. MORALITY AND STRUCTURES PAGE 139

3.3. SOLIDARITY PAGE 141

4. *Morality and economic activity* PAGE 142

4.1. THE COMPLEXITY OF THE PROBLEMS PAGE 142

4.2. OWNERSHIP AND USE OF THE GOODS OF THE EARTH PAGE 143

4.3. PROFIT AND MORALITY PAGE 146

4.4. ECONOMIC RULES AND MORALITY PAGE 147

PART THREE

Morality and development PAGE 151

7

Hunger, a challenge to united development PAGE 153

1. *The problem* PAGE 155

2. *Faced with the starving* PAGE 156

2.1. IF YOU ARE ABLE, YOU MUST GIVE HIM SOMETHING TO EAT PAGE 156

2.1.1. *GIVING SOMETHING TO EAT* PAGE 156

2.1.2. *THE RELATIONSHIP* PAGE 157

2.1.3. *THE CONCRETE GESTURE* PAGE 157

2.1.4. *«IF YOU ARE ABLE TO DO IT»* PAGE 157

2.2. HIERARCHY AND URGENCY OF VALUES PAGE 158

2.3. JUDGMENTS AND PRE-JUDGMENTS PAGE 159

2.3.1. *SELF-PRIVILEGE* PAGE 159

2.3.2. *DIRECT AND INDIRECT OPPORTUNITIES* PAGE 160

2.4. SOCIAL RESPONSIBILITY PAGE 160

2.5. QUESTIONS ABOUT FOUNDATIONS AND MORAL FORMATION PAGE 160

3. *Faced with hunger in the world* PAGE 161

3.1. THE GOODS OF THE EARTH PAGE 161

3.2. THE COMMON DESTINATION OF GOODS PAGE 164

4. *The responsibility of Christians and the Church* PAGE 165

4.1. INTERPRETING HISTORY THROUGH FAITH PAGE 165

4.2. LIVING THE EUCHARIST PAGE 166

4.3. PARTICIPATING IN TODAY'S EFFORTS PAGE 168

4.4. FORMATION OF CONSCIENCE PAGE 169

4.4.1. *EDUCATING THE INNER SELF* PAGE 169

4.4.2. *EDUCATING TOWARD THE COMMON GOOD* PAGE 170

8

Toward an ethic of development PAGE 171

1. *Development* PAGE 173

2. *Development of the South* PAGE 174

3. *Ethical problems in North-South relations* PAGE 175

4. *The possibility of development and ethical responsibility* PAGE 177

4.1. THE COMPLEXITY OF THE PROBLEMS PAGE 177

4.2. PEOPLE AND SOCIETY PAGE 178

4.3. PERSONAL MORALITY, MORAL CUSTOMS, STRUCTURES PAGE 178

5. *Human values and moral value* PAGE 180

5.1. THE CONTRIBUTION OF CHRISTIAN FAITH PAGE 183

5.2. NORMS, CODICES AND MORALITY PAGE 184

PART FOUR

The story of evil, the story of good PAGE 187

9

Moral evil PAGE 189

1. *Evil as an ethical and theological problem* PAGE 192
2. *The evil that comes from the human person: Genesis 2-3* PAGE 193
3. *Evil in a story of relations: 2 Sam 11-12* PAGE 199
   3.1. THE SIN OF DAVID PAGE 199
   3.2. DAVID'S CONVERSION PAGE 203
4. *The humanity of Jesus in a story of sin* PAGE 205
   4.1. THE WAY OF THE INCARNATION PAGE 205
   4.2. THE KILLING OF A JUST MAN PAGE 208
5. *A story of good* PAGE 209

10

Structures of sin PAGE 211

1. *The strength of evil and the temptation to avoid responsibility for it* PAGE 214
2. *Sin and relationality* PAGE 217
3. *Sin and the structuring of human co-existence* PAGE 219
4. *Structures of sin* PAGE 222
5. *Conversion of people, conversion of structures* PAGE 226

11

Punishment, morality, and the common good PAGE 211

1. *Personal morality. Being honest* PAGE 234
2. *Simple and complex structured relations* PAGE 237
3. *The common good and the goal of social life* PAGE 239
4. *Behavior judged by the penal code* PAGE 241
5. *The victim* PAGE 242
6. *The guilty* PAGE 243
7. *Society, punishment, and the common good* PAGE 244
8. *Conclusions* PAGE 247

12

The reaction to evil PAGE 249

1. *A type of relating* PAGE 252
2. *What justice?* PAGE 255
3. *The Christian interpretation of the human: the memory of Jesus* PAGE 259
4. *Opportunities and restrictions in ethical cultures and faith traditions* PAGE 262
5. *Faith tradition and conscience* PAGE 265
6. *Responding to evil with good: how effective is it?* PAGE 268
7. *Toward truth and good* PAGE 271

PART FIVE

Morality and the structuring of relations PAGE 275

13

Conscience: autonomy and community PAGE 277

1. *Personal moral conscience* PAGE 279
2. *The formation of personal moral conscience* PAGE 284
3. *Faced with the historic force of moral evil* PAGE 290
4. *The role and task of the Christian community* PAGE 294

14

Freedom and responsibility in family life PAGE 297

1. *Family structure and socio-cultural diversity* PAGE 299
2. *The role of mediator in regard to human society* PAGE 301
3. *The role of mediator in regard to the church community* PAGE 306
4. *Advantages and difficulties in generational encounters* PAGE 312

15

Authority and obedience PAGE 321

1. *The analogous use of terms* PAGE 323
2. *Authority as a social reality* PAGE 324
3. *Authority as meaning* PAGE 325
4. *Obedience to human authority* PAGE 326
5. *The foundation of authority and obedience* PAGE 328
6. *Authority and obedience in the church* PAGE 330
7. *Free and responsible communion-edification* PAGE 333
8. *Temptations* PAGE 336

16

Freedom and responsibility in the ecclesial community PAGE 339

1. *Unity and growth in the church* PAGE 341
2. *Christ, foundation and hope* PAGE 343
3. *Unity-communion as criterion for discerning charisms and tasks: why a criterion for discerning the good* PAGE 344
4. *Ecclesial life as social life of a believing community* PAGE 346

Bibliography PAGE 351

Introduction

The critical nature of the problems of justice, within individual nations and on an international level, has captured significant attention because of the serious consequences that impact the lives of so many people. In this context, in religious circles there has been reference to *social sin*, or *sinful structures*, and such phraseology has also been utilized in the Encyclical *Sollicitudo rei socialis*. The reality of such grave evils caused by human beings (not just by natural disasters), without being able in every case to identify a guilty party, raises questions about the relationship between personal moral responsibility and social responsibility. The dynamics of this phenomenon need to be understood within an ethical reflection presented in an organized and constructive manner, which, without confusing the various levels, can identify the areas of responsibility of each person as well as each person's room for freedom.

Over the course of a number of years various occasions have led to the individual interventions related to morality and social justice that are brought together in this book. Their unity lies in the fact that they focus attention on the issues to be presented and the role that interpersonal relationships assume in the ethical experience and the experience of Christian faith.

The chapters within the book have been organized according to a unified complementary plan, indicated by their subdivision into five parts. Individual chapters have a unity linked to the various circumstances for which they were written, and thus it will be quickly noted that there is some repetition within them.

Part One: Believers present in the life of society. In this first part, there is an examination of how the reality of social life for believers might be an area of responsibility in which humanity can build and grow in history. Individuals and the community of believers are committed within the social sphere, so that the love of God may bear the fruits of salvation through their life in human history. As believers we know that we are called to live in this life according to the intentionality of God, building fraternity as disciples according to the beatitudes, and with the experience and the discernment necessary to identify the criteria and paths to be traveled in social life.

Part Two: Morality and social life. Social, political and economic life is a reality constituted by relationships. The complexity of phenomena should not permit us to forget that at issue always is people's responsibility for people. Our concern is never just a matter of «functional» questions and issues, because the outcome of political and economic decisions touches people's lives. Morality and social interaction are closely connected, the common good must represent a non-exploitable aim, the economy must be examined with reference to the human quality of the relations it realizes, and life is not shared without sharing use of the necessary means for living.

Part three: Morality and development. The extreme difference in living conditions from region to region and within the various regions of the world raises a most serious moral dilemma. Finding viable solutions is difficult and complex. The ethical requirement in this case is developed within its fundamental references of meaning, through the serious co-responsibility that the problem implies. The difficulty arises when the issue is publicly recognized, but practically deferred to the level of non-importance and non-urgency by the priority choices that continue to be made and that continue to aggravate the very situation of objective injustice. Famine continues to be a challenge for our humanity, and development does not appear in fact to be animated and guided by justice.

Part Four: History of evil, history of good. We live in a history in which moral good and evil are effective through the very structures of life to which men and women dedicate themselves. Thus, even our way of understanding justice, when faced with someone who acts unjustly, could be characterized by a mindset that intensifies the force of evil. We will look at the dynamics of the effectiveness of sin and its significance in determining the structures of social life and the need to react to evil without assuming its own rationale and its criteria of effectiveness.

Part Five: Morality and the structuring of relations. The structures of social life, even when institutionalized, are never completely fixed and do not work in an automatic way. The freedom of the person who lives in them produces their true outward appearance, and can also significantly modify them from within, and even before their possible institutional modification. Of primary importance is the formation of responsible freedom in the true context of relations: the network of freedoms maintains relations in a process of permanent structuring, even within the soundest of structures. We examine personal responsibility within a believing community, in the relationships of family life, in relationships of authority and obedience, and in the visibility of the relationships between the faithful who carry out their different tasks entrusted to them in the church.

What is most deeply personal within us is that which forms and structures our relationships. It is in this that our history is interested, a history that will become more human as our consciences become more free and responsible.

Part One

Believers present in the life of society

Chapter 1

The earth and the human person

BASTIANEL S., ABIGNENTE D., «La terra e l'uomo. Vita politica, vita morale, fede cristiana», in *Theologica & Historica.* Annali della Pontificia Facoltà Teologica della Sardegna, XI. «Miscellanea in memoria di P. Sebastiano Mosso S.I.», Cagliari 2002, 129-151.

The Encyclical *Sollicitudo rei socialis* explicitly states that the social teaching of the Church legitimately claims to be the fruit of the reflection of moral theology[1]. The question arises: what does the Encyclical's statement mean? It would certainly seem reductionist to think that the aim is simply to justify the Church's social teaching, in its variety of expressions and continuity of meaning, within a particular category[2]. Rather, the text notes the fact that this teaching arises out of the question of the free and conscious responsibility of people and groups in the face of historically important values and is able to assist in developing a critical reflection on Christian praxis, according to the purposes and specific character of an ethical-theological discipline[3].

The intervention of the ecclesiastical Magisterium in the social sphere is always driven by real-life problems, where at issue are values, human rights and duties, with problems and positive possibilities affirmed or contradicted, due to cultures of relationships and economic, social and political structures, in differentiated historical circumstances. The question about free and conscious personal and social responsibility will require, then, the most *objective* reading possible of the facts, situations, and problems and therefore it cannot disregard the critical tools offered by the different competent disciplines that are suitable for delineating, describing, and defining the various elements at issue. Sociology, economics, jurisprudence and law, and the political and psychological sciences will all be needed. Also required will be that complex of reflections that have not yet become theories, but are already critical readings of the «signs of the times», in which the historical present is very rich. At the same time, however, one must be aware that the results of these scientific investigations should be interpreted through an ethically-based and conducted critical reflection. No scientific conclusion, in fact, is by its nature immediately transferable into an

1 «The Church's social doctrine *is not* a "third way" between *liberal capitalism* and *Marxist collectivism*, nor even a possible alternative to other solutions less radically opposed to one another». Constituting a unique type of reflection, it belongs «to the field, not of *ideology*, but of *theology* and particularly of moral theology» (JOHN PAUL II, Encyclical Letter «Sollicitudo rei socialis», n. 41, in *Enchiridion Vaticanum 10*. Documenti ufficiali della Santa Sede 1986-1987, Edizioni Dehoniane, Bologna 1989, 1799. On the meaning of the magisterial statement, cfr. BASTIANEL S., «Dottrina sociale della chiesa come teologia morale», in BERNAL RESTREPO S., *Teologia e dottrina sociale. Il dialogo ecclesiale in un mondo che cambia*, Piemme, Casale Monferrato 1991, 51-73).

2 As perhaps the English translation of the original text would suggest. The Latin «*proprium ac peculiare genus*» has in fact been translated, in a way that is not at all clear, using the expression «a category of its own» (*Ibidem*).

3 As «*accurate formulation* of the results of a careful reflection on the complex realities of human existence... in the light of faith and of the Church's tradition», the Church's social doctrine has as its «main aim» to «*interpret* these realities (...) thus to *guide* Christian behaviour» (*Ibidem*).

ethical conclusion. To reach conclusions, and prior to that, moral interpretations, it is necessary to reflect on the meaning of the human person and of living side by side on this earth (therefore one needs to be mindful of anthropological support). Specifically, it is necessary to reflect on that meaning which comes to people's lives through the exercise of conscious and free responsibility of consciences. This is also essential when it is a matter of discerning in faith the complex reality of existence in reference to revelation and the church's faith tradition. In this case as well, it is important to address specific ethical questions: Why do we speak about values and on the basis of what criteria do we judge their effective worth? For whom are they effective and how can they be recognized and assumed? What are the aims understood by people and social groups in proposing and pursuing the realization of certain goods?

By examining lived experience, with the interpretations given to it, from the point of view of the free and conscious responsibility of consciences, the ethical and ethical-theological reflection can exercise a *critical, stimulus*, and *integration* role[4] even toward what are held to be basic criteria and categories of social and personal life. It is precisely through an analysis of the problems that a responsible assessment can be encouraged.

It is in this context that the significance of our reflection comes into play. It aims to focus critically on the categories, apparently taken for granted, by which we understand social interaction, moral life, existence, and the significance of structures and institutions in their relationship with consciences. To assist the maturing of *consciousness* within the structures and shared life styles, which is denounced today with particularly compelling force by many within technological-capitalist societies, it is perhaps necessary to not count these categories as a foregone conclusion, even in their simply terminological clarification. Moreover, without consciousness there can be no assumption of honest social *responsibilities.* Pressure of circumstances is not enough, nor even the emphasis placed on the affirmation and defense of human rights, because the issue is actually about politics and ethically-socially correct praxis.

Naturally, we will focus only on some points, some essential ways of thinking, with a necessarily limited reflection. In the light of the knowledge of God in Jesus Christ, we will ask ourselves about the meaning of morality and social interaction

4 Such roles of moral theology and church Magisterium in determining the direction of an innerworldly ethics are clearly expressed in AUER A., *Morale autonoma e fede cristiana*, Edizioni Paoline, Cinisello Balsamo 1991 (orig.: Düsseldorf 1971), 186-199.

in their mutual relationship, trying to discern the intentionality that emerges from biblical revelation, in the memory of the Lord's gestures and words.

1
Morality, social interaction, politics

Perhaps we have become too accustomed to speaking about social or political issues and asking ourselves what might be the ethical implications. Similarly, we are accustomed to speaking about the ethical-political relationship as a central question of our time, and we do it largely in reference to themes or problems concerning the structures and institutions of human society. The emphasis placed in modern times on «political responsibility» as the nucleus and fundamental role of ethics[5] was tragically called into question precisely within a western context that vaunted its clear theorization, above all, by the massacres of the wars and absolutism. However, it was also reinterpreted in the last century, both at the level of social and political praxis and in explicit philosophical, religious and economic reflection, and it finds an undeniable harmony with the consciousness assumed and proclaimed by the church's social Magisterium[6]. In our

5 In truth the claim is much older than its modern formulation (in the religious field, but also in the lay philosophical-political field: who hasn't read Plato's *Crito* or is unaware of the vitality of Greek theatre, the indications of Stoic ethics, the teaching of Seneca?). But the passage from a religious foundation of ethics to the autonomous roots of responsibility, with the respective conviction that the ethical claim of responsibility is absolutely the highest manifestation of human life, has given great strength, in modern Europe, to the innerworldly commitment. One can already see the writings of U. Grozio and above all the paper of KANT I., *Perpetual Peace*, (English translation by MARY C. SMITH), Cosimo Inc, New York 2005, the first text, perhaps, that alludes to international law as having constitutional standing. But the central ethical task of political responsibility has been affirmed perhaps even more by the theories, and historical, social, economic, and juridical praxis of modern Europe. One thinks, especially, of the experiences that in the eighteenth and nineteenth centuries led to the birth of national constitutions and declarations of the rights of man. Naturally, the major limit of modern European ethical-political thought, strongly denounced by the critical theories of Marxist society, has been that of taking and imposing, in a universal model of rationalized co-existence, that middle class-capitalist thought, first Eurocentric, then «western». Cfr. MARCUSE H., *One-Dimensional Man*, Beacon Press, Boston 1964; RIZZI A., *Crisi e ricostruzione della morale*, SEI, Torino 1992.

6 We note, among others, some contemporary authors who, in the current context have argued authoritatively for the need for an ethical-political, ethical-economic, ethical-religious reformulation of personal and world responsibility in a technological-capitalist era. Cfr. HABERMAS J., *Legitimation Crisis*, Beacon Press, Boston 1975 (orig.: Frankfurt am Main 1973); JONAS H., *The Imperative of Responsibility. In Search of an Ethics for the Technological Age*, University of Chicago Press, Chicago & London 1984 (orig.: Frankfurt am Main 1979); SEN A., *Etica ed economia*, Laterza, Bari 1988, (orig.: Boston 1980). On a number of occasions in recent years the church's

present time, by virtue of the radical structural change in world societies, the relationship between ethics and world economic policies seems to have become not just the principle object but also the privileged criterion of moral and theological reflection. If the make-up of conflicts and the responsibility toward future human life seem to place themselves as the first task of justice[7], moral reflection must not only be careful about reasoning theologically, with a perspective of consequential evaluative wisdom, but must also learn to consider with priority not individual actions and players, but rather collective players and actions: public politics of an economic character above all[8]. Naturally, at the origin and expression of explicit reflections in the shared way of understanding and evaluating, there are entrenched ways of thinking. Under those circumstances what happens is that one often hears talk of world societies, of financial politics and responsible globalization, and yet the questions that are raised about them often continue to be ambiguous, both on the personal and institutional levels, by virtue of the very use of the terms «moral», «social», «political», and the meaning and aims that characterize their interpretation.

The question about the ethical meaning of collective action and public politics certainly requires consideration of the existence and meaning of models and processes of social action, social structures and institutions, and the *modus operandi* of these structures, together with the collaboration of specific expertise. But there is also a problem that is not related to specific expertise but that affects everyone: *How* to be present within social and political life? How is moral responsibility involved in the structuring of relationships that make up human

social teaching has not only encouraged, but urged reflection in the same vein. One thinks especially of the Magisterium of JOHN PAUL II and his constant reminder of the actual responsibility of justice. Cfr. MOSSO S., «Il rapporto fede-giustizia. Il Magistero di fronte ai problemi degli ultimi 15 anni», in *La Civiltà Cattolica* 141 (1990/I) 546-558; ID., «Etica, economia e sviluppo nell'insegnamento episcopale», in *La Civiltà Cattolica* 146 (1995/III) 472-484.

7 Cfr. RAWLS J., *A Theory of Justice*, Harvard University Press, Cambridge, MA 1971).

8 The statement of H. Jonas in this regard is clear, and is not exclusive to this author: if through the technological revolution «the realm of making has invaded the space of essential action, then morality must invade the realm of making (...) and must do so in the form of public policy» (*The Imperative of Responsibility*, 9). In his critique of traditional ethics, H. Jonas notes that its essentially anthropocentric content was limited to the immediate field of action. This certainly included interpersonal relations, but limited them to a restricted circle of action, controllable by agents, in which the human good, known in its universality, was caught in the contemporaneity of time, thus leaving in the shade the consequences of human action, which prove to be uncontrollable by subjects even though they are fruit of well-intentioned present decisions. In the vision that characterized the traditional ethic «the short arm of human power did not call for a long arm of predictive knowledge» (*Ibidem*, 6).

society? With what type of presence can one basically build a «human» civil society? We begin, therefore, with consideration of the relationship that exists between *social interaction and morality*. In what way and at what levels, covering the field of experience indicated by the term *moral*, do we come across something that belongs to the social dimension of our life?

1.1. AN INTERSUBJECTIVE EXPERIENCE

Personal moral experience is not a social addition, because it is essentially relational. We can state that the condition of every conscious human experience is precisely its being present in an intersubjective environment in which the individual human person is born and through which he/she becomes a conscious person, free and responsible, communicating and sharing with others the aims and perceptions of values, judgments, models and criteria of behavior, knowledge, and normative experiences. Of course, the fact of living with others and by virtue of communicating the human story with others is not a sufficient condition to give rise to personal morality, if a response of conscious and free responsibility is missing. However, it is true that the individual subject, born in history, develops and matures in a social context that is not just external to him/her, but *makes him/her* be so, informing his/her way of understanding and acting. This dynamic of social sharing belongs to the forming and becoming of a culture, of the various moral cultures in their historical application.

If the context of the maturity of a personal morality already expresses the essentially relational character of morality, the internal connection between «moral» and «social», which lies at the root of moral and social life, stands out when we consider the essential character of moral necessity. By nature, this is averse to letting oneself be guided by events, by circumstances, by the expectations of others that are determined by current habits, such as the authoritative needs external to conscience. In describing *moral value* in its distinctiveness and its necessary relation to other human values, we are accustomed to indicating the threshold of morality and its original place in that dimension of life which is *the encounter with the human «you»*, the human being in relation to the other person, to others. To this experience is linked the meaning of truly human *freedom*, the meaning of personal conscious *responsibility*, the meaning of *gratuitousness* as essential content of the properly moral response. To become morally responsible means accepting the fact that the encounter with the other person redefines the horizon of existence and the whole of one's life; it means accepting the presence of the other person as reason and fullness of the meaning of one's own freedom, assuming the other not as an object with which to build an exploitable relationship if and how it may be of use, but as a person, as center of meaning and generation of meaning, in a relationship redefined by the possibility of living as *«indebted-acknowledged»*[9].

Moral responsibility is not about tolerating the presence of others or attempting to render that presence harmless or less costly by the use of force or various forms of «pacts» and regulation of subjective rights, which are in themselves ambiguous because they are based on competiveness and mutual defense. The mere fact of being with others becomes genuinely «moral» when one takes on the experience of being *fellow humans* as the meaning of one's own life and chooses the realization of one's own freedom in making oneself consciously responsible.

If that is the case, then every personal responsibility is identically an experience of *co-responsibility*. Each of us can see how one's own responsibility may be made possible and conditioned by the multiple relationships that he/she has had, by the concrete forms in which human life is structured, and by the values and hierarchy of shared values. On the other hand, in the concrete exercise of his/her freedom, each person contributes to make possible or hinder, curb or liberate, the opportunities of others with respect to their living in free responsibility. This means that in this history each of us is not only *conditioned*, but also *conditioning*, receiving opportunities and limitations from others and offering to others possibilities and limitations, by virtue of values recognized or non-recognized, realized or contradicted. This history is about opportunities and limitations established by human relations in history, a co-responsibility that creates *children-parents* out of this history in its various cultural expressions. In this sense we can say that *solidarity* is first of all the free and responsible assumption of our intersubjective life as people oriented to making such life «human».

Given this fact it seems evident that the term «moral» is closely connected to the term «social», and yet moral and social are not the same thing. Just as the mere presence of the other person does not determine the quality of my personal response, since I can take on or deny that presence as a radical option, so also the social fact and the assumption or interpretation of just social rules are

9 Cfr. BASTIANEL S., *Teologia morale fondamentale. Moralità personale, ethos, etica cristiana, (for students'use)* PUG, Rome 2005, 27. For lengthier treatment of the originally relational character of the moral experience cfr. ID., *Autonomia morale del credente. Senso e motivazioni di un'attuale tendenza teologica*, Morcelliana, Brescia 1980.

still not sufficient conditions of morality[10]. What is morally qualifying is not the fact of social life, but the way in which co-existence is assumed and guided as a place of responsible freedom and personal creativity.

1.2. POLITICAL LIFE

The necessary distinction and at the same time the obvious connection between the spheres are made clear if we reflect on the meaning of the term «political». Normally, the term «political» indicates a specialist activity: that of a person who, as in a paid or voluntary profession, dedicates him/herself to the running of the state, primarily in the legislative or administrative field, as distinct from others who carry out different activities. This use of the term «political» is not incorrect, since it refers directly to the significance, strategies and functionality of the *structures* that regulate and coordinate the life of a social group. However, it is not completely exhaustive, and in fact, we all have experience with the difficulty of charting the boundary of the «political» reality.

The life of the *polis* is a broader reality than the institutional dimension or legislative, governmental, administrative activity. Communal life is everything that belongs to the common fabric of encounters and human experiences; everything that in the manifold dialogue of daily relationships is communicated, accepted, rejected, modified; everything that creates sensitivity, ways of thinking, life styles, judgments about what is of value and what isn't, what is preferable and what is to be avoided. Communal life is everything that *forms* personal consciences, indicating consciousness, particular choices, and the global planning of life, and therefore, the objective conditions for the exercise of free responsibility. The life of a social group makes reference to much broader «life worlds» than the various social «systems». It is comprised of a reality which, prior to the structures, through and beyond external structures, profoundly structures ways of thinking and sensitivities in the manners of perceiving and reacting, in the values, norms, evaluations, and preferences exercised. Moreover, even when the term «political» refers largely to the various functional activities of an institutional system, one cannot avoid considering the rational criteria and parameters of a given social system, underpinned by the same manner of understanding

10 Clear in this regard is the judgment of naïveté and reductionism that, even within the tradition of the critical theories of society, J. Habermas addresses to K. Marx. Cfr. *Knowledge and Human Interests*, Beacon Press, Boston, MA 1971 (orig.: Frankfurt am Main 1968).

and living, at the various levels of presence, in the life of human society[11]. The question is central and, even if dealt with in a variety of ways, has always been a matter of interest to the church's social teaching[12].

In this sense the term «political» does not define simply an aspect of social life, but indicates an ever-present dimension of human life, as already well-noted by the Aristotelian definition of the human being: *politicon zoon, social animal.* Every activity and every word, every silence and every omission, every decision, every gesture, is placed necessarily within a relational context, by virtue of which in fact they contribute, positively or negatively, to confirm or modify consciences, structuring *co-existence.* The mode of (political) social life belongs to the cul-

11 One sees in this sense the clear distinction that J. Habermas makes between *lifeworld* and *system* in understanding the life of a society. According to the author the limitation of traditional sociology has been precisely that of the unjust identification betwen society and the lifeworld. Cfr. *The Theory of Communicative Action II.* Beacon Press, Boston, MA 1987 (orig.: Frankfurt am Main 1981), 697-809. It is a matter of not thinking simply about the systemic effective functionality of the different expressions and social communications. There can be specialist political participation, but also the same co-responsibility toward political life experienced in the production of values and normative life styles, established through the word and silence, through presence and absence, in the explicit field of formation of consciences, but also in the care of prayer, praise, and the praying memory. Cfr. BASTIANEL S., «Rapporto carità e politica. Aspetto etico», in MARINELLI F., BARONIO L., EDD., *Carità e politica. La dimensione politica della carità e la solidarietà nella politica*, Dehoniane, Bologna 1990, 223-241.

12 Within the tradition and social teaching of the church, to the meaning of political activity is often linked the debate about political power, its limits, its justification. The debate is very old and was already noticeably present in the biblical Old Testament tradition. One thinks, for example, about the problem of the birth of the monarchic tradition within the Israelite biblical tradition. On this matter, cfr. FOHRER G., *History of Israelite Religion*, SPCK, London 1973 (orig.: Berlin 1969). If one then refers to the criteria for evaluating human society and the moral correctness of political action, one recalls in particular the criterion of the *common good* constantly reasserted within the social and moral teaching of the church, in close relationship with the intentionality of revelation, and the idea of *natural moral law*, paradigm of non-directly scripturalist interpretation, which had already arisen in the sphere of Greek philosophy through instances of evaluation and objective judgment based on reason, but interpreted not without problems in the course of the centuries. In this regard we cannot but recall that theological social moral teaching, despite its positive applications, has demonstrated some weaknesses in the elaboration of the idea of natural moral law, especially when it basically identified the *societas christiana* with the *societas humana* or when, in the same line of thought, it interpreted signs and systems of human values in a legalistic, naturalist or biological sense (especially in the modern era). Even from this point of view what should be remembered is the critical insistence from the recent social Magisterium of the Church which, evaluating more decisively ethical and sociological phenomenological and historical categories, prefers to speak of *interdependence*, as a condition of human co-existence and of the category of *solidarity*, as its moral interpretation. Cfr. JOHN PAUL II, *Sollicitudo rei socialis;* BASTIANEL S., «La fame, una sfida allo sviluppo solidale», in *La Civiltà Cattolica* 148 (1997/I) 330-343; CHIAVACCI E., *Teologia morale,* 2, Complementi di morale generale, Cittadella, Assisi 1980; MOSSO S., «Bene comune, struttura di peccato, solidarietà. *Categorie centrali del Magistero sociale della Chiesa.* I», in *La Civiltà Cattolica* 142 (1992/III) 355-364.

ture of a human group and expresses it. Therefore, there is no human activity that is not political, including that which is most eminently spiritual. If it forms consciences, if it is concerned with consciences, even the presence of the priest in the confessional impinges upon public life, with the understanding, as Habermas would say, that comes from the exercise of «communicative reason»[13]. This does not signify a claim of «confessional» direct political action on the part of the church. It is not about claiming specificity of governance or administration; rather, if personal life always has a public dimension, what touches consciences will be something that touches life[14].

Politics as communal life, social interaction as communication between consciences means, therefore, that people's moral responsibility is always played out in a social and political dimension. This does not mean that moral responsibility is identified with social issues and the political sphere, nor that a personal gesture carries the same weight and has an equal possibility of outcome as those of a well-established structure. Nevertheless, there is an intimate connection between personal decision and structures of co-existence. The relationship is similar to that which exists between implicit and explicit, interior and exterior, transcendence and substance. Thus, socio-political structures, likewise, are not realities that come about of their own accord, or exist on their own, regardless of that spiritual reality which is the life of consciences and the relationship between consciences. On the other hand, the same well-established structures contribute to the formation of consciences through the «social» arrangement

13 Distinguishing the «strategic-instrumental» rationality (proper to the language directed to the «success» of the affirmations, to the convictions of the other person and the environment, to the effective reaching of an *understanding*) from the «communicative rationality» (to which, rather, the *telos* of *coming to an understanding* is immanent), J. Habermas notes: «this concept of *communicative rationality* carries with it connotations based ultimately on the central experience of the unconstrained, unifying, consensus-bringing force of argumentative speech, in which different participants overcome their merely subjective views, and owing to the mutuality of rationally motivated conviction, assure themselves of both the unity of the objective world and the intersubjectivity of their lifeworld» (*The Theory of Communicative Action* 1. Reason and the Rationalization of Society, 10).

14 The term «public» should not be understood in the sense of opposed to «private». N. Bobbio rightly notes that the term «public» rather means «evident», in the sense of opposed to every «invisible» power. The distinction concerns the character and fundamental reason for authorities and democratic societies. Democracy is considered the ideal of good government precisely because it proposes to make transparent the very goal of establishing within human societies the visibility and transparency on which they were originally founded. Visibility of power means that the very care of the common good, in directing means to the understood end, is entrusted to the whole political-social community with the diversity of its roles, functions, and specific competences. Cfr. *Il futuro della democrazia. Una difesa delle regole del gioco*, Einaudi, Turin 1984.

of shared life. Naturally, it is precisely an awareness of the connection that exists between *social-political-moral* that should recall the importance of the moral aspiration as *spirit* and criterion for verifying the authenticity of social life and should be a reminder that it will always be in the *arena* of social interaction that we live out our free responsibility[15].

1.3. WHAT IMAGE OF CONSCIENCE?

An ever-hidden temptation, with ever-new guises and expressions, is to *privatize* the ethical experience (and, for the believer, to privatize at the same time the faith experience). The temptation is accepted wherever essentially, even without explicit theorization, we create a separation (not just a distinction) between the ethical and social spheres. If the sphere of morality is defined in terms of my intimate relationship with my conscience, without interference from others, then in reality I assume a figure of moral conscience radically marked by disinterest in the other person. This focusing of one's own morality on oneself is at the root of immorality, since it fundamentally contradicts the specific meaning of the moral life; that is, giving oneself up to another in free responsibility.

It is not possible to privatize the ethical experience. In the way in which we experience social interaction we offer an image of conscience through actions. That means, for example, that if I pretend to be honest and in fact put forward my honest pretense, while at the same time I am disinterested in the person who is my neighbor, or if I resort regularly to my own exclusive opinion in the search for correct solutions, then with my worldly-wise attitude I am communicating a message-program of life based on the dichotomy between moral and social. Whoever knows me and is aware of my behavior will see in me a figure of conscience centered on the self that is thoroughly selfish, not fraternal and not open to the search for the good *because* it is good. There is no need for a discourse or theorization about the separation between public and private life; it is sufficient that I in fact live out that separation, and thus my presence will mediate an understanding of existence that justifies at its roots an *honest disinterest* in the other person.

This way of living and perceiving the experience of conscience, which at heart is dichotomous, touches consciences and impacts upon their formation, creates or maintains a basically individualistic style of relationships, contributes

15 Cfr. BASTIANEL S., «"Strutture di peccato". *Una riflessione teologico-morale*», in *La Civiltà Cattolica* 140 (1989/I) 325-338.

to the formation of ultimately individualistic and, to the very roots, violent structures. Consequently, relationships and structures will come about and develop inspired by a functional rationale in the search for the proper good of individuals or groups, so much so as to reduce even the common good to a tool for the private good. It is obvious that in this way the victory of the strongest will be justified, and a way of thinking based on criteria of competition, defense and privilege will be confirmed.

1.4. WHAT IMAGE OF GOD?

Where there is an internal and lived dichotomy between the spheres of conscience and social activity, between the primacy of the «sacred» and the marginality of the «profane», between care for the soul and care for public life, in its diverse cultural and social expressions, at issue is not just an image of conscience but also an image of God[16]. This aspect addresses whoever declares oneself to be a believer in a way that is not at all of secondary importance. In fact, merely by expressing at the same time a profession of faith, the believer who experiences this internal dichotomy states that the God he/she believes in is not interested in the life of human beings, in communal life, in the life of one's neighbor. If faith is consumed in an intimate, private relationship, in gestures and words that concern self and God alone, then in the witness of daily life one is testifying to an image of God not interested in inter-human relationships; essentially human life is not important for him. In such a way, the image presented of God is radically contrary to that which we find in the Scriptures: this God is not the Father of Jesus Christ, is not the one who reveals himself working within human history, who from the outset is «interested» and certainly not indifferent to the fate of peoples, the poor, and the weak.

On the positive side we can say that the believer's conduct, his/her way of being present in social life, his/her taking on appropriate responsibility insofar as is concretely possible for what concerns human life, mediates an image of God; it is testimony that truly *makes* the human story in its being oriented toward God, understanding and welcoming the God of the covenant and of salvation.

16 Cfr. FUCHS J., «Our Image of God and the Morality of Innerworldly Behaviour», in ID., *Christian Morality: The Word Becomes Flesh*, Gill and Macmillan, Dublin/Georgetown University Press, Washington, DC 1987 (orig.: *Stimmen der Zeit* 109 [1984] 363-382), 47-78.

Emphasizing the intimate connection that exists between the *figure of human relationships experienced and the image of God presented*, also means remembering the concern of this testimony of the God who acts in the cultural context in which one lives, even before and beyond possible explicit awareness. This relates to the unity of personal experience and the de facto unity of our common belonging to a *land*, in being mutually linked by bonds of solidarity that touch all the levels of our living in a common history.

2
Communion with God and interhuman communion

We have attempted to provide an overview of the fact and meaning of living in relationship, in the world and in history. We will try now to discern its significance in the light of faith, discerning the intentionality of God that emerges from the foundational moments of biblical revelation, and in light of the experience we have of this our world, bearing in mind the evil as well as the hopes present in the humanity of which we are a part. The «*sub luce Evangelii et humanae experientiae*», indicated by the conciliar constitution *Gaudium et spes* as a fundamental hermeneutic criterion for ethical-theological reflection[17], requires first of all that in the unity of moral, personal and social experience morality and faith not be separated. By our decisions and attitudes, our presence or absence, we in any case build the common life. In the light of revelation, the contribution that moral experience offers as responsibility to the conscience of each person does not change nor find guarantees or opportunities to flee negativism, but precisely as a requirement of responsibility, is part of the meaning of the human response to the work of God[18].

In the explicit awareness of one's own faith, the Christian recognizes that attention in all conscience to history, in its complexity, and the search for truly human solutions, belong to his/her role of *making oneself a neighbor* to those with whom one lives. Having at heart the testimony of the Lord, he/she knows that precisely from the moment when one is truly a neighbor one can also proclaim in a credible fashion the closeness of God who saves.

17 ECUMENICAL SECOND VATICAN COUNCIL, *Pastoral Constitution on the Church in the Modern World «Gaudium et Spes»*, n. 46.

18 FUCHS J., «Vocazione e speranza. Indicazioni conciliari per una morale cristiana», in *Seminarium* 23 (1971) 491-512.

We can recall historical moments and elements of explicit ethical reflection documented in the Scriptures[19]. The principal allusion is to that experience of the relationship between God and us which, as a unifying criterion of meaning, runs through the whole span of biblical history, in its diversified conditions and expressions, right up to the fullness of God's self-revelation in the humanity of Jesus Christ. From the original tradition of *Exodus-Sinai*, God's self-revelation is experienced and understood as self-communication and a call to share his intentionality of communion. Gradually in a more explicit and reflected manner, and also by virtue of the events experienced and the contributions from the peoples and historical cultures encountered, Israel understood the relationship given by God as a radical experience of reciprocity and, assuming an interpretive category linked to the Middle Eastern cultural environment of the III-I millennia B.C., indicated such a relationship with the term *covenant*. In time the juridical-literary form of the word *covenant* has assumed semantic values and varied ethical, juridical, and religious meanings. The specific term, even considered in its historical evolution of meanings, therefore needs to be understood with reference to the broader biblical vocabulary expressing the *meaning* of human life in the light of a fundamental *relationship* with God in an historical space of *relationships* given and granted[20].

God *reveals himself in action*. At the beginning there is neither a noetical-conceptual definition, nor a religious discourse. God communicates himself by intending, deciding, working out the personal and social liberation of real people in a real history. Establishing a specific relationship with the direct interlocutor

19 For an historical-genetic plan of the biblical ethos, cfr. BASTIANEL S., DI PINTO L., «Per una fondazione biblica dell'etica», in GOFFI T., PIANA G., EDD., *Corso di Morale*, 1, *Vita nuova in Cristo. Morale fondamentale e generale*, Queriniana, Brescia 1983, 75-173.

20 For an understanding of the term and its theological meaning, and for a theology of the Old Testament through the category of covenant, cfr. BEAUCHAMP P., «Propositions sur l'alliance de l'Ancien Testament comme structure centrale», in *Revue de Sciences Religieuses* 58 (1970) 161-193; BONORA A., «Alleanza», in ROSSANO P., RAVASI G., GIRLANDA A., EDD., *Nuovo Dizionario di Teologia Biblica*, Edizioni Paoline, Cinisello Balsamo 1988, 21-35; EICHRODT W., *Theology of the Old Testament*, 1, trans. J.A. Baker, SCM Press Ltd, London 1961. More than from the term, or its etymology, the theological significance stems from the experience reflected on and described. In this sense a biblical theology of the *mutual relationship* assumes conceptual vocabulary, culturally conditioned, even seemingly very distant from that ethical-juridical understanding of the covenant (very much present above all in the prophets) and, however primary, equally significant. One thinks, in particular, of the theology of the «origins» present in *Gen* 2-11, and invaluable texts such as *Ruth*, *Tobias*, *Wisdom*, and Johannine theology, etc. Cfr. LOHFINK N., «Il concetto di "alleanza" nella teologia biblica», in *La Civiltà Cattolica* 142 (1991/III) 353-367.

(Moses, a figure of personal mediation) and with those to whom he was sent, he reveals his name (*Exod* 3), making himself neighbor and liberator. His speech and his actions are intimately linked in a decision that is absolutely free, unconditional, and gratuitous. The various biblical theologies, in particular Deuteronomy, will keep alive the memory of it. At the outset it is gift! The foundation of Israel's faith and call lies in this story of gratuitous kindnesses carried out, revealing God irreversibly committed to the weak, wanting nothing other than the liberation of the oppressed, author and promoter of their very own capacity for peace and life in a fraternal space of blessing. It is the promise of a reciprocity that knows the diversity of the partners, but that nevertheless is true reciprocity and therefore involves faithfulness[21].

On the one hand the understood experience is that of being the *goal* of the relationship that God establishes. On the other hand, the very gratuitousness of his gift is the foundation of a *moral requirement*, suggesting a responsibility to respond. It is this people, whom he declares to know, wishing to take on its destiny, that God asks to be «his» people. To know God becomes recognizing «this» God, wishing to be «his» people, born from him and entrusted to him, but in the freedom of a decision of solidarity. To understand his gift is at the same time a call to assume it; to recognize being freely saved is, for those who have the experience of it, awareness of the ability given to assume in oneself the very intentionality of God. In that extraordinary passage from the «prologue» to the «fundamental declaration», evident in the structure of the biblical covenant, the meaning of a possible communion is stated, preceded and generated by a liberation that is not just exterior, but interior: a liberation now freely *granted*[22].

21 In the «structure» of the covenant, reconstructed in various Old Testament biblical texts, historical and prophetic, on the basis of the relationships with the treaties of Hittite or Neo-Assyrian vassalage, the two first moments are characterized by the «preamble» of the self-presentation of Yahweh and by the «historical prologue» of the good deeds carried out by him in an absolutely unconditional manner on behalf of his people. Cfr. MCCARTHY D.J., MENDENHALL G.E., SMEND R., *Per una teologia del patto nell'Antico Testamento*, Marietti, Torino 1972; LEPORE L., «La *b'rît* come obbedienza e come comunione», in *Rassegna di Teologia* 42 (2001) 867-890. As a significant element in this regard see the text of *Josh* 24. For an examination of this text, cfr. DI PINTO L., *Fondamenti biblici della teologia morale. Tracce e integrazioni ad uso degli studenti*, Napoles 1998-1999.

22 Within the Old Testament covenant texts, both in the minor literary units (microunity) and in the greater literary units (macrounity), the fundamental ethical moment is highlighted by the central passage from the «historical prologue» to the «fundamental declaration», that is, from the narrative recollection of the works carried out by Yahweh on behalf of Israel (kerygma) to the effective proposal of decision (relationship response). The passage is significantly expressed by the phrasal adverb *w'attah, so now*, which here has not just logical-juridical, but also chronological-axiological value. It is a key term for illuminating the *foundational* relationship that

Knowledge of God is connected to knowledge of the other person, of history, of the future. The response that engages consciousness cannot be simply faith manifested in word and cultic celebration. Life itself, too, must respond at the same time, in its accustomed manner of making concrete decisions and daily gestures. The «believing» manner of the concrete gesture will be that which aspires in the human interpersonal (therefore in the *social* and *political*) sphere to being the realization of the intentionality itself of the divine intervention: *to create a fraternal relationship*, a *family* of people, in a blessing of solidarity, toward a real *land* of *communion*[23].

Regarding a morality-social interaction-«land» concept, in the experience of the Old Testament covenant, just as in the young community of *Acts*[24] that

exists between the gratuitousness experienced by Israel and the possibility of her response (very eloquent, for example, in *Josh* 24:14: «So now, fear Yahweh and serve him perfectly and sincerely...»). Cfr. DI PINTO L., *Fondamenti biblici della teologia morale*, 101-107; L'HOUR J., *La morale de l'alliance*, Gabalda, Paris 1966. Naturally, it is the significant experience, much more than the term *so now*, which highlights the fundamental ethical movement present within the experience and the Old and New Testament biblical Scriptures. In this regard, one recalls the relationship between kerygma and conversion emphasized in the gospels, but also the gospel presentations of conversion «figures» and the profound core of Pauline theology.

23 The whole dynamism of the covenant leans toward this *land* originally designed and thought through by God as a place of peace. The *blessing* that inhabits the place will be, however, also the result of the free human response and, precisely because of that, will also be able to endure rejection of the gift, too, specifically, the reality of a non-meaning, a non-peace and non-fraternity, therefore a *curse*. This meaning of the «earth», and the importance of the forms of blessing and curses at the end of the covenant (highly valued above all in the theology of Deuteronomy), emerges from the examination of the structure of the «agreement». Scholars note the similarity between the moment of the memory of God's gratuitous activity («historical prologue») and the form of «blessing» (extraordinarily underlined also by the opposite response of the «curse»). In both moments the gratuitousness is valued, as foundation of life and perspective of a people's future. But there is a difference between the «first» gift, emphasized in the «historical prologue» and due to the exclusive initiative of God, and the gift of the «earth». Now the people is asked to inhabit and cultivate the place of the gifted relationships with the same perspective as God's activity: the *earth*, not just as a physical-exploitable space, but «human» and «theological», is entrusted as a place of desirable and possible *communion*, of *sharing* and common reaching out toward the *common good*. On this earth God himself will live «with» people: his promise is sure. From this point of view we remember, together with Deuteronomy, the moments and motives of the prophetic criticism regarding the pretense of entrusting the whole of one's response in worship of God, while instead, *knowing God* is the reality that involves the works of justice and is expressed in them (cfr. *Isa* 1-2, etc.). There is an interior connection between the truth of knowing God and the truth of recognizing the other person as other. In this sense, see also the connection between the prologue of the *Decalogue*, which recalls God's saving work, and the normative content of the individual commandments, which recall the places of relationship in which a people of brothers and sisters is established (*Exod* 20:1-21; *Deut* 5:1-22).

24 See above all, the summaries of *Acts* 2:42-48; 4:32-35; 5:12-16 that accompany the narration of the first establishment (in reciprocity of witness: *Acts* 1:12-14) and the first autonomous decisions in faith of the young Christian community. On the theological meaning of these «frames» for the whole Lucan work, cfr. HORN W.F., *Glaube und Handeln in der Theologie des Lukas*, Vandenhoeck & Ruprecht, Göttingen 1983.

arises from the mutual witness of Jesus Christ, awareness of the profound unity between the form of the relationships that are experienced and the image of God that is presented is clear, as is the free and responsible search for this unity. On the other hand, in response to the question of *how* to find the realistically correct manner for the response in life, one must recognize (for the ethical indications contained in Scripture, as well) that it is *the moral experience of historical reality* that offers the content of the answer, namely, the experience of what is good and what is evil, of what constitutes interhuman solidarity, of what makes people live together in peace, of what becomes realization of communion because it is realized through sharing. The moral decision to establish a people of brothers and sisters did not mean, both in the witness of the Old Testament and even more so by virtue of the incarnation, a search for and drawing up of values or «specifically» Israelite or Christian ways of responding; instead, human experience provided the material to identify the commandment[25], and the intercultural encounter «made fruitful» the land of the relation-covenant.

2.2. THE LOST «LAND»

The relationship with the other person is present at the origin of the moral experience and at the origin of the experience of faith, at the foundation of their specificity. The viewpoint suggested here thus far is the essentially social dimension of people's lives, both in good and in evil. Whether it is the good that comes out in people's lives, the story of positiveness that makes human life possible («blessing»), or the evil that we can consider to be present in it («curse»), they are *facts*. The personal existence of each person, with his/her own sin or with his/her own reciprocating to God's gift, is placed essentially within a story. We exist because we are co-existent; an actual solidarity links one person to another and we are responsible for our participation in a story greater than the individual one. The «account of the origins» in *Gen* 2-11 compares human sin and its consequences with God's creative intentionality (and with the faithfulness of his redemptive intentionality). The theological interpretation of history that these texts offer has its roots in Israel's long experience as the people of God: a social co-existence established in the awareness of the founding presence of God who saves, but a co-existence in which injustice is present.

25 As symbolic case, see the presence and origin of the «catalogue of virtues and vices» within the Pauline letters. Cfr. BASTIANEL S., «Assunzione di formule e paradigmi etici nel nuovo testamento», in *Servitium* 14 (1980) 32-41.

The long tradition from which the text comes[26] senses the need to explain the presence of a *land* that is hostile and to link it with creation, knowing it is not possible to attribute that hostility to God himself. There is a need to understand, in faith and in the discernment between good and evil, the true reality of sin not as something inevitable or «natural», almost as a consequence of the creative will of God, but as a reality that attacks people's responsibility. Thus one perceives the personal moral dimension of sin, but one already senses how this personal moral dimension is not limited to only individual realities. The «land» has become «hostile», that is, humanity which is fulfilled therein has become the agent of hostility. We enter into a world already established by decisions, behavior, ways of thinking, sensitivities, in which sin is present and which therefore are such as *to be inclined toward* evil, furthering the actual possibility of personal sin.

It is interesting to see how such ancient ethical-theological traditions are already careful to grasp the historical forcefulness of sin, which in its strength conditions the experience of people and human cultures. Behind this attention there is an historic significance, the perception of a genuine historical dynamic of the burden of sin, a sensitivity capable of grasping the historical genuineness of good and evil and the responsibility entrusted to consciences. This historic sense and this sensitivity also challenge us believers today, precisely in the capacity to read as believers, conscious of freedom of responsibility, the reality of the world, and the reality of the church in the world as well. More than once, in fact, in reference to sin one repeats: «We are human!», almost giving the impression of finding what happens regularly to be «normal». At this time of bloodshed and shameless arbitrary acts carried out on the poorest of the world, we often call this inhuman humanity «natural». Is it not actually also a profound attitude of self-justification that leads us to understand in this way? Despite God's continuous interventions, despite the prophetic preaching and the repeated proclamations of the covenant, despite the fact that Israel had known of the blessing of the «land», in structures and the cultures developed on the level of

26 The text of *Gen* 2-11 has long been considered one of the more important nuclei of the *Yahwistic Tradition*. Current historical-critical research of the Old Testament biblical text raises many doubts about it. Attacking the classical documentary hypothesis, authors have radically reviewed the composition, date, and even existence of the Yahwistic document. Some consider the texts of *Gen* 1-11 to be later than the Deuteronomist and located in the time of the Exile. For this matter, cfr. SKA J.L., *Introduction to Reading the Pentateuch*, Eisenbrauns, Winona Lake, Indiana 2006. Cfr. also FANULI A., «Due recenti introduzioni critiche sulla composizione del Pentateuco. Un primo bilancio su un'ipotesi gloriosa», in *RivBibIt* XLIX (2001) 211-225.

social, economic and religious development, it had not escaped the Old Testament biblical tradition that within a people which dearly sees itself as the people of God, sin has not disappeared. In fact the most difficult observation is that not only are there still individual sinners, but that sin is present in a serious and verifiable manner even within the institutions and the way of administering justice, that is, even when legitimate authority and legitimate administrators steer decisions by the arbitrary use of lawfulness. How is such complicity with sin possible despite the understood and shared experience of the covenant?

The account of «original sin» reminds us that inhumanity is not «natural» (and is not unchanging!). Man and woman, as created by God, are able to recognize good and live it; they are not necessarily sinners. Sin is present in the world due to people's free decision, with results not limited to the lives of individuals. From the point of view of the relationships between Adam and Eve and therefore, in perspective, the internal relationships within the human family, there seems to be a bond of solidarity in the complicity of understanding and realization of the gesture arising from the suspect (*Gen* 3:1-8). However, as soon as Adam feels himself challenged and questioned about his behavior, he feels the need to defend himself. Complicity gives way to self-defense, the relationship breaks down and Adam accuses: «the woman you put with me» (*Gen* 3:12). The cause is the other person, it is the woman. It is like saying that you and the woman you gave me have made me a sinner. The *rationale of defense* becomes the root and the manner of self-justification. To defend himself, God and the woman are *simultaneously* made enemies and declared to be such, and defense suddenly becomes attack: to attribute guilt to the woman is to wish that it is she who should pay to resolve everything. Nor will it be any different with Eve, soon after. The logic of defense-suspect has produced its effects and the blame is placed on others!

The historical consequences of this are the breaking of communion with God, with the woman, and with the land. What is indicated to us as a «curse» is the internal consequence of sin itself, which in the subsequent chapters is recounted as the history of sinfulness, with the gradual strength of its forcefulness at the various levels of human co-existence (*Gen* 2-11). The result of sin is a divided life, which in the continuity of the texts stands out even more in implicit contrast to what has been narrated before (*Gen* 2). The creator's intentionality is the «garden», the «land» as a place adapted for life and the sharing of goods and relationships. Humanity can live in relationship with the land, cultivating it. With harmony between people broken, the relationship with the land becomes a relationship of domination, a relationship guided by the rationale of possession and defense: spasmodic violence for possession, lying defense from one to the other.

The text of *Gen* 2-11 goes on to explain the history of humanity living in not inescapable sin, division, and possession generated by our battling and defending ourselves, in a rationale of death[27]. It is a story in which people, instead of living according to the intentionality of the creator, make themselves masters of themselves and their history, as far as *Babel,* as far as the internal incapacity to understand themselves, as far as the lost reciprocity, the broken word. *Gen* 11 recalls it with clear eloquence. «Throughout the earth men spoke the same language, with the same vocabulary» (*Gen* 11:1). Is there a degree of irony or perhaps awareness of a diversity of gifts, of languages, of cultures not seen as gift, but as waste? This is not an incapable humanity. God's creating faithfulness continues to make us humans capable of intelligence, organization, complex choices, and sophisticated, precise, and functional projects. But how are these choices made? Pacts, alliances, unity are put to the test, but in that unity God is not present and there is not a *true* meaning. The meaning is what we decide because we decide it, and there is no one above or in front of us. So, even when one forms a partnership, it is done in order to better defend oneself or to make self-defense, defense of groups and of one's own interests more effective. Everybody wants to obtain the greatest advantage possible, and the common good is understood, looked for and experienced *as the private good*, not the search for good as good, not a rationale of communion[28].

«Now Yahweh came down to see... let us go down and confuse their language» (*Gen* 11:5.7). What happens when in this way one builds the city; what happens to the skill? Actually the rationale that functionally unites causes unity to crumble. Even aligning ourselves with others sets us against others, in the exclusive plan of protecting ourselves from the other person and from God. The «common» project actually betrays the rationale of a radical looking at the other person and God as rivals, so that even when pronouncing the same words, one per-

27 Cfr. ALONSO SCHÖKEL L., *Dov'è tuo fratello? Pagine di fraternità nel libro della Genesi*, Paideia, Brescia 1987 (orig.: Valencia 1985).

28 The moral social teaching of the Church recalls, in the wake of Thomas Aquinas, the very meaning of virtue beginning with the horizon of the common good: if a certain exercise of life is genuinely virtuous it can be seen from the common good it intends and produces (cfr. *Summa Theologiae* I-II, q.90). Therefore, if not directed toward the common good, if it is not consistent with the common good, a good «is really not a good and the virtue in question, really, is not a virtue» (MOSSO S., «Bene comune, struttura di peccato, solidarietà» 361).

son's *meaning* and another person's *meaning* will be «confused». There is a search for the sharing of existence on the earth, but with a divided heart, not because making others live belongs to the fulfillment of one's own existence. This is exactly the opposite of God's intentionality. It is an incapacity to dialogue; it is the lost «land»; it is «scattered» (*Gen* 11:9).

The actual land (the «human» one) is therefore not there for us; it is «lost land». The «garden» has been lost: this is our reality. The land we know is this: hostile, not just incidentally or *per accidens*. The human being we know (that is ourselves) is *of this land*. And yet our humanity continues to be accompanied by the presence of God. God does not cease to speak to Adam, to humanity. He speaks to us and can be understood and receive answers. Even after sin he makes himself present in the breeze of the day (*Gen* 3:8-9). He continues to be creator of closeness in this story. Not only and not so much through extraordinary events, but with the «yes» of people capable of producing good, and the sharing that is *possible* on this earth.

2.3. THE KINGDOM OF GOD ON THIS EARTH

The reality of the earth can well explain, in its expressions, the relationship between God and people and the historical social relationship. Onto this reality of the earth given and hostile, promised and lost, comes the New Testament proclamation of the kingdom of God, the center of the gospel message. In Jesus Christ this kingdom is *already present;* it is already a reality for us; in him is the foundation in which the *earth* has the possibility of becoming a *garden* again. Remember how, from this point of view, the evangelist Luke allows Jesus to proclaim, precisely at the moment of his death, the same word that in *Gen* 2 indicated the *garden*, now a metaphor for the *land* of the restored relationship. To the thief who entrusted himself to Jesus, calling him by name: «Jesus remember me when you come into your *kingdom*», Jesus replies: «Today you will be with me in *paradise*» (*Luke* 23:43). The parallel places the emphasis even more on fulfillment, extraordinarily underlined by the fact that in this case, the proclamation of the resurrection happens even before the death of Jesus. Having come to make possible *on the part of humanity* the relationship with God, Jesus returns to the Father's house with man, with the sinner who in him has found life. Just like the thief condemned to death, who dies having «seen» in Jesus, in the truth of his life and the grace of being close to him, the kingdom of God not just as desirable, but present and victorious over death, we too cannot say today what the *earth* is without mentioning the presence of Jesus Christ as an already active, already significant, already salvific presence in our co-existence in this world. It would not be true to speak of our history without speaking of the Passover of Christ Jesus, the son of God with us, the man of Nazareth who experienced our true story, in the manner of concrete human, cultural, historical relationships.

We can call to mind the experience of the disciples[29]. What image of relationality, social interaction, of «land», did they have in their time while following Jesus? While sincerely holding onto the relationship with Jesus, while valuing their lives as *companions*, while desiring a free land, they nourished expectations that were not in accordance with the understanding, evaluating, and feeling of Jesus. In its rationale of non-fraternity, this land that we have called «lost» also conditioned the life of the disciples, no different from others, no different from us. Up to the moment of Jesus' passion, even during the Last Supper, we see them transform the *common life* into a space of private, self-affirmation for each of them. They are not among the authorities, capable of making their prestige felt by their own means, but they share with them the same criteria of evaluation and judgment: not fraternity, solidarity, sharing, but the measure of *first* and *second*, the cleverest and the least clever. Precisely by virtue of these rationales of relationality and discipleship they also reached the point of being scandalized by Jesus. In the hour of the passion they were not able to accept him, someone even sold him, someone else fled or denied him. Jesus seemed to them a loser, his passion a scandal. In a «land» in which one kills the other person while even affirming his/her own space of arbitrariness, to live and decide as Jesus has, led to his condemnation. And yet it is precisely this, his authentic manner of *giving oneself up*, even to taking on his shoulders, in extreme unconditional faithfulness, the fruit of an earth cultivated according to a rationale of sin, which has brought to life these disciples, that thief, and us human beings. In the gift of the Eucharist, in his giving himself as our bread, in the free daily life up to the shedding of blood, Jesus gives us the unique pathway in this story of overcoming a rationale of competition, violence, and death. The disciples will remember that, even in the face of his imminent death, Jesus continued to make possible with his gift of self a life that is liberating in this salvation story, precisely when he refuses to ac-

29 For the conversion «figures» of the thief and the disciples, cfr. ABIGNENTE D., *Conversione morale nella fede. Una riflessione etico-teologica a partire da figure di conversione del vangelo di Luca*, Gregorian University Press-Morcelliana, Rome- Brescia 2000.

cept limits on the gift of self[30]. The fulfillment of the *resurrection* has become possible at this beginning of human existence and we are born into a story that *already* lives under the sign of the Passover of Jesus Christ. If we cannot see this we must ask ourselves about the authenticity of our faith. Have we known the Lord? Have we met the Living One? Do we understand ourselves individually, or do we understand ourselves fundamentally incorporated into communion with Christ?

It is true that sometimes it is difficult to see *how* good operates in history, but that should not mean denying it. The history of salvation, which in Jesus Christ has found its fulfillment, is entrusted to us. It is not a matter of putting into action just symbolic gestures, nor just exemplary models; instead, it is matter of «cultivating» the earth, making it become a kingdom of communion, and learning to recognize the historic forcefulness not just of evil, but also of good. Of course, the historic dynamic of the positive does not with one stroke cancel the dynamic of sin on the earth, but it opens out to conversion, raises questions, arouses hope, and generates in others the experience of a possible communion. The expression *historic forcefulness* also recalls the fact that our outlook on the world, the current situation, society, must be animated internally by the experience of faith. This means to live the experience of faith not as a relationship with Christ as a *person from the past*, but as a relationship with Christ present, an experience of salvation present and active today in history.

The theme of the garden, the theme of the land, is the theme of newness as the authenticity of humanity made possible for us by the fact that it is already present with Christ, and through him, by the strength of the Spirit, it is already present in history, even when the historic consequences of sin, from the point of view of social visibility, are still very much present (with the experience of evil and injustice), and for which newness is not a simple «cancellation» of sin and its effects. Even in the face of the permanent force of sin, we affirm that nevertheless the newness brought by Christ (and visibly active through the presence of believers) is not a reality that one expresses alone or chiefly in precise moments or in «moments of grace». It is the *story* of grace, the story of *salvation*.

There remains, in the manner of realization of the effectiveness of redemption, something that we cannot see, that we cannot confirm, but that we believe

30 On the meaning of the Eucharist as foundation and fulfillment of an authentic moral life, cfr. BASTIANEL S., *Vita morale nella fede in Gesù Cristo*, San Paolo, Cinisello Balsamo 2005, 153-171.

through the word of the Lord. Just as salvation by nature touches everyone, it also is a reality that belongs to the realm of mystery. We say therefore, that from the point of view of responsibility of the individual and of the community, this salvation passes through relationality to the way of free and conscious personal responsibility. People's *collaboration* in the work of God is like human beings established in communion with him, capable of doing what God's intervention wished to realize. In this profound sense, to build on our earth, in our history, a *rationale of communion,* means making the hostile earth a *garden*; it means living the rationale of the *kingdom.* This supposes understanding and acting according to a rationale of communion that is not inherent, in other words, by being a neighbor, which is contrary to a rationale of possession-defense-death. It means having an interpretation of what is human, and therefore of history, which does not hide in idealism (as if evil did not exist), but which is not resignation to evil (as if it were inescapable), realizing relationships that are recognized as *free* because they are *liberating* the other person's freedom. It means not living with the other person as an adversary and thus not living under the dominion of the *fear of death.* It signifies a liberated moral experience by virtue of *faith in the resurrection.*

Chapter 2

Responsibility for the other person

BASTIANEL S., «"Dov'è?": la domanda di responsabilità», in *Servitium* 110/3 31 (1997), 147-161.

«*Where is your brother Abel?*» (*Gen* 4:9). The question is not about a law, but rather it is a question about the relationship. It extends into consideration of a fundamental reality: the personal moral life is essentially open; it is not an individual and private question. Moral responsibility concerns a person's decisions and life, not as if they existed «alone», but in the historic reality of his/her relationships. The relationship with the other person is present at the origin of the moral experience as such, at the very root of its specificity. The point of view suggested here relates to the essentially social dimension of the moral life, both good and bad. Both the good that is realized in people's lives (positivity, which makes human life possible) and the bad that we can confirm as being present in life (negativity, which opposes authentic human life) are part of *history*. The personal life of each person (positive or negative, with one's own sin or with one's own reciprocating with God's gift) is essentially placed within a story. That is the nature of our existence on earth. A true solidarity binds us to each other, and we are responsible for our participation in a story that is greater than our own individual story.

«*I do not know. Am I my brother's guardian?*» The attempt at self-justification would like to appeal to freedom. But the question about the relationship recalls the very meaning of freedom: what type of freedom makes you just? The way of exercising freedom reveals a human meaning fulfilled or denied. The brother's being is for Cain the possibility of living as a person; it is the gift of a possible humanity. Specifically therefore, if his freedom creates fraternity, he fulfills his existence. If the exercise of his freedom is denial of fraternity, at the same time he denies his own humanity, the fulfillment of his own person.

The assumption of responsibility in the relationship with the other person is an internal requirement of the experience of personal freedom; it is a requirement of human meaning and truth. Cain cannot «be free from his brother». With this delusion, he loses his brother and loses himself as brother. This failure is not the failure of a particular objective; it is the failure of his own existence as a person.

The horizon of meaning of all that belongs to the sphere of morality has its focal point: a relationality qualified by gratuitousness, acceptance, and fraternity. The internal consciousness within the experience of freedom requires a liberating relationship, that of one who assumes one's own liberty as responsibility for the life, the freedom, and the good of the other person. The internal unity of consciousness, freedom and responsibility (that is, the person as moral conscience) is positively realized as creation of humanity.

In the many challenges that the problems of our humanity are always creating, our actual abilities to respond (and therefore our actual responsibility) are always extremely limited. It is always a matter of «just» doing the good that is concretely possible; but to discern this concretely possible good is not something arbitrary or with no criteria. It is always a matter of identifying what is truly a creator of fraternity. To respond to the other person is to make him/her be brother /sister. To respond to God is to be on his side in looking at the brother/sister.

1 *Genesis 2:4b-3:24: sin enters into the world*

The most obvious sign of sin enters into history through Cain: murder. It is the animosity that is consumed in a place of fraternity. It is the denial of that communion between people which belongs to God's creating intentionality.

God's faithfulness is expressed in his continuing to address his word to the sinner, and it is a word that evokes the meaning and value of life. Cain's response of self-justification echoes the arbitrary will of Adam. This outlook on history thus interprets the non-meaning of division and the meaning of the communion that God continues to offer, to make possible, to suggest to human reason. *Gen* 2:4b-3:24 narrates the meaning of human sin and its consequences, comparing it with the «before» of God's creative intentionality (and then with the «after» of his redemptive intentionality).

The Yahwistic tradition sees the need to explain the disconcerting reality that the evil caused by humankind, the injustice and its consequences, are heavily present within this people, which nevertheless sees itself as the people of God. It is the need to understand, in faith and discernment between good and evil, the true reality of sin, not as something inescapable, or «natural», almost as if it were a consequence of God's creative will, but rather as the work of humankind. Along with that, one already senses how sin is not just an individual reality: *the earth* has become hostile, that is, *humanity*, which fulfills itself through the earth, has become an agent of hostility.

One can see in this context that personal sin certainly attacks personal responsibility, but it is not just personal. Personal sin, at the moment at which it is carried out, is something that others have in some way encouraged. It can be the classic theme of *concupiscence*, that is, we enter into a world already constructed through decisions, behavior patterns, and ways of thinking, and sensitivities, in which sin is present. Therefore this world is such as to *incline* toward evil, to encourage the concrete possibility of personal sin (we recall the tree «pleasing to the eye and desirable» of *Gen* 3:6).

From this point of view, the account of original sin recalls the fact that sin (that of people in general and that of Israel in particular, the injustice present within the people of God) is not to be attributed to some evil divinity or to some power higher than humanity, but to people's very hearts, but that does not mean, however, attributing it to their «nature». The Yahwist recalls that man and woman, as created by God, are capable of recognizing good and living it. In communion with God and in communion between themselves, Adam and Eve are placed in the «garden», in a land adapted for them.

It is through their free decision-making that sin enters into the world, which is not just from the individual person and does not lead to a sinful outcome just for the same individual person. Already present in the account of original sin is the sense of an actual historic dynamic of the burden of sin. Such a dimension is indicated in the result of the relationships between Adam and Eve, in what is narrated as a curse, as an internal consequence of sin itself, which in the chapters following Genesis 3 is recounted as a story of sinfulness with it forceful strength, beginning with Cain's fratricide.

Between Adam and Eve there seems to exist a bond of solidarity, which leads them to decide on and carry out the sinful act together. But, as soon as Adam feels challenged and questioned about his behavior, he feels the need to defend himself. The rationale of defense becomes the root and means of self-justification. In order to defend himself, God and the woman are at the same time declared enemies. The woman you gave me is the cause of all that has happened. You and the woman you gave me, you have made me thus (cfr. *Gen* 3:12). Defense suddenly becomes animosity, which does not hesitate to strike: attributing the fault to the woman is to demand that she should pay.

These are precisely the historical consequences of sin. It is the contemporary rupture of communion with God and between people. With sin there enters into humanity's history a divided life, which in the account stands out particularly in contrast to what was narrated before. The result of creation is the garden, the place adapted for the life of human beings, the place in which people (men and women, the couple, humanity) can live together their relationship with the earth, cultivating it. Their humanity, in this life on the gifted earth, is continually accompanied by the presence of God who speaks to them and can be heard and can receive answers. With sin the earth is no longer the garden. With harmony with God and between people broken, the relationship with the earth will be a relationship of dominion, a relationship guided by the rationale of possession of the earth and defense of one person from another.

The text of *Genesis* goes on to show how that brings forth the fruits of death. Beginning with the symbolic fratricide, the work of Cain, people live dividing and fighting between themselves. Humanity lives in sin and division. A story is produced in which people, instead of living according to their nature, that is, according to the intentionality of the creator, want to place themselves in control of themselves and in control of their history. And therefore it is a violent story.

2 *The gift of fraternity*

Fraternity, as a figure or paradigm of communion on earth, is presented in the Bible as a gift of God. It belongs to the act of the creator and the creative intentionality. It therefore belongs to the very nature of humankind; it is that which constitutes a person (cfr. *Gen* 2) as someone made capable of recognizing him/herself in such fraternity. The word of God, his will, and his commandments express themselves in all the ways capable of arousing in people an awareness of their own personal stature and the task of realizing it within the framework of relationship.

The presence of the other person is a gifted opportunity of personal existence: in the gift of the other is the gift of the creator God. But this gift must be recognized and welcomed. Even in the face of disregard and non-acceptance, the word of God continues to indicate the meaning of life, saying that it is possible.

Genesis 4 presents a farmer and a shepherd. Each has his sphere of life. In this land that is no longer the «garden»; the division of trades seems like the division of the «vital territory». Each is defined by what he does. But this definition still does not indicate who the human being is. To determine who Cain is, it is not enough to speak about his relationship to the land and to animals. That would present the image of a person as a *homo faber*, someone who constructs one's own life through realizing the opportunities offered by his/her world. Personal life, with the totality of individual decisions, would seem then to be somewhat like proceeding along the path of free self-expansion.

As long as the person-to-person relationship is not considered in its specific value, each reality that actually appears on a person's horizon is a reality that is offered to his/her free disposal. «Keeper of flocks» is a relationship of dominion, a practical ability, an exploitable relationship; but this is not sufficient to explain the person.

A new relationship issue is raised when the object of a relationship is a personal subject. Then it is a matter of a «you», which with his/her subjectivity walks alongside in the world. That other has his/her way of understanding and taking one's bearings, his/her horizon of evaluation and planning. He/she does not offer him/herself as a tool. With his/her inherent subjectivity and freedom, he/she refutes every possible pretense at dominion over him/her and the possibility of simply being integrated inside someone else's horizon of understanding and decision-making.

The person I meet does not accept being functionally integrated into my plans. He/she resists the presumption of being commanded. This shows me the impossibility of directing someone else's subjectivity toward the planning of my own existence, as if it were a useful relationship, one to be used. I cannot give that person the name that I wish. In the encounter with a living subjectivity, his/her *interpretive* being already belongs to his/her presenting him/herself as subject. Each of the two presences is an affirmation of meaning, is a proposal of a universe of values. This means that to each is given someone else's life, interpreting, valuing and planning. To each is offered the possibility of assuming the interpretive being of the other. It is the opportunity to re-qualify one's own horizon of understanding and evaluation with the help that comes from the interpretation of someone else. It is the opportunity to perceive and build one's own life with the collaboration of the life of someone else.

The appearance of the «you» on Adam's horizon with the creation of Eve (*Gen* 2:21-23) is this experience of radical novelty in his being finally «with someone», a reality understood and assumed as *the gift* that comes to his life from the life *of the other person* beside him. The level of his own personal life is qualified by the fact that he has the opportunity of a relationship in which the subject not only speaks a meaningful word, but also receives a meaningful response. Thus the relationship to the world is not entrusted to his own solitary interpretation and activity, but rather entrusted to a reality of response. That also means that in all human activity in the world there is present a call to *respond*.

The otherness of a subject specifically suggests a dialogical relationship. His/her being present on my horizon of understanding is an *original* way of being present, precisely due to the claim of providing me with meaning. I am appointed his/her interpreter. There is a reality of *word* that reaches me and that I return to him/her, a relational reciprocity, both being interpreters and interpreting. Choosing the manner in which to implement the relationship, both state the significance of the other, beginning with oneself and the significance of self as coming from the other. Decision-making cannot escape the presence of the other person. Decision-making (the choice of a relationship) is, however, affirmation of the meaning that one wishes to give to the being of the other; it is response to his/her presence, even when it is a relationship of exclusion.

The reality of taking part in a conversation, constitutive of the interpersonal relationship, is necessarily a relationship of reciprocity. His/her presence says something about me, about the meaning of my life, on the basis of my telling him/her something about his/her significance.

If from within myself I can state that my relationship with the other person is good, it is because I recognize his/her confirmation (response) of the meaning I acknowledge of him/her. And this is not because the other vocalizes it, but because in the meaningful word that I pronounce, in deciding on the relationship, at the same time I state what is the essence of the person and his/her being, both his/hers and mine. I explain my meaning in affirming his/hers. I refute my meaning in refuting his/hers. I state or refute my personal being in accepting or denying the personal being of the other. It is negation of his/her personal being if I desire that person to be simply an available reality, arbitrarily directing it toward my own life. However, in doing so, one also affirms oneself as constituted by the relationship to things and not as people in a person-to-person relationship. Thus, it would be to refute the specific gift that comes from the presence of another subject. It would refute the level of being person, which is given by virtue of interpersonal relationships. The meaning of the non-availability of the other person is not only, or primarily, in an experience of boundaries, but rather in the experience of the gift offered by his/her presence: a gift that can only be truly so if welcomed as such in the specificity of its offering.

The presence of the other person, offering him/herself to the reality of the free relationship and taking part in a conversation, suggests a meaning of life that is life as person-to-person, life by virtue of a relationship of word given and word welcomed, by virtue of a relationship that is a giving over to the presence of the other person and acceptance of his/her presence. The request or need that the other suggests through his/her being is a human life in the world (from understanding up to decision-making), not in the manner of solitary individuals in the middle of things and dominating things, but rather in the manner of people who understand and plan their own lives fundamentally understood as interpersonal. It is about re-qualifying and re-defining one's own horizon of understanding, planning and decision-making.

It is a matter of perceiving life on earth, understanding and deciding concrete relationships in this world as *our* life and not *my* life. The value proposal that arises from the encounter with a «you» is not simply one of many values, that is, one of the many relational possibilities that everyone evaluates, interprets and assumes in the order of their own being. Rather, it is the value of being with others in recognizing and assuming meanings and values in this world. In other words, the «you» is not suggested to me as an object of my possible decisions, but as co-subject of my understanding and decision-making. The truth of deciding about myself faced with another person, the truth of the relationship I establish with him/her lies in this assumption of co-subjectivity (interpersonality) as an interpretive reference point for all that I value on the earth, for all that I can arrange in a project of humanity and personal human fulfillment.

In the field of moral experience, the encounter with the other person thus suggests a reality that can re-qualify the global meaning of one's own life, from the depths of the innermost being to its concrete expression. It is the reality of reciprocity and recognition. It is the original locus of responsibility and therefore the original locus of morality.

In the internal unity of conscious and free responsibility the experience of moral conscience matures and it expresses itself in the judgment of goodness or malice, a judgment that stems from the quality of the relationship established with the other person, that is, an assumption of responsibility for the life and freedom of the other (goodness), or arbitrary decisions that do not take his/her presence into account (malice). Arbitrary freedom is precisely the freedom of the one who makes him/herself «arbiter» and not «responsible».

3

The risk of fraternity (failure)

When fraternity becomes demarcated, when partial solidarity is established, in reality the claim is that it is done as an extension of the search and defense of self. The result is an apparent fraternity that builds animosity. This is true also for fraternity taken as rightful and a foregone conclusion, fraternity aspired to or vindicated on the basis of belonging or «rights». Experienced within defined boundaries, it sanctions them and justifies enmity. But the arbitrariness of the boundary becomes arbitrariness in moving the boundary according to one's own will. One decides at will who is the brother, or what is due to the brother. «Am I my brother's guardian?» (*Gen* 4:9).

We are rightly accustomed to conceiving personal freedom as belonging to every person, because it is foundational to the essence of person. But at the same time we are inclined to understand it as if it were possible and sensible to start from the subject and consider just the subject as an individual. We say that freedom is a human right, but often discussion about human rights is limited to the individual aspect. Thus, one runs the risk of speaking about responsibility as an exercise of freedom in which it is also necessary to respect the rules in order to preserve one's own individual liberty.

The fact that rules are needed for human co-existence is beyond doubt, since it is part of being in a socially structured life. It is important, however, to know what basis we give to the very significance of personal freedom. If one says that the liberty of each person has limits placed on it by someone else's liberty, one could mean by that (as is often the case) that per se personal liberty can be defined without comparing it with the reality of the encounter with the other person. The encounter with the other would suggest simply adaptations, necessary so that the exercise of each person's liberty might be guaranteed. The subject would thus be defined in the essence of his/her being person, beginning with his/her subjectivity and not interpersonality. But we would then be describing that arbitrary subject who is defined by his/her relationship with things. It is as if by his/her nature he/she is master of the world, and only afterwards, and therefore in an extrinsic way, finds him/herself having to accept a requirement (more correctly, a constraint) on the basis of the need for co-existence, as if to say *unfortunately there are others and they need to be taken into account.*

The presumption of arbitrarily understood subjectivity emerges also from the experience of sin in *Gen* 2-3. It is the arbitrary freedom of the person who wants to give a name to everything *and everyone*. It is the presumption of declaring that good is good because I say that it is, without having «to answer» to or about anyone. It is the desire to make oneself arbiter of good and evil. With this pretense, with this rationale of subjectivity identified with the essence of the person (since the person would be completely defined starting from the individuality of his being subject), the other is necessarily a rival. He/she is the one whom it is necessary to take into account in order to survive, in the face of whom one is forced to try to harmonize one's own plans with extraneous plans.

Consistent with this way of reasoning is the rationale of defense, possession and death (of «killing»). From the outset the other person, the competitor, is basically an enemy from whom one has to defend oneself, both in a direct relationship and in an indirect one that comes about through the use of the goods of the earth.

It is possible to have a concept of morality based on an individualistic interpretation of subjectivity, as if the person can be defined completely beginning only with his/her being a single, individual subject. Morality would then consist in respecting the same right to subjectivity for everyone. It would be rather like a pact between people, which on a moral basis could be expressed thus: since there are other people, each person must respect the rights of others in the same way that he/she demands that his/her rights be respected. To determine a code of behavior and respect, it would be the responsibility of each person to ensure the possibility of pursuing one's own plan, within the limits of the given situations.

However, on the basis of an understanding of people as necessarily enemies between themselves, the best result that one can hope for is that they establish pacts of non-invasion and agreements to not kill each other. It is true that, if then one also succeeds in «useful» cooperation, so much the better, but fundamentally each person will keep his/her eyes on the other, knowing that he/she must defend him/herself and hope that this might be possible without too much cost and to great benefit. Would this be morality? This way of looking at the other person is precisely the fundamental problem. Even if one could construct a highly refined and internally consistent «rational» ethic, but on the basis of the presupposition that the subject, individually and beginning with him/herself, can determine the entire meaning of his/her life and can plan it, the result would already be an expression of what we correctly call «sin».

One does not kill only with the sword, but also by asserting that the meaning of someone else's life is functional in relation to one's own life. To accept the other at a functional level does not necessarily mean that at every moment one is attempting to use him/her with a view to one's own ends. It means, however, that one accepts or rejects him/her under certain conditions, that is, on the basis of his/her submitting or not to one's own plans. The ways of relating to the other person will, however, be determined in view of that person's being useful to, serving (or at least not being a risk to) one's own previously determined life plan. This means stating that the other person is worth as much only as he/she is useful. In fact, presence that constitutes a risk or an obstacle is rejected. The relationship to the other would, however, be understood as exploitable for one's own ends.

In this sense, it must be said that any mode of acceptance conditioned by the other is not acceptance, but rather an attempt to make him/her an instrument, that is, insofar as it depends on me, you do not exist as a person, but only as a possible instrument in my life. As noted above, on the contrary, the presence of another as such makes possible and demands that the universe of understanding and planning be qualified and defined beginning with the acceptance of his/her otherness. This means desiring that the world be the world *of people* and not *my* world, in which people also exist.

The experience of the encounter radically raises the issue of freedom as a call to make oneself responsible, which in some manner always means «giving oneself over to the other person», as true acceptance of the other as person, without any reservations about him/her and without privileging oneself. The way in which we often justify *conditional* acceptance is, in fact, linked to the fear that the other's freedom can be an enemy of mine, that the life of the other can be an enemy of my own. The person in his/her freedom to understand by understanding him/herself, to plan by planning, to decide by decision-making, is implicated by the presence of the other in the search for what is best for one's own life.

Thus, the alternative is set up between two opposite rationales, that of the gift and that of denial. The first implies that freedom makes itself responsible by freeing the other by making of one's life a presence that makes possible the life of someone else. The second, instead, usually plays on the conditional acceptance of the other person: if you do no harm, if you seek my good, then I will accept you. In other words, you must enter into my plan in my way or otherwise I have no choice but to reject you. Such an attitude is arbitrary in that I declare myself judge and origin of the legitimacy of my judgment about the right or non-right, dignity or non-dignity of the other person, and therefore about his/her presence.

The moral experience suggests a radical requirement through the rationale of the unconditional gift. Opposed to it is the fear of being exposed to the risk of succumbing or being exploited. In fact there appears to be a widespread and strong pre-understanding of self and the other person that tends to legitimize the fear of losing one's own life.

Regarding this objection one can note that the placing of prior conditions on the acceptance of the other person always bears fruits of violence. Throughout history the assertion of dominion over the other, by an individual or a social group, has never been motivated by the need to defend oneself or to secure one's own life against the possible superiority of the other. Conditional acceptance, made with reservations, means always instituting (if it's not already there) or radicalizing (if it is there) a rationale of violence; and the pretense that with this rationale one can build fraternity has no foundation.

When we speak of Christian conscience, or love of neighbor even so far as to love one's enemies, or of the radical nature of the gospel or discipleship of the Lord, we are speaking about a reality that is at the root of people's lives and feeling, understanding, and evaluating. At issue is the *human* interpretation of morality itself. The *Christian* interpretation of morality needs to be built on the basis of a correct and not reductive understanding of that which is human.

These interpretive elements about conscience, freedom and personal responsibility have their own strength in structuring ethical discourse; that is, they are at work in all the thinking that we do about moral values. One could understand the meaning, value and dignity of freedom, beginning with a «definition» of person that identifies the person with the individual. But with such an understanding, all that belongs to the commandment, to the ethical need however it may be formulated, would in fact be radically understood as constraint of freedom.

One could reason on the basis of the freedom and dignity of the person, saying that a value is morally important and normative when it serves the true realization of the human being, while at the same time understanding that the value of freedom, per se, would be that of the free personal growth of the subject searching for him/herself, beginning with him/herself. If that were the case, one would have to conclude that everything that presents itself as a requirement or moral norm, since it implies objectively a limit to the free growth of the subject, in reality is against the subject and damages personal freedom.

Where is your brother? In that he depends on you, what have you done for him? Have you made him your brother? Who are you? Have you been a brother?

In this story we know that the premise for our work is not the communion already established and to be safeguarded. In a story of animosity and division it is about creating opportunities for communion. The faith traditions (Old and New Testament) recall the presence of God who always and again makes possible and asks for fraternal communion, in communion with him. At the same time, the same traditions recall and indicate in this gift of God the possibility of understanding and assuming the task of fraternity as fulfillment of one's own personal existence in history. The intentionality of communion supports and explains God's activity in all his interventions, from the creative word to the word made flesh, from the Mosaic covenant to the new covenant in Jesus Christ. His intentionality makes people capable of communion and re-forms them as such from their condition as sinners. God asks human beings to recognize the intentionality of his work and to take it on in their own work, in free responsibility.

Even to Cain God still speaks. He invokes his conscience, stimulates his intelligence, calls for reflection, asks that meaning and values be recognized, and that life and conduct be ordered rationally.

The Christian, beginning with the specific gift of explicit faith, from the gifted experience of conscious communion with God in Jesus Christ, will remember the undertaking of a love like that of Christ. For the Christian, too, and precisely in order not to misunderstand such a task, it is a matter of putting into operation the criteria of choice suggested by the figure of humanity of the Good Samaritan in the Lucan parable (*Luke* 10:25-37). We see that it is a matter of recognizing the good that is truly possible and doing it because it is good. It can be recognized by looking at the objective conditions of the other and examining one's own objective opportunities. Genuine personal freedom must «respond» to the presence of someone else, becoming responsible for his/her life and good inasmuch as one truly can. It is becoming a neighbor that creates closeness; it is freedom that liberates; and it is responsibility that welcomes the human and gives him/her a face in history.

Chapter 3

The ethics of the beatitudes

BASTIANEL S., «Un'etica delle beatitudini per la cultura contemporanea», in COMPAGNONI F., PRIVITERA S., EDD., *Vita morale e beatitudini. Sacra Scrittura, storia, teoretica, esperienza*, (Teologia morale. Studi e testi 8), Edizioni San Paolo, Cinisello Balsamo 2000, 182-207.

The message of the beatitudes, as they resound in the Matthean version of the Sermon on the Mount (*Matt* 5-7) and in the Lucan version of the Discourse on the Plain (*Luke* 6:20-49), finds its context of meaning precisely in the biblical traditions, a context of faith; that is, in the kingdom of God that is fulfilled in Jesus Christ.

This new reality, which is realized in the history of humanity, is absolutely the Lord's gift[1]. The beatitudes proclaim the sovereignty of God as a present reality, not just a future expectation, and a decision that God makes in his total freedom, with a gratuitousness unconditioned by human initiative: *the Lord has decided on the salvation of humankind and is carrying it out here and now.* In the words and actions of Jesus of Nazareth this proclamation as good news reaches the poor, the marginalized, and the excluded. They are blessed because, if on their shoulders weighs the sin of humanity that makes them poor, through the sovereignty of God present they will be the first to be relieved of their condition; their lives are blessed because they are in the hands of God who loves and saves[2].

This same context of faith interprets the history of people and the *meaning* of being human. The message is not only for those *belonging* to the Judaeo-Christian faith traditions; rather, it is founded on God's working for the salvation of humankind and calls for taking on in one's own free responsibility, in the concreteness of history, the very intentionality of the Lord. What corresponds to his word and his gratuitous action is proposed as a «beatitude» of existence,

1 Old and more recent studies have strongly emphasized the fact that the beatitudes should not be understood as simply a moral exhortation, but rather as proclamation of a *kerygma.* That proclamation is not about highlighting the conditions to enter and be part of the kingdom, but rather it is the proclamation of the gospel of grace that is absolutely and disproportionately the fruit of God's initiative and that wants to develop in the existence of those who knew Jesus and recognized in him the saving presence of God. As an expression of the gifted reality of God's sovereignty in the historical existence of humanity, of each person, the whole of Jesus' discourse in which the beatitudes are placed assumes the value of an essential reference point of meaning and life for every generation that understands itself in relation to Christ, beginning with him. On the origin and the material of the Lucan discourse (closer, it seems, to the original tradition) and that of Matthew, and above all on their significance, see, in addition to the commentaries relating to the text in the versions, the ever-valid monographs of DUPONT J., *Le Beatitudini, 1.2,* Edizioni Paoline, Rome 1972, 1977 and of MERKLEIN H., *Die Gottesherrschaft als Handlungsprinzip. Untersuchung zur Ethik Jesu,* Echter, Würzburg 1978, and the studies of KERTELGE K., ED., *Ethik im Neuen Testament,* Herder, Freiburg-Basel-Wien 1984, 50-118; MESTERS C., *La Parola dietro le parole,* Queriniana, Brescia 1975; SCHNACKENBURG R., *The Moral Teaching of the New Testament,* 1, *Jesus' Moral Demands,* Burns & Oates, London 1965, with the bibliography indicated; SCHOTTROFF L., STEGEMANN W., *Jesus and the Hope of the Poor,* trans. Matthew J. O'Connell, Orbis, Maryknoll, NY., 1986; THEISSEN G., *Sociology of Early Palestinian Christianity,* trans. J. Bowden, Fortress Press, Philadelphia 1978.

2 Cfr. MESTERS C., *God, Where Are You?,* Wipf & Stock Publishers, Eugene OR 2003.

as a path for the fulfillment for humanity's history. From it comes an indication about the very identity of Christians, in their interpretation of the present story and living it as people of the kingdom of God, who know the beatitudes[3].

Not through a perspective of self-improvement, but through this perspective of reflected awareness of God's saving love, experienced and recognized in the reality of human circumstances and experiences, does it make sense to speak about an ethic of the beatitudes for contemporary culture. This will begin with two series of questions: To whom and how were the beatitudes proclaimed? To whom and how was this proclamation and the one who made it remembered? In other words: What happened in the story of humanity when the beatitudes were proclaimed and remembered? What happened in people's lives on earth under the profile of ethical questions, that is, from the point of view of the exercise of free and conscious responsibility?

We know that through the term «beatitudes» reference is being made to Jesus' proclamation. We know the texts well. But the questions become: How did Jesus live on earth? What impact did his concrete existence and his word have on the culture surrounding him, on the ways of thinking and life styles present in his environment? We also know that the texts we read were formed by virtue of the testimony of those who lived with Jesus, his disciples. But those, who remembered the words of Jesus, when and how did they understand this «blessed», and the person who said it, in relation to their culture? How did those disciples live in relation to the beatitudes and to Jesus[4]?

These questions cannot remain simply in the background if we wish to understand the meaning of the beatitudes and their centrality for our ethical discernment as believers today.

3 Cfr. BASTIANEL S., «Conversione e sequela nel Nuovo Testamento. La "Magna Carta" del discepolo», in LORENZANI M., ED., *La morale nella Bibbia*, Edizioni ISSRA, L'Aquila 1996, 67-81; SCHNACKENBURG R., *The Moral Teaching of the New Testament*, 1, *Jesus' Moral Demands*, Burns & Oates, London 1965.

4 On the lifestyle of Jesus' disciples in relation to their culture, see the recent study by the brothers STEGEMANN E., STEGEMANN W., *The Jesus Movement: A Social History of its First Century*, Fortress Press, Philadelphia 1999, 169-417.

1
Jesus and the contemporary way of thinking

At the beginning of Mark's gospel we find a concise recapitulatory formula of the preaching of Jesus: «The time has come and the kingdom of God is close at hand. Repent, and believe the Good News» (*Mark* 1:15). The word is clear: The reality of the kingdom of God is present. Change minds and hearts and entrust yourselves to God who loves and saves. Believe in this gospel.

Why change minds and hearts in order to entrust oneself to the gospel, to take seriously the proclaimed word of salvation? And who has to convert? Just some people or everyone? From what is said to us it seems that it is not just some. «Repent and believe» is said to everyone: to the public sinner and the holy faithful, to the one who does not justify his/her sin, to the one who looks for justification in his/her presumed justice, to the one who is a long way off, and to the one who is more well-known to Jesus. A number of times in the gospel accounts it emerges that even those closest to Jesus —his disciples— need to change minds and hearts. Even Peter, the disciple who is spoken about more than the others, is someone for whom entrusting himself to Jesus and his word means not just following and listening to him, but changing his own way of understanding, evaluating, interpreting the true story and the choices to be made[5].

We can ask ourselves what reaction the beatitudes aroused in Jesus' hearers. Presumably they sounded a bit strange, even to those expecting the kingdom of God. We calmly state that this message must have seemed almost paradoxical to those who heard it, in reference to the reality of things and because it was suggesting an upheaval of the framework of values usually shared[6]. But, if this had happened, obviously it would be because the contemporary way of thinking at the time of Jesus was already not consistent with the beatitudes.

In addition, the resistance encountered in the face of this proclamation was the same as that provoked by Jesus' way of life. Both the gospels of Matthew and Luke, just before presenting us with the discourse of the beatitudes, give us a

5 Cfr. BASTIANEL S., «Conversione», in COMPAGNONI F., PIANA G., PRIVITERA S., EDD., *Nuovo Dizionario di Teologia Morale*, Edizioni Paoline, Cinisello Balsamo 1990, 153-154.

6 One often hears talk of an «alternative world» in regard to Jesus' programmatic discourse. Cfr. STEGEMANN E., STEGEMANN W., *The Jesus Movement: A Social History of its First Century*, Fortress Press, Philadelphia 1999, 357-358.

glimpse in the account of Jesus' temptation, presented in the style of a dramatic narrative (*Matt* 4:1-11; *Luke* 4:1-13), of what represents a place of resistance to the word of God, a place of scandal in the face of the model of human existence that Jesus suggests[7]. In the context of the desert and the time of prayer, what stands out with particular intensity is the contrast between Jesus' transparent intentionality and the hostile test to which he is subjected. But the questions, there posed in that way, actually seem to suggest that they are the same ones that Jesus hears being suggested every day of his life by his own environment, right up to the point when he breathed his last on the cross. It is not a matter of open incitement to dishonesty or imprudent egoism, as, for example, would be the advice to enrich oneself at all costs to the prejudice of others.

The proposals put to Jesus, and observed by him as «temptations» in his humanity, are instead understandable in their significance and their apparent «logical» plausibility beginning with what the disciples felt, too. The gospels tell us that these men struggled to understand that adversaries do not have to be thwarted and annihilated. They are unable to understand why Jesus does not defend himself and does not ask to be defended, faced with those who are taking advantage of his disposition in order to ruin him, and faced with the discourse Jesus gives on the necessity of his passion and death, they remain perplexed and bewildered. They believe in Jesus; they are ready to trust in him, but they struggle to understand a salvation that in Jesus is not asserted by means of the reckoning of this earth or the power of the potentates of this world. They struggle to such an extent that, in fact, Jesus is called to one side by one of them and reprimanded just after having prophesied his imminent Passion: «Jesus said all this quite openly», writes Mark, «then, Peter, taking him aside, started to remonstrate with him» (*Mark* 8:32).

Not only those who are far off, but even Peter thought that Jesus was making a mistake, that he should not talk in that way, that he was a bit naïve to say the things he was saying and to expose his humanity in that way. How could he speak about the humiliation of the Messiah? Hadn't he learned from his faith traditions that the Messiah would defeat all his enemies? Just as in the desert, so on the road to Caesarea, even on scriptural grounds Jesus is reminded that what he is saying is wrong and the choices he is making are wrong.

7 Cfr. BASTIANEL S., *Vita morale nella fede in Gesù Cristo*, San Paolo, Cinisello Balsamo 2005, 114-118.

For the contemporary mindset at the time of Jesus, for the ethical, social, religious culture of his environment, by virtue of the expectations reinforced by the way of interpreting the same tradition of faith, there is something scandalous in what Jesus says and the way he freely chooses to live. It is the fact that *the just dies for being just.*

For us it is the same. The scandal is in thinking that the person who lives a virtuous life has no reward, cannot be truly happy on this earth, and cannot be blessed. And this, together with the no less scandalous fact (even if at times unfortunately the risk is that it concerns us less) that even today the overpowering strength of unjust structures and the historic efficacy of evil, continue to create poor, martyred, marginalized, persons and peoples deprived of fundamental human rights.

The scandal that Jesus' way of life and words causes does not lie simply in the proposal to lead a virtuous life that draws its strength from the principle of a previously shared reciprocity. How could a personal and social life that is based on a free interpersonal relationship not appear convenient, if the value of making oneself mutually responsible for each other was recognized and shared by everyone on this earth? How could the invitation to recognize the value of the «you» in the objectivity of his/her placing him/herself as autonomous subject not appear useful if people were certain of being recognized in turn in their proper dignity and meaning? The scandal of Jesus' life, which fundamentally is the same scandal of the authentic moral life, is provoked by his word and his life of *gratuitous* acceptance, because that means *unconditional acceptance*, that is, without any previous guarantee of being accepted and respected[8].

If on this earth one accepts the other person without being concerned about setting guarantees depending on self-defense, does not one run the risk of losing one's own life? The rationale of defense stems from this fear of losing and losing oneself—a fear that certainly cannot be explained without the effective yielding of the abuse of power of the strong over the weak in this world, but that, at heart, becomes itself food for scandal and an obstacle to the truth of human relations. Because of that fear, in fact, that worldly criterion, which insinuates itself like a temptation, tends to justify itself and appear plausible, «logi-

8 On the encounter with the «other» as primary opportunity of morality and on the application of gratuitous giving over of self as the meaning and measure of the ethical need, see BASTIANEL S., *Autonomia morale del credente. Senso e motivazioni di un'attuale tendenza teologica*, Morcelliana, Brescia 1980; RIZZI A., *Crisi e ricostruzione della morale*, SEI, Turin 1992.

cal». It implies that one can live on this earth, that one can realize something good, which genuinely means something, only if one goes through the «necessary» imposing of oneself on others with the inability to give respect to those who don't count and the ability to satisfy oneself in the face of the other person. Moreover, this way of reading reality is actually considered as human by virtue of such plausibility, reaching the pretense of indicating what living the virtuous life on this earth means, which is that one is «wise» when one responds to the other person only on condition, that is, with guarantees of a prior acceptance on the part of the other. Naturally, by that, and we will not be sincere without stating it explicitly, one means a criterion of *human* and a criterion of *prudence* founded, in fact, on the prior guarantee of self, that is, on the privilege and defense of ourselves.

When, therefore, according to this rationale, we read «blessed are the poor», «blessed are you poor», is it not strange that we ask ourselves, in a rather perplexed manner, what is being suggested to us with this phrase? Do we perhaps need to leap from the understandable to the incomprehensible, from a plausible rationale on this earth to a real and true paradox, from conscious common sense to a voluntaristic endeavor? With what courage can we read the beatitudes proclaimed and lived by Jesus saying at the end «This is the word of the Lord» if, after all, that word is scandalous for us? And then, how can we explain to the objectively marginalized what we mean when we say «you are blessed»?

2
The experience of the disciples

The proposition of Jesus' good news does not seem to imply renunciation of the conscious realization of self on the part of the human being, nor some sort of voluntarist asceticism accustomed to mortification. This we can state with assurance, remembering exactly the disciples' experience. These were men who, right up to the unique and great institution of the Eucharist, and still immediately afterwards, were capable of arguing about who counted the most and who the least, about which of them was the greatest (cfr. *Luke* 22:24-27). Therefore, how will these disciples remember the beatitudes pronounced by Jesus and all those words that are so similar to them? What happened?

These people nearest to him saw that the salvation of Jesus of Nazareth—in a manner that was different from how they thought and valued, different from what they held to be most clear in their interpretation of faith—was not asserted through power, victory over the enemy, or self-affirmation. Present at the words and actions of Jesus, the disciples were accustomed to seeing him meet those who opposed him, without annihilating them and without «shouting out, or breaking the bruised reed» (cfr. *Isa* 42:2-3). It was this way up to the moment of the passion, when his enemies, instead of being annihilated, were in fact put in a situation of taking advantage of his not defending himself, right up to the cross. The Messiah the disciples had encountered in Jesus of Nazareth was not, therefore, what they had thought he would be; his way of living on earth was not what they had imagined.

Faced with the arrest of Jesus, when their master was taken and events accelerated, it is not difficult to understand how these people felt themselves to be plunging downwards headlong. That question about «the greatest», asked shortly before, gave way when faced with the dismay, emptiness, and bitterness at not having understood and supported him. The death of Jesus thus signified their death, too.

With the death of this Jesus, the disciples died to their expectations, plans and certainties. This means, however, that they had expectations in which the worldly, sinful dimension, rooted in a rationale of power and a way of thinking so far away from that of the Lord, had reached the point of interpreting the significance of their very vocation, their very role as people called by Jesus and sent by him. With the death of Jesus they experienced death; they saw him condemned, crucified, dead, and buried. However, this was not the last word of their life, their actual living, because that crucified and buried master they then met alive, beyond death and their failure, and they were helped to understand the existence on earth of this Jesus of Nazareth whom they loved, in whom they had believed, and whom they had sincerely followed in their own way.

In the encounter with the living Christ the disciples were helped to remember Jesus, his human existence on this earth, his relationship with them, and to understand the full meaning of his life and the real meaning of their discipleship. They understood that Jesus' surrendering of himself did not begin with his final giving over to death, but corresponded to the lived intentionality in the unity of his life. They understood that their entrusting themselves to him was sensible. It was not mere ambition; it was not a mistake. And so they were able to recognize in him the Lord, the *Kyrios*, the Savior. Beginning with this recognition that God's plan was truly fulfilled in a man, his Son who on earth had lived thus, had spoken thus, had died in this way, they were able to understand the meaning of a beatitude.

What does it mean to understand the proclamation of Jesus, to *understand* the meaning of beatitude? As long as Peter saw only humiliation in Jesus' giving himself over, he was unable to understand. As long as any disciple, who even knew Jesus, thinks that someone who is killed is necessarily a failure, he/she will not be able to understand the meaning of that «blessed are you», you who weep, you who are persecuted with him or for him. When in this Jesus of Nazareth the disciples *recognized* the Lord, when they were able to *understand* that Jesus' *human* existence on earth, in the way in which he lived it, was completely fulfilled, only then were they able to *understand* the evangelical word thoroughly. We cannot skip over this passage, because it is about being able to see that the very existence of Jesus of Nazareth shows the way of living in a fulfilled, completely human manner on the earth.

Moreover, believers recognize that in Jesus the fulfillment of human living is possible for human beings. We must not forget how much the gospels convey this message to us. In comparison with the one who reconfirms the tempting rationale of the worldly mentality, saying to Jesus, «If you are the king of the Jews, save yourself!» (*Luke* 23:37), the evangelist Luke places exactly at the crucial hour of Jesus' death the image of a different human way of looking at and understanding Jesus and one's own life. There is a man crucified next to Jesus, someone who is not just, not godly, but whom everyone has recognized as a wrongdoer, and even he recognizes it. He entrusts himself to Jesus even as far as saying, «Remember me when you come into your kingdom» (*Luke* 23:42). He did not have the explanations of the disciples, and we are not told if he had known Jesus for some time. Yet it seems that God speaks to him factually through what is happening to Jesus and in words that seem to be scandalous to many people. Luke tells us of this man's reaction of conversion and faith. In Jesus he does not see a scandal, but rather the reality of the sovereignty of God, finally come down to this earth[9].

9 On the conversion of the good thief crucified next to Jesus, cfr. ABIGNENTE D., *Conversione morale nella fede. Una riflessione etico-teologica a partire da figure di conversione del vangelo di Luca*, Gregorian University Press-Morcelliana, Rome-Brescia 2000, 87-104.

We know Jesus' reply to him: «Today you will be with me in paradise» (*Luke* 23:43), a reply of confirmation and consolation announcing the reality of a relationship with him that will never end. Exegetes recall that this expression, in all probability, is used here deliberately by the evangelist. The extraordinary repetition of the Greek term *paradeísos* would be, in fact, the LXX translation of the term *gan,* which indicated the garden in the account of *Gen* 2-3. The life of communion that corresponds to the original intentionality of God has become possible now, through Jesus, on the part of humanity, on the part of sinners.

3
The new covenant in Jesus

The wrongdoer confesses Jesus as true Lord even before his resurrection. In Jesus, in his human way of living and dying, he recognizes the complete accomplishment of God's plan and encounters salvation, according to that long-expected promise mediated by his tradition of faith. The proclamation of the beatitudes, likewise, should be understood in this context of God's intentionality expressed in his creating, revealing word, which is made flesh in our human history.

At the origin of the Yahwistic religious traditions, at the origin of the Old Testament religious traditions, there is the unity of the Exodus-Sinai event, the liberation from Egypt and the gift of the covenant. God's self-revelation in the concrete activity of the liberation of his people, making himself close to them and Savior, constitutes a unity with his self-revelation in calling this people to be a people of brothers and sisters, and making them capable of so being. We know that in the Israelite tradition everything is interpreted in the light of this foundational Exodus-Sinai event. The long and complex historic formation of such a tradition develops in reference to the understood experience of the Lord *speaking* and *acting*, in the personal affairs and history of the people, in a reality of liberation at the same time external and internal[10].

The knowledge of God who takes the side of the weak and the experience of a reciprocity that certainly knows the difference between the two partners in the relationship (God is creator of the relationship), but that nevertheless is true reciprocity and therefore will involve faithfulness, gradually nourish awareness

10 Cfr. AUZOU G., *Dalla servitù al servizio, Il libro dell'Esodo*, Edizioni Dehoniane, Bologna 1976; EICHRODT W., *Theology of the Old Testament,* 1, trans. J.A. Baker, SCM Press Ltd, London 1961.

of the Lord's free gift, of one's own identity, and history, and responsibility. Even the story of the fathers is re-read beginning with this historic experience of liberation, in the knowledge of being constituted in a loyal unity as people. God reveals himself liberating a people and asks this people to be so, that is, to become «his» people living as brothers and sisters, as a united family before him. The word that reveals God's action, that speaks of his intentionality and the purpose with which he works, is the word that asks that this plan, this purpose, this intentionality be assumed in conscious and free responsibility.

In this way is interpreted the future of the life and freedom of the people called by God to solidarity, and in this way is interpreted the origin, the meaning given to human life by virtue of the action of God the creator. The creating word makes humanity in communion with God and the human being is created as God's interlocutor, capable of listening to his word, of recognizing it as a creating word, and of responding. And he/she is created in communion with other human beings. The image of the human couple, as we know, provides the perspective of the personal life in the true sense that is realized in a fraternity of life, not Adam on his part, not the individual on his/her part, not an existence defined simply by its relationship with things (cfr. *Gen* 2:18-23)[11].

God's intentionality, from creation to liberation and to covenant, in the perspective of the *eschaton*, is therefore an intentionality of communion: communion with him and, in this communion with him, fraternal communion. This Word, this intentionality of God, is recognized by the continuity of his action. Here there seems to us to be an important reference providing the interpretive criterion, the meaning and the reality of the human being and what contradicts it, beginning with that reality which we call sin and which consumes itself precisely in breaking the relationship, as is recalled in so much of the Scriptures and in the account the book of Genesis already describes to us (*Gen* 3:1-19)[12].

11 On the interpretation of this text in reference to the moral newness of the encounter with the other person and with God, see BASTIANEL S., *Teologia morale fondamentale. Moralità personale, ethos, etica cristiana*, (for students' use), PUG, Rome 2005, 23-36. On the anthropological newness of the interpersonal relation, see BUBER M., «Io e Tu» in ID., *Il principio dialogico e altri saggi*, San Paolo, Cinisello Balsamo 1993, 59-146; MERLEAU-PONTY M., *Phenomenology of Perception*, trans. Colin Smith, Routledge & Keegan Paul, London 1962.

12 The text presents a theological interpretation of the story that has its origins in Israel's already lengthy experience as «people of God». The account of original sin and its consequences is placed in relation to the «before» of the creative intentionality (and then with the «after» of the redemptive intentionality). It responds to the need to explain the reality of a «hostile earth», injustice and violence, where such injustice and violence derive from falsified human relations and not from an inescapable negativity of human «nature». Cfr. BASTIANEL S., «"Dov'è?": la domanda di responsabilità», in *Servitium*, n. 110 (1997) 27-41.

The breakdown in communion begins when the image of God that one has within oneself begins to be one of suspicion: Who knows if it was really necessary for these things to be imposed on me? Who knows if it really is for my good? This breakdown is expressed in a reality of distance from God, in which the human person distances him/herself, hides, and, in a reality of defense from the other person, he accuses the other in order to save himself: «the woman you put with me» (*Gen* 3:12). The radical contradiction, the «breakdown» from the rationale of communion to a rationale of possession-defense, of self-guaranteeing, of self-sufficiency, of arbitrary freedom, does not involve just the interpretation of the relationship with God, but, at the same time and identically, both in terms of logic and meaning, the interpretation of the interhuman relationship. We well know that the third chapter of the book of Genesis reveals the story of division (cfr. *Gen* 4-11), in which the *gan*, the garden of the relationship, is no longer a garden. This not only because of the material hostility of the earth, but also because of the condition of the human reality as in fact it has become through that suffering inherent in the very rationale of division, which in turn creates division and possession, and mutually possession and division, so that in order to possess the earth, we separate and divide, right up to struggle and death.

These are stories we know because it is our story, too. Even when one doesn't speak about God, even when there is no religious interpretation, this story of division, struggle, murder, today could probably not be honestly recognized by anyone as the story of humanity, because its inhumanity seems obvious.

The solidarity that comes from God, and God's love for the people whom he creates in his own likeness, make them capable of gratuitousness and communion. God's creating word (not creating as an instant in time but as giving meaning and purpose to the human condition) remains, because he is faithful. The Lord continues to render people capable of goodness, capable of gratuitousness, capable of being creators of solidarity. However, the experience is that this human capacity is badly played out by human beings, and in the historical reality what appears to be dominant is not a capacity, but rather a profound incapacity to assume faithfulness to the covenant. Therefore there needs to be a new, decisive intervention from God, so radical as to overcome every precedent, an intervention made possible within humanity that is capable of generating within humanity a faithful response to God's action, consistent with his intentionality. It is what the disciples see happening in Jesus of Nazareth, in his way of being in full and transparent communion with the Father precisely in his being a neighbor to people, without waiting for the answer of reciprocity before surrendering himself. He is the Word made flesh; he is the new covenant, because his whole existence, from the beginning to the resurrection, is lived in a rationale of free communion on this earth.

One recalls that to Jesus it was suggested, not just by the tempter but by those close to him and those far from him with whom he came into contact, that he utilize the rules usually in force in worldly relations if one wants to succeed, be effective, and do something good on this earth. But the rules in force are those established by great shows of strength and impositions on the weak: those rules according to which it is necessary to make oneself the strongest of the strong in order to be capable of doing good, because good must be imposed and one's own desire for good, in order to be effective, must be imposed, too. Even salvation is thought of in this rationale of affirmation of strength, affirmation of power. Moreover, even before reaching the explicit suggestion of subjugation to the worldly sovereignty of the mighty, the first of the temptations proposes that Jesus intervene in the affairs and events of the earth using to his advantage his status as son of God, that is, that if you have opportunities that others do not have, if you have a role that others do not have, why not make them serve you above all?

But instead, «no». Jesus will not use his being son of God to escape from the human condition. The incarnation means precisely that God operates in communion between human beings in the manner proper to the condition of human beings, in the rationale of the human story. From such an assumption of united humanity without exception, can the story of humanity's faithful response to God begin.

This faithfulness led Jesus to condemnation and death; for this faithfulness he was led to the cross, because in a world in which the powerful are powerful, he who does not make himself strong, as Jesus did not make himself strong, is not vouched for in his offer of free closeness. It is not said that gratuitousness is met with gratuitousness, or that a person who does not use strength will not find the other person using it against him. And yet, from this faithfulness of the son of God on this earth the disciple, who has encountered him and lived in familiarity with him, discovers him/herself «changed within», that is living a «new life», also indicated with words such as «rebirth», «regeneration», and so on[13].

13 Terms that appear above all in the Pauline writings and that evoke the same experience as the apostle.

The disciple's newness of life and faith develops precisely with the recognition that this Jesus, who lived and died in this way, is not just living beyond death, but is the one who has made the disciple capable of life, of having a new mind and heart, capable of seeing, in this life thus gifted, the meaning of human life on the earth and the full meaning of one's own life. Recalling Jesus, the words and concrete ways of relationship that Jesus lived, the disciple can recognize in his/her very own experience the maturation of a reality of beatitude. *Jesus making himself a neighbor to him*, his patience, his care, his gestures, his repeated explanations, his reproaches, can basically be understood as opportunity given to be made capable of closeness. For the disciple to state that Jesus «made himself a neighbor» also means saying: «Jesus has made me be a neighbor, similar to him».

4
«Blessed are you»

The newness brought by the presence and preaching of Jesus, the newness brought by the message of the beatitudes, concerns the first and direct interlocutors of the gospel, that is, those disciples who were next to Jesus, but it also concerns the second and indirect interlocutors, that is, we who read the gospel[14]. The gifted reality of God's sovereignty, what God *does*, is in fact reality that demands to become *effective* on this earth through the intentionality of human beings. Every person who has known the gift of the Lord is called to be similarly a creator of closeness and communion, precisely by virtue of the communion given.

In this sense it should be said that the «Sermon on the Mount» (or «on the Plain»), of which the beatitudes form a part, should also be understood in its specifically normative moral value, that is, from the point of view of the demands it places on the conscience of believers. Even so we can ask ourselves: in what sense do we understand such *normativeness* for our life and our Christian morality? When we listen to these words do we think of the «beatitude» in the light of the «commandment» or the «commandment» in the light of the «beat-

14 Although there is a different point of view and communitarian concern in the Matthean and Lucan versions of the message of the beatitudes, it is possible to state that the discourse directly concerns the disciples of the historical Jesus as representatives and mediators of the wider and more diversified number of disciples of future generations. On this question see SCHÜRMANN H., *Il vangelo di Luca*, 1, Paideia, Brescia 1983, 531-534; SCHOTTROFF L., STEGEMANN W., *Jesus and the Hope of the Poor*, trans. Matthew J. O'Connell, Orbis, Maryknoll, NY., 1986, 118-124.

itude»[15]? This is not just a question of different shades of meaning. Instead, the question is about the very understanding of morality and the truth of our experience of faith. To grasp the importance of it we can again recall some figures from the gospel, for example that of the Samaritan (*Luke* 10:25-37), with the ethical model of interpreting existence suggested there, or the rich aristocrat (*Luke* 18:18-23) and the rich tax collector (*Luke* 19:1-10), with their different reactions to the encounter with Jesus. Considering these last two figures in particular, we ask ourselves: Where is the profound reason for this diversity? Why, faced with Jesus and his word, does the first go away while the second is converted?

The figure of the rich man appears with variations in the different synoptic accounts, even though in all of them we are presented with a person who effectively seems to have tried to live honestly according to his understanding of the commandments of the Torah[16]. Finding himself faced with the Master[17], he clearly expresses the intention of an answer of basically complete faith, and we must think that the intention is sincere. Precisely because he perceives this sincerity and recognizes the observance of the commandments affirmed by this man, Jesus tells him: the only thing that really counts, which you lack, is now possible for you; you can live with me, like me, on this earth[18].

15 The statement that the beatitudes are central to the preaching of Jesus, for their moral value, too, apparently seems unquestioned by textual scholars and by the theological and pastoral traditions of the Christian Churches. On this question, cfr. SCHNACKENBURG R., *The Moral Teaching of the New Testament, 1, Jesus' Moral Demands*, Burns & Oates, London 1965, 91-107. However, the truly *normative* character of this message is not always grasped with transparency with respect to other scriptural texts recognized for their morally binding character. For example, it is noted that some stipulations are paradoxical, others illustrative, others geared toward indicating an ideal of perfection. In this way, however, every attempt to recover the genuine ethical value of the text is compromised, due to a model of normativeness inspired by the legal model of the formulated norm, and so the conscience of believers is still left with the question: are we really convinced that «blessed are the poor» or «blessed are you who are poor» is morally binding for every disciple? Cfr. BASTIANEL S., «La normatività del testo biblico», in FERRARO S., ED., *Morale e coscienza storica. In dialogo con Josef Fuchs*, AVE, Rome 1988, 197-203.

16 Cfr. FUSCO V., *Povertà e sequela*. La pericope sinottica della chiamata del ricco (Mc 10,17-31 parr.), Paideia, Brescia 1991. One recalls that the figure of the rich man in his dialogue with Jesus appears at the beginning of the Encyclical *Veritatis Splendor*, as an argumentative starting point for the whole discourse. Cfr. GIOVANNI PAOLO II, *Veritatis Splendor, I fondamenti dell'insegnamento morale della Chiesa*, Piemme, Casale Monferrato (AL) 1993, nn.6-22.

17 Luke does not say how he found himself to be in front of Jesus. Matthew says he «came to him» (*Matt* 19:16) and Mark even says he «ran up, knelt before him and put this question to him» (*Mark* 10:17), as if to emphasize this man's initiative and searching.

18 Note that the Lucan passage, composed in a concentric manner, finds in Jesus' suggestion in v. 22 the center of meaning: to the «one thing» that this man lacks and that recalls the «God alone» of v.19, corresponds the «follow me» said by Jesus, to which later on corresponds the image of «making their way into the kingdom of God» (v. 24). Cfr. MEYNET R., *Il vangelo secondo Luca. Analisi retorica*, Edizioni Dehoniane, Rome 1994, 508-512. Also in this passage, therefore, atten-

What proposal can be more consoling than this? Does it not appear to be, on the part of Jesus, an offer of full and trustful communion, equivalent to that made to the closest disciples? And yet what this man understands is something completely different. He seems to notice only the fact that he has been asked to sell his goods and give everything to the poor and thinks that, therefore, in this way he has lost; Jesus' suggestion seems humiliating to him.

The gospels explain that it is the obstacle of richness that deludes this man, even though he is sincere. But in what sense is he deluded? It is because he is persuaded that possession of goods is *the good* and is what really counts on this earth, and in this way he is not free to listen to and understand what Jesus is saying to him and that to live with him, like him, would in reality be the fulfillment of what he has always looked for all his life. It has not been sufficient for this man to obey the commandments in order to see the beatitude in Jesus' suggestion, something that, strangely enough, another rich man, a heartless sinner, at a certain point, somehow sees.

How does Zacchaeus see what the rich aristocrat could not? Because he realizes that Jesus is interested in him and does it in such an obvious way that it threatens his own public image just to establish a genuine relationship with him, exposing himself, a religious man, in front of the holy religious leaders of his time, who in fact aren't slow to grumble and be scandalized: «He has gone to stay at a sinner's house!» (*Luke* 19:7). Zacchaeus sees this, senses in the gratuitous closeness of Jesus a relationship not only not sought after by him, but not even thought possible or desirable, and yet real and truly given. In the manner of this relationship, in the way Jesus' humanity is mediated in this relationship, he now understands that to live freely, to live like Jesus is living with him, means to live in fullness on this earth[19].

What happens in this encounter is what we call grace. From the point of view of the ethical experience, Zacchaeus understands that the gratuitousness is a reasonable way of living on the earth, which in that way is worth living, that now it is possible for him, too, to live like that.

tion is placed on the reality of God's reign that is realized not only in the person of Jesus, but also in the following of him made possible by his gift. And yet worldly logic based on possession and self-concern, even before making the exercise of responsibility difficult, seems to inhibit in the person development of his/her awareness and, therefore, of his/her freedom.

19 Cfr. BASTIANEL S., «Conversione e sequela nel Nuovo Testamento. Figure di incontro con il Signore», in LORENZANI M., ED., *La morale nella Bibbia*, Edizioni ISSRA, L'Aquila 1996, 86-93.

Until now the tax collector knew there was a commandment that forbade fraud but he didn't keep it, because he figured that it had no significance for him. What has now changed is the fact that he sees as the meaning and fulfillment of personal freedom making oneself responsible for the other person, in a similar fashion to what Jesus did for him. He sees that this is good, that it is the beatitude of existence. He understands that he has been offered the opportunity to live it and find in his own way the manner of realizing this given opportunity, with a rationale that comes out of gratuitousness. The rich tax collector thinks: I am wealthy and there are people I have defrauded; I cannot gauge how much I must give them and be satisfied according to the measures foreseen in the law; if there is someone who is needy and I have goods, I can use these goods for those in need. The account does not say that Zacchaeus was given a command, and yet it emphasizes the seriousness of the tax collector's commitment. He seems to detect an interior need that he did not detect before, not because of some legal bond, but by virtue of the experience he has had of communion with Jesus. What signifies Zacchaeus' conversion is the meaning recognized in this encounter. The criterion of communion, seen and understood in Jesus, «overwhelms» him[20] in his new outlook on life and drives him now to make himself a neighbor.

Thus it is for Zacchaeus, heartless sinner, but it is the same for every believer. The newness of life for the disciple is his/her understanding and assuming, from within his/her own personal inner life, that it is not a matter of loving one's neighbor simply to fulfill a precept established by God, but it is because love of neighbor speaks about the meaning of human life on earth beginning with the reality of the relationship experienced in the encounter with Jesus and gratuitous love. He is the creator of communion and makes one truly live, according to the intentionality of the active word of God. And that is not all. The disciple is the one who has experienced that this Word is not just desirable, but has become possible for him/her because of this Jesus of Nazareth who has met him/her, loved him/her, created with him/her a relationship of closeness that does not come to an end, that is reality enduring and founding a life of beatitude by virtue of the Lord's faithfulness.

20 One can state this in the perspective expressed by Paul in *2Cor* 5:14.

«Love your enemies, do good to those who hate you» (*Luke* 6:27)[21]. In this phrase of Jesus, the disciple understands the «blessed» and that is what is the meaning of life, not what is the command, if by this term we mean a legalistic interpretation of the very word of God, which puts as secondary or does not necessarily presuppose the experience of the personal conscience in its conscious freedom. The normativity of the *commandment* to love freely is understood in the light of this *experience of beatitude*, that is, beginning with the inner bond of a freedom that understands itself liberated by the encounter with Jesus to become responsible.

Moreover, if God's activity in history from the beginning, from all points of view and at all times, is a work of communion, it would not be true that he loves us and he wants us with him if he were not to ask us to recognize him and make communion our interpretive criterion for everything to do with life on earth. This is normative, this binds us in conscience, not in the way of a formulated norm, but in the manner of conscience, in its truth, in its liberty and responsibility.

On the basis of the experience of the gratuity and closeness given by the Lord, that means *to understand* that we are able to be on God's side in looking at reality, in the way of reading the history of humanity, in recognizing and preferring the paths to truly building communion on this earth. That means not being happy at loving «for» love of God, as a type of justification for humiliating the life of the other person and the reason for one's free love, but loving the other, because and as he/she is, «in» the Lord, that is, basically with the eyes of the Lord, even when the other is not necessarily a friend, or perhaps is even a person who wants to do evil or who does evil to me.

5
The privilege of the weak

How does one move from the assumption of God's intentionality to translating it into action? And what does it mean to activate fraternal closeness objectively in this human story?

21 Cfr. *Matt* 5:44. Note that, while in Matthew love of enemies is placed as a supreme requirement at the end of a series of antitheses (*Matt* 5:43-48), in Luke the same commandment is placed at the beginning of Jesus' discourse following his proclamation of the beatitudes (*Luke* 6:27-38), as if to place every need, manifested there, within the horizon of the gift: the gift of God and the gift of selves.

First of all one calls to mind the parable of the Good Samaritan (*Luke* 10:25-37). If we re-fashion ourselves like the figure presented to us there, we can sense the normativity of an ethical model in which the correctness of fraternal love is not simply affirmed, but in which an interpretation of existence according to Christ on this earth is also proposed[22].

We recall that the parable responds to a question from a doctor of the law committed in conscience in his religious faithfulness, a bit like the rich aristocrat (cfr. *Luke* 10:25 with *Luke* 18:18). It is interesting that the theologian is urged by Jesus to see precisely in the reply of a Samaritan, a man who in his eyes will certainly not appear to be motivated by reasons of orthodoxy, the image of accepting God's intentionality, which is basically a full and proper acceptance, through the moral transparency of his conduct. In what does the Samaritan's objective transparency consist, recognizable and communicable beyond the specific religious traditions? We can also ask: in what does that truth of conscience that becomes the gospel of God's intentionality on this earth consist?

Asking the question «who is my neighbor?» (*Luke* 10:29), the doctor of the law reveals a way of thinking shared in his environment (and not only there), a way that, while affirming the centrality of the commandment of love of neighbor, tends to interpret it in a partial manner, as a duty of solidarity toward some people, toward those on one's own side. Naturally, according to this way of thinking, even subconsciously, the tendency is to specify who is the neighbor that we are to accept, or at least to end up establishing, in one way or another, the conditions of acceptance, specifically, that the other person is accepted only if he/she responds to those requirements that justify the judiciousness of handing oneself over to him/her.

In such actions there is a problem, not only with the correct understanding of the «you» of the neighbor, who is in truth never definable and never integrable in my horizon, nor dependent on my understanding, because he/she in him/herself is center of meaning and value. Here there is also actually a denial of free personal responsibility, because fundamentally the question would be this: up to what point am I obliged?

22 Cfr. BASTIANEL S., «"Dov'è?": la domanda di responsabilità», in *Servitium*, n. 110 (1997) 27-41; RIZZI A., *Pensare la carità*, ECP, San Domenico di Fiesole (FI) 1995.

The answer that comes to us from the Good Samaritan is very clear, precisely in the rationality of the behavior presented[23]. It is like saying to whoever is listening that faced with the other person, you are obliged, in conscience and always, to carry out that good which is actually possible for you. To translate actively the Lord's intentionality, of course will also mean deciding something, but precisely what is to be decided is not the significance of the other person and his/her dignity, but rather what is it just to do here and now to respond to the objectivity of a need. This will mean knowing the other person, the situation, the true conditions, and also the proper objective conditions of the response, using tools to analyze the goods and values at issue and carefully evaluating the consequences that might derive from one or other course of action.

It is the link to objectivity that obliges the Samaritan, in his moral goodness, to look for the good that is really possible. It is the same link to objectivity that binds the life and person of the disciple. This means that, if in our story the objective conditions of poverty, in all the ways in which the person is humiliated and opposed, are objectively the result of human activity that opposes the work of God, there will be no objective acceptance of the sovereignty of God and an effective search for justice *if it does not favor the weak.*

The centrality of the Samaritan's care of the unfortunate victim reminds us that to live in gratuitousness of conscience on this earth cannot be limited to a generic affirmation of love of the other person that never dares to have preference for the weak. After all, the parable is clear and the message of the beatitudes is clear. Addressed precisely as an announcement to one who is weak, it reminds not only the disciples of Jesus' generation, but every disciple, that in an historical condition in which there is the first and the last, weak and strong, justice will not be true if I do not privilege the weak; that seeking fraternity will not be true if I do not try to put the other person in the condition of being a brother/sister. It is not true that there can be communion when choices do not prefer the weak, beginning with the weakest. The sometimes difficult interpretation of weakness and its «measure», like the difficulty of discerning the good that actually is possible, must not become the pretext to evade the criterion that is suggested to us.

23 On the comprehensibility of the commandment of love, cfr. GINTERS R., *Valori, norme e fede cristiana. Introduzione all'etica filosofica e teologica*, Marietti, Casale Monferrato 1982, 98-116; SCHÜLLER B., *La fondazione dei giudizi morali. Tipi di argomentazione etica in teologia morale*, San Paolo, Cinisello Balsamo 1997, 79-148.

In this sense we must say that the message of the beatitudes is entrusted to us as a reality that the Lord makes possible, but also as a provocation and invitation to our responsibility. Before God for what are we responsible? If we are responsible for the brother/sister and freely so, we will be responsible first of all for the poor, for those who are weak and objectively in need of help. So the word «blessed» will sound like the question: «Where is your brother»? (*Gen* 4:9)[24].

With respect to the virtuous life, what does this mean? What do the beatitudes say? Perhaps, above all, it means the fact of accepting the activity of God and allowing that, through one's own free responsibility, this work may be effective on the earth. This means not searching for communion only if and when circumstances appear propitious, but because God is here and at work and it is a matter of accepting him.

Obviously this acceptance, even understood in its meaning as a disciple, can appear onerous when one finds oneself effectively persecuted or humiliated. In that regard the beatitudes remind us above all that these conditions of humiliation are part of life and that, precisely regarding such conditions, there is a need to better understand who God is and who we are, who wish to be with him. Not only that. The Lucan version of the beatitudes says «blessed are you», with a clear reference to those who not for any motive whatsoever, but precisely for the fact of being with the Lord in this world, are persecuted. If to live according to a rationale of charity on earth means to be humiliated in various ways, the word of the Lord does not tell us that we will be blessed one day, as if to the constraint of the present there would be almost in restitution a reward for heroic conduct in life. «Blessed are you» reminds us that, in a story in which the efficacy of evil is present, to live in fullness of communion with Christ now, that is, to live this life in basic fullness in the human sense, means like him to go to meet even the cross.

The disciple who wishes to be neither masochistic nor heroic has understood this. Precisely because of this, for no reason in the world will the disciple consent to create division, struggle, death, and suffering, but in the historical concrete relationship with the «you» of the other person, who even may possibly be hostile, he/she will tend to recall a love that bent down to him/her and a capacity to love that was given to him/her. He/she will remember a word of beatitude pronounced over him/her and will him/herself be able to pronounce it. It

24 On the meaning and centrality of this question for the moral life of the believer, see the monographic edition of *Servitium* n. 110 (1997) entitled «Dov'è tuo fratello».

will be a matter of accepting the necessary patience of time and the restrictions of not just external conditions, but also those within ourselves. In these conditions we are asked to live not as people resigned and ready to self-justification, but rather by trusting in the Lord and configuring our lives to his.

6
An ethical culture

The evangelical message of the beatitudes indicates something that is at the root of Christians' identity in their understanding of and living in the present reality. Out of it comes, also, as a consequence, the necessity of translating the message, interpreting in relevant terms the problems and possibilities of our time, indicating the paths of humanity, and contributing to building more human ways of thinking and behavior on this earth.

It is relatively easy to say that the newness of the Christian ethic is Jesus Christ, but obviously that implies interpreting the meaning of human life in historical contexts in which *the human* (that which is of value, that which is proposed as good) is always culturally communicated and also in which the reference to Jesus Christ can only assume cultural forms, even if we well know that no cultural understanding is immune from the risks of a worldly mentality. The problem, then, is that of assuming such understanding with critical awareness and ensuring that Christian morality, Christian moral theology, is truly a critical theory of the praxis of Christians, of their lived experience, with the criteria of judgment and the values considered in an ethical context.

Speaking, in this sense, of the ethics of the beatitudes for contemporary culture, we must not think that there is an ethic that Christians live and then also live within a certain culture that is beside it or opposed to it. Culture, human cultures, are those within which we live as Christians, with understandings of values that condition, in the meaning of their limits and opportunities, our very knowledge of the Lord, and the purpose and expectations of our discipleship. For example, we should not be too surprised if in a dominant culture, not only at the time of Jesus, but likewise in a thousand different guises today, too, the point of view of the temptation that tends to thwart the *meaning* of the figure of Christ often does not appear as open refutation of Christ, but rather as a generally shared system of self-justification. At the same time, however, we should know how to appreciate that manifold witness of the gospel that, passing through cultural understandings, brings its efficacy to bear beyond the confines of explicitly belonging to the Church.

The first Christians, receiving an already existing Israelite inheritance, showed themselves to be very attentive to this type of witness. Just to look at one example, think of the term *virtue*, so dear to the Stoic and general Hellenistic environment (but present also in the Jewish environment), and how it entered into the New Testament writings. We know that the Stoic ideal of the virtuous life carries within itself a connotation of self-sufficiency and self-salvation. To assume this concept of a virtuous life within the context of a Christian proclamation, that is, interpreting it beginning with the awareness of being saved by virtue of the merciful goodness of the Lord and not through any other means, while defusing that pretext of self-salvation, is to allow one to glimpse an attitude of conscience recognizable in its meaning and value even by pagans[25]. For these, also, it is important to attend to their honesty without being a judge of others, without becoming superior, without pretending to be the guarantor of life. Similarly, with everyone it is important and urgent to understand solidarity not in a partial manner, as something that fundamentally is still affirmation of the privilege of a group, but rather in a basically human and unconditional dimension.

For the message of the beatitudes, also, it is worth the possibility and therefore the responsibility to carry out a careful cultural accommodation. If, then, one affirms the correctness of the *privilege of the weak* at the level of interpersonal relations, this same perspective should go so far as interpreting the major questions at an international level and those concerning the internal life of a nation, for example the meaning and value of peace; relations between the north and south of the world; relations between the various state bodies with their respective powers and those between the different social parties; the ethical criteria for an economic globalization that respects the different cultural elements of the world populations; and other important questions that concern the present life and the future of humanity. At the same time the purpose of communion with the other, built through acceptance of the weak, should be present in the manner of facing specific problems. One can think of the family, education, tax, genetic experimentation, health assistance, protection of minors, and information.

25 Cfr. BASTIANEL S., «Assunzione di formule e paradigmi etici nel nuovo testamento», in *Servitium*, n. 9 (1980) 32-41; SCHELKLE K.H., *Theology of the New Testament*, III, Morality, Collegeville, Minn. 1973, 227-229; WENDLAND H.D., *Etica del Nuovo Testamento*, Paideia, Brescia 1975, 78-83.

There will be tools to use, but not just in any way whatsoever. What will allow the means to be prepared and adjusted in an adequate manner will always be clarity of purpose, because the desired result will not be achieved using a tool internally contradictory to the end. With regard to the purpose of communion, in the contemporary cultures one can certainly identify the strengths. To provide examples: the growing feeling for peace and solidarity, attention focused on human rights, the increasingly active interest in the many initiatives of a humanitarian nature, or even the public debate about issues of justice. In the same cultures there are also weaknesses. Among them, in particular, we can note a strong individualistic-positivistic tendency in interpreting and demanding rights and, at the same time, a lasting difficulty in making impartial and basically universal the search for solidarity in the face of the excessive power of the economy[26].

In this context the idea would be that of seeing what are the possible strengths in contemporary sensitivity, actually in the sense of being able to indicate in them the methods of a human existence qualified in its humanity, that can bring results in life and lead to the basic overcoming of conflicts, poverty and injustice. Necessarily alongside these indications, one should carry out critical discernment on praxis beginning with the critical discernment of Christian praxis. This theme concerns us as disciples of the Lord and the church as community of believers.

Within the church the primary need, of a precisely ethical nature, to which the message of the beatitudes calls us, is certainly that of a personal experience of faith sufficiently mature to be able to understand the beatitudes as *beatitudes.* That presupposes placing some emphasis on the plan of *formation*, on the level of care for the capacity of each person within the church, in the roles in which they find themselves, to live that gifted communion that is made possible for us by God and that from within us the Spirit moves, in order to identify the ethical problems and find ways of Christian life and interpretation. We must not forget, from this point of view, that the opportunity to make a gospel understanding of humanity pass through our present cultures, even beyond the confines of ecclesial belonging, obviously depends on genuine inner acceptance of the gospel message, on one's sharing in the church, on the *intellectus fidei* of the believing community, and therefore also on the effort of discernment within moral theology, with the preciousness of its insights and even of its present difficulties.

26 Cfr. JONAS H., *The Imperative of Responsibility. In Search of an Ethics for the Technological Age*, University of Chicago Press, Chicago and London 1984, 3-32.

Naturally, the affirmation of the beatitude of the poor finds one of its main places of verification or misrepresentation in the very structuring of the church, in the way in which it sets itself up and its visible expression. The institutional and visible reality brings its specific weight to bear on the cultural impact of the life of the church and in the very formation of consciences. Of particular import is the way in which the church structures its internal relations (roles, tasks, functions) and the way in which these relations are usually lived, explained, and justified. The way of conducting relations between the institutional church and civil society, the way of weaving international relations with states and peoples, is also a specific crux of the cultural impact that verifies or misrepresents the gospel message through its own efficacy. Certainly we cannot forget that the way in which the average Christian, known as such, lives and explains his/her social, political, economic relations is the locus of his/her contribution to the cultural interpretation of the values and criteria of behavior on which the reality of history feeds.

At the time of Jesus' proclamation of the beatitudes and the recollection of them on the part of the emerging church, the gospel message was intended as not homogeneous to the worldly mentality of the listeners, be they public sinners, or be they those who believed themselves to be, and to a certain extent who effectively were, holy and just. To them the beatitudes called for an upheaval in their previous scale of values and their interpretation of life, even if it was a religious interpretation. It wouldn't be strange if that should happen to us Christians, as well, and for the church today.

The newness that the beatitudes propose, with respect to our way of thinking and our theological culture, also calls us to ask ourselves about the meaning of human life and what we value in fact as *success* in personal, social, ecclesial life, in cultural contexts in which simple success is often seen as a measure of good. It is not about thinking of the beatitudes, in contrast to this way of seeing things, as an ethic of failure. Instead we must remember that even humanly, the perspective of success as legitimate ethically, in whatever way and as the first thing to attempt is seen as illusory. It is true, in fact, that many people, not only Christians and not only believers, find it reasonable to renounce something, even considerable, in order to achieve an important objective in terms of meaning, in terms of human value and free and responsible relations. Certainly, if at heart we do not recognize the perspective of the beatitudes as of value and think we do not have the tools to show what is humanly of value, we will not be able to establish the efficacy of the gospel beyond the confines of the adherence of explicit faith. But perhaps the difficulty of witnessing and explaining would have as a not-occasional companion an equal difficulty in identity and Christian life. What is at issue at the same time is our understanding and living in true adherence to the Lord as a way of fulfillment of our existence.

The conversion that the proclamation of the beatitudes calls for is that of a radical gospel conversion. This does not consist in heroic ideals; instead, it is the indication of an unconditional adherence to Jesus Christ (and to truth, to good) and to being with him on this earth. To try with him to understand human existence on this earth, to assume a perspective of life with Christ and to live it in him and by virtue of him, is neither humiliating nor illusory. It is a utopian perspective; always prospective and never ending, it states the meaning of the disciple's life and offers the criteria for it, and so calls a person to be guided, as a perspective of beatitude and equally as a responsibility, along the path of human personal moral conversion in faith.

Chapter 4

The church's social doctrine as moral theology

The Encyclical *Sollicitudo rei socialis*[1] states that the Church's social doctrine belongs to the field of moral theology. While recommending «a more exact awareness and a wider diffusion»[2], the text also describes briefly of what the Church's social doctrine is comprised. The formulation of it is reached through *reflection* on the complex reality of social life, a reflection guided «by the light of faith and the Church's tradition». The purpose of the Church's doctrine is to *interpret* social realities, so that the behavior of Christians may *be correctly guided* in a coherent way with the meaning of human life understood in faith[3]. We must ask about the precise meaning of the statement according to which the Church's social doctrine is moral theology. It is a question about the meaning and way of «reflecting», «interpreting», and «guiding».

The text of this Encyclical notes that it is a teaching concerned with complex problems, which are the object of analysis and study by different disciplines. We are told that it is necessary to reflect in order to interpret the data of these various complex problems in the light of revelation, therefore with a criterion that is not just human reflection (consequently it belongs to theology). It is also stated that the aim is correct behavior (consequently it belongs to morals). The phrase used for this last statement indicates that correct behavior is not just an individual precise act, but rather a constant disposition and a consciously formed way of action *(habitus)*, based on an aim correctly pursued.

In this regard one could recall another phrase from classical language, that of *ordering one's life*, aware of its aim and acting in such a way that everything is really directed toward that end[4]. That means good personal morality and the help

1 AAS 80 (1988) 513-586.

2 Quoting the Instruction on Christian Freedom and Liberation (CDF, *Libertatis conscientia*, 22.03.1986, n. 72: AAS 79 [1987] 586) in regard to the Church's social doctrine, the Encyclical states: «In today's difficult situation, a more exact awareness and a wider diffusion of the "set of principles for reflection, criteria for judgment and directives for action" proposed by the Church's teaching would be of great help in promoting both the correct definition of the problems being faced and the best solution to them» (*Sollicitudo rei socialis*, 41).

3 The Church's social doctrine is «the accurate formulation of the results of a careful reflection on the complex realities of human existence, in society and in the international order, in the light of faith and of the Church's tradition. Its main aim is to interpret these realities, determining their conformity with or divergence from the lines of the Gospel teaching on man and his vocation, a vocation that is at once earthly and transcendent; its aim is thus to guide Christian behavior (*ut christianus sese gerendi habitus recte dirigatur*). It therefore belongs to the field, not of ideology, but of theology and particularly of moral theology» (*Sollicitudo rei socialis*, 41).

4 This is the sense in which one should perhaps understand the English translation («guide behavior»), which would otherwise be too far removed from the official text.

of a correct morality[5]. With its teaching about behavior in the social sphere, the church intends precisely to offer to the personal morality (to the «good will») of Christians, and indeed everyone, the assistance of moral correctness.

1

Moral theology and scientific expertise

The connected problems are linked to the relations between different fields of knowledge, which need to maintain their specific roles and be integrated in a united and coherent cognitive and assessment process. At a first level, there is knowledge of the empirical reality, as proper knowledge of the sciences. Then there is the interpretation of the empirical reality, as an operation proper to philosophy (interpretation in relation to humanity). Finally, interpretation of the empirical reality «in faith» involves an explicit revealed reference, which is understood and assumed within a faith *traditio.*

A specific problematic peculiarity comes from the fact that the scientific knowledge here at issue is not that of physics or mathematics; it is about sociology, economics, politics, and so on, sciences that directly impact upon behavior, choices and decisions, and that therefore are immediately connected to morality. Morality then (as experience and also as reflection, as understood moral experience) is not the exclusive patrimony of moralists and experts, but a common patrimony of every person. Whoever conducts a scientific reading of the empirical reality as a sociologist, economist or political scientist, does it having—rightly— the conviction of knowing what is «moral», and that will mean that he/she will not conduct merely a «vapid» reading regarding morality. Therefore, there is a specific problem in the relationship between morality and science with regard to the field of social problems. Moreover, even though without a specific role in the field, the moralist lives and knows something about social, economic and political problems. He/she, too, in reflecting from the moral point of view, has a way of understanding society, the economy, and political life.

5 Following the common usage in moral theology, I speak about *morality* to indicate the moral experience, or the conscious exercise of free responsibility. What is at issue is the moral *goodness*, the personal relation to what is good (and is known as such). I speak about *morals* to indicate the reflection leaning toward an organic whole of principles, values, norms, indications of hierarchy and urgency and criteria for identifying them. What is at issue is moral *correctness*, the precise indication of what it is good to do.

Speaking of conscience and interpretation, we are confronted here with a cluster of problems in which knowledge is already close to assessment, at least in the sense of what one might «call» assessment. Therein lies the sensitivity of the relations between the various levels of understanding and the way in which one reaches an assessment that one wants to be «conclusive».

1.1. MORAL THEOLOGY

Our reflection concerns «moral theology», not inasmuch as it draws up its first principles, but rather inasmuch as it reflects on the ethical life in reference to a specific compass of behavior, with which social doctrine is concerned. Since the social dimension is in some way always implied in human behavior, we can state that the specific problems at issue are those concerning social life as it is «structured».

The moralist who wants to develop a reflection on «social morality» finds that he/she must assess data interpreted theologically, comparing their objective value (comparing the various elements in their objective worth) in relation to the Christian meaning of human life in society and attempting to formulate what is morally important in those data. It is a matter of pointing out the human values that have to do with consciousness, liberty, and personal responsibility, since where personal conscious free responsibility in decision-making is at issue, there is the moral problem. It is also a matter of identifying the hierarchy of values, and perhaps the urgency of values as well, in specific contexts.

Doing this means in each case implying meanings that are not just partial, but that refer to a meaning/goal of life itself (and therefore of human life), in order to be able to indicate in which way one can and must order the various partial purposes to this non-biased end, both in individual and collective decisions.

1.2. THE AUTONOMY OF DIFFERENT FIELDS

A fundamental problem that theological-moral reflection must face arises in relation to the other disciplines. Recognizing the diversity and specificity of the fields, one must recognize their relative and relational autonomy. Let us attempt to clarify the meaning.

Autonomy proper to science. In the first place there is a need for recognition and true respect for the autonomy of science and the diverse scientific disciplines. This means recognizing that each individual science has its own experience base and its own practical «laws», its own methodology. Consequently, it will be on the basis of these specific experiences and laws, not on the basis of other elements, that *its* conclusions can be verified or disproved.

Scientific knowledge cannot therefore be substituted by philosophy, or by theology, or by morality. Stated in these terms, recognizing the autonomy proper to science is none other than recognizing the effective specific identity of every science. It also means that scientific knowledge, with its results, cannot substitute philosophy, theology, or morality. No scientific result is directly transposable into a moral argument or conclusion. Scientific knowledge is not the last word about knowledge or life, or knowledge for life. It has its sphere, its autonomy therein, its dignity, its function in relation to the whole field of knowledge and life.

Autonomy proper to philosophy. Philosophy, too, has its experience base (experience of meaning, of the human) and its own «laws», its own methodology; on the basis of these *its* conclusions will be verified or disproved. It cannot be replaced by science, theology or morality; nor can it take the place of science, theology or morality. It is not the last word about knowledge, or life, or knowledge for life.

Autonomy proper to theology. Theology, too, has its experience base (the experience of faith —or meaning in faith) and its own «laws», its own methodology; on the basis of these, in its specificity, *its* conclusions will be verified or disproved.

There is *intellectus fidei,* in the double sense of the objective and subjective genitive: *intellectus* wishing to understand faith and *intellectus* of the reality and history by virtue of faith, beginning with faith. For this, too, its proper identity and autonomy refer back to its «partiality», to its being part of knowledge, with its constitutive relation with other competences, which it cannot substitute and by which it cannot be substituted.

Finally the *autonomy proper to moral theology* should be noted. It has its experience base and its own «laws», its own methodology; on the basis of these *its* conclusions will be verified or disproved. It is *intellectus fidei* about human behavior as conscious, free and responsible.

Such autonomy concerns the relation to the sciences, beginning with the data on which one reflects, which are never *only* those offered by the sciences, since at the same time they converge with the data proper to ethical experience itself. But moral theology, precisely in order to be that which it is called to be and in order to make its contribution, must maintain its necessary autonomy also with respect to the disciplines with which it is even closely linked, such as the other theological disciplines (dogmatic or fundamental theology, for example) and philosophical ethics.

If it is a matter of a discipline «of meaning» (the search for meaning, in order to assess), then it is a hermeneutical discipline that constantly reviews the various aspects implied in its considerations. As interpretation it will be necessary therefore to have the rules for interpreting philosophy: if one reasons, it must be a reasoning according to the requirements of logic. As interpretation «in faith», it is necessary to show coherence between reasoning and the foundation of faith, showing the contribution of one and the other, without confusing the levels. If it is interpretation in faith of the reality of conscience, that is, of the experience of free conscious responsibility, then respect for these elements must show its reasoning and its being enlightened by faith.

1.3. INTERPRETIVE CORRELATION

As long as the autonomy of each discipline is affirmed in theory, each one is respected and everything proceeds well. The problem comes when one tries to put together the data from disciplines that are in fact different. At any rate, it should be immediately considered that where moral problems are concerned, at the basis is knowledge of empirical data, because if these are omitted one does not know that realities are being discussed, and everything is questionable. However, it should also be noted that the problem of respect for reciprocal autonomy and the ability to listen reciprocally is not a linear problem; apparently it is a matter of clarifying first the scientific discourse, then the philosophical one, and finally the theological one. In reflection on ethical problems, on the problems that relate to conscious free responsibility, there is always a pre-understanding at work in this reflection as well. When we begin to reflect directly, we do so with a mental inheritance, and not just a mental action that is ours alone; we begin by already having a reference vocabulary, speaking to people whose vocabulary we know. It is a culturally determined understanding, result of a history in which scientific, philosophical, and moral knowledge is present to make reference to the terms that interest us directly. When we begin to reflect on morally important questions, we already have this pre-understanding, which is the fruit of the story in which we are placed and in and to which we actively contribute. This culturally determined pre-understanding is personally assumed, in the sense of being the result of one's own personal story, both as one's own experience and understanding, as well as through questions that from time to time are raised. When I reason on the validity of democracy, or of another form of government, even if it were the first time that I reflect knowing how to do it, I am not beginning with a «nothing» understanding of the problem, even from the point of view of personally assumed experience and understanding. This is to say that there must be an «*ascesis*» of study and philosophical reflection (that which the treatise of E. Huber reminded us as necessary «at a distance»). Knowledge of one's own scientific, philosophical, theological and moral presuppositions is necessary. This is not always so obvious in the exercise of reflection and interdisciplinary discussion.

It is necessary to assume the critical requirement that comes from the exercise of the individual disciplines, whether scientific knowledge, philosophical and theological reflection, or specifically moral reflection.

Given the pre-comprehensions at work at any rate and given the increasing specialization of the various disciplines, the necessary critical requirement seems to need genuine communication between the various disciplines. Such communication would not only be timely, but beautiful. If there is not such communication, the result arrived at, or believed to have been reached, would suffer.

Furthermore, given the historicity of our knowing reality and reflecting on it, and given the change in actual conditions, with the actual opportunities and restrictions for decisions and action, and keeping in mind the demand of the critical requirement, it seems as if these realities can never be overcome; that is, we can never presume to have reached a level of knowledge about something that can be considered to be comprehensive and exhaustive. This clearly raises problems with respect to the possible claims of moral theology, calling for a conscious differentiation in its results. It also has its impact on the opportunities that the Magisterium has in speaking about specific issues in social morality, in the sense of the necessary care in qualifying the interventions, their meaning, and their importance.

2
The contribution of Christian faith

The problems recalled necessarily impact upon the commitment of whoever cares to interpret social reality in reference to the gospel, in order to guide behavior. With respect to them, the question about the way in which the specific contribution that comes from Christian faith and revelation works could be usefully placed alongside the revealed texts themselves, to see how questions about what we call «social morality» are treated in the arc of the history of faith as testified by written revelation. By way of example, we will consider some references in order to see how there is also a similar process in terms of moral theology and the authentic contemporary Magisterium. We also need to be able to identify explicitly those recent elements available to us for interpreting the concrete, the partial. It is about recognizing the foundation and meaning that we attribute to human social life understood in faith.

J. Schasching's treatise recalls some of what could be considered foundational principles. They are already «specific» elements, which concern the social sphere, indications for this sphere of principles or more fundamental values. Let us first consider from Sacred Scripture a basic element that is foundational for the whole of biblical moral interpretation, without which one would not understand «social moral principles»; secondly, we will consider two situations in which these «specific» principles can be identified in the social field.

2.1. THE GIFT OF THE COVENANT

The characteristic element, which runs throughout the whole of the Old and New Testaments, for interpreting the reality of social life is expressed in the theology of the covenant, which in the New Testament is presented as «fulfilled» in Jesus Christ. It is the experience, understood in faith, that God makes himself neighbor and creates and calls for closeness. He «comes down» to Egypt to liberate his people, reveals himself present in his liberating work, creates a people, and asks that this intentionality (the intentionality of his action, making himself a neighbor and creating a people) be assumed in intentionality precisely by those who recognize themselves as saved by him. The children of the covenant must be «Yahweh's people»; it is God himself who makes them his people and asks them to be so in free and conscious liberty, as a family of brothers and sisters before God, recognized as their father. The commandments, the will of God, are always interpreted in this manner. It is seeing how, with respect to the particular situations and life's various problems, to be that which God has made us to be and calls us to be responsibly. We can phrase it thus: in answer to God who calls and saves, we are to assume in conscious free responsibility the very intentionality of the saving work of God. This can be stated in terms of communion: communion given and with which one is made responsible (before the giver); communion with God and, by virtue of it (in him, therefore) reciprocal communion. The founding event of Israel's faith is the liberation from Egypt, the unity of Exodus and Sinai, together with the revelation of God's name.

Developing on the basis of this tradition of theology expressed in terms of covenant, creation itself (the meaning of human beings, their nature) then becomes interpreted and formulated in terms of covenant. The human person is created by God in his image and likeness and is placed before him, made interlocutor, capable of listening to what God says, capable of hearing from him about the meaning of life on this earth, in this garden, a garden created by God as a place of living and at the same time in communion on the part of this human family (the first couple and humanity in perspective), by virtue of the gifted communion with God himself. They are his interlocutors, therefore in dialogue among themselves, in a place that is called to be a place of interhuman communion.

This is the theology that comes down to the New Testament indicating, in Jesus Christ, the fulfillment of the salvific will of the Father. It is revealed in the Passover of Jesus Christ, by virtue of his ultimate and definitive making himself a neighbor, which is becoming the Word made flesh, and in the creation of a group of disciples that becomes the church, which is the reality of this communion given in Jesus Christ, and which has communion as precisely one of its tasks (charity-communion). We say therefore that charity, in the sense of love like that of Christ (discipleship) is the principle and foundation of every moral bond for the Christian; it is the interpretation of the very morality of the Christian in all the fields in which it is expressed.

The first interesting thing to emphasize, in the context of our discourse, is perhaps precisely the fact that what is presented as the meaning of morality in terms of faith has no need of any «addition» to be able to include the social dimension. The social dimension is proposed to us right from the outset, when it speaks to us of morality understood «before God». We remember that the individual commandments of the Decalogue, when they are assumed in the covenant according to the formulation of *Exod* 20, are proposed with the interpretation of a prologue, which is the affirmation-reminder of the liberating event that God placed at the beginning of and foundation of the covenant: «I am Yahweh your God who brought you out of the land of Egypt, out of the house of slavery» (*Exod* 20:2). The interlocutor to whom the word is addressed with the «you» is the people, considered in its unity. Through this reminder-foundation is proposed the request to be *his people*, in reference to him and in the unity of the people, before and according to the table of the law. In the New Testament, from the Passover of Jesus Christ, is born the community of the new covenant: in remembrance of the Lord, and by virtue of the personal relationship with him, interpersonal relations and the structuring of community relations tend to translate into praxis according to the rationale of communion, of non-privilege of self, of sharing[6].

2.2. THE INSTITUTIONS: THE MONARCHY IN ISRAEL

Let us consider an example focusing on the problem of social institutions, perhaps the one most widely described in its manifold implications: the institution of the monarchy in Israel[7].

In the long process of unification of the various tribes, in the time of pre-state Canaan, there is a period in which the difficulty of aggregation and the novelty of the situations, while they united in a coherent way, change the life style from a semi-nomadic people to a stable people on this earth. They encounter models of organization of life different from those of the patriarchal family and more adapted to the sedentary life, the models of small city-states with their king, and they too have questions about centralized government and problems accepting it; during the whole time of the Judges only an occasional unifying leader was accepted as a function of defense from the enemies who arose from time to time. Thereupon the monarchy was in fact installed and continued, even after a whole series of problems, which were expressed in criticisms of the monarchy.

We may ask what the moral faith judgment is that Israel slowly gave. It is possible to recognize it looking at the outcomes of the various problematic trials, which arose in various ways and in different situations, in connection with the establishment of the institution of the monarchy. It has to be said that at the level of genuine motivation the most rational motivation from a functional point of view prevailed. It was really no longer possible for this gradual unification toward becoming a truly united people to continue without government centralization and a state organization. And yet they had seen the different kings from nearby peoples, even before the installation of the monarchy, just as they were also seen afterwards (now including those of Israel), and the evils linked historically to this institution had also been seen.

6 By way of illustrative references one thinks of the accounts of the institution of the Eucharist and their contexts (*Luke* 22; *Matt* 26; *Mark* 14; *1 Cor* 11), the pictures of the first community in Jerusalem (*Acts* 2:42-48 and 4:32-35), the Sermon on the Mount (*Matt* 5) and the Lucan parallel (*Luke* 6:20-38), as well as all the specific texts on charity and discipleship.

7 Cfr. *1Sam* 8-11.13.15; *Judg* 9:8-15; *Deut* 17:14-20.

The theological interpretation also raised questions about the compatibility of the monarchy with Yahweh's sovereignty, in that the unity that forms this people is not because of great gestures of a leader (Moses, despite the greatness of his figure, does not represent such a model as «founder» of national unity). Instead, this people arises from God's liberating action and understands itself as such and recognizes its origins as such. The response to such types of questions is that this is the most suitable institutional solution to make this «people» this particular people. But be careful. We interpret in faith the reality of «people», not like the various peoples of Canaan or how Egypt interprets its being people. For us «people» means a community of brothers and sisters before God. So the king will be one of the brothers of this people and not above the people. His reign must be transparent of the reign of Yahweh, therefore at the service of this becoming a people of brothers and sisters.

There is recognition of the human value of an institution and the request that such same human value of the institution be interpreted by virtue of one's own faith, not juxtaposed. Among Israel's institutions strongly criticized by the prophets the monarchy seems to be second only to worship. And yet not properly highlighted is the question about the institution itself as such; its value, or lack thereof, should be revealed by the facts. What is at issue is the manner of reigning (like the manner of celebrating Yahweh, or administering justice), and the evaluative criterion is always in reference to the covenant: the gratuity of God who loves and saves needs to be assumed as gratuity of the relations between those who know they are brothers and sisters. At the point where, if the king can make himself heard more than the others, his voice must be in defense of the weak; his true reign can be expressed nowhere more fully that in his doing justice for the weak. This is a theme that is found throughout the Old Testament.

This controversy about the proper role of the monarchy was, therefore, a very long and differentiated one about the validity of the monarchical institution and a response that is truly of faith and that is not replaced by human assessment of what best serves the social functioning of a state institution, but which desires that, a state's being a state, the national unity of this nation, be understood in terms of faith. It is the desire that the human worth of the rules that sustain this people's internal relations be understood in light of the meaning of the covenant.

2.3. SLAVERY IN THE LETTER TO PHILEMON

From the New Testament we consider a somewhat problematic issue: the question of slavery, as it is understood and interpreted in the short letter to Philemon. The Pauline letter, if considered with our actual criteria, seems at least not to place much value on the negative import of the institution of slavery publicly recognized as legitimate. It does not seem to have perceived as a moral social problem the fact that there are slaves and masters. This type of relationship is not indicated as a social evil with such moral importance that one must work for its abolition. The assessment that we would probably give to the same problem today does not belong to the sensitivity and moral understanding of the time, not even on the part of Christians.

There seems to be present in the letter to Philemon a perception of the value, discreetly implied and advised, of a gesture on the part of the master of liberating the slave (vv. 14-16, 21). However, it is not stated as something necessary, as a duty of justice, nor as a necessary expression of charity.

With regard to his relationship with the slave who fled and returns, the recipient is asked to remind himself of Jesus Christ, to remember that he (Philemon) has been saved, to remember his communion with Paul himself in this matter of salvation, and to treat this man as a brother. What is asked of him is not something small; it is the gospel in its radicalness. Perhaps we might think that, if this radicalness, which is fraternity, were fully lived by believers, their understanding as well, about the institution of slavery would have needed fewer centuries to develop. The fact remains, however, that in the field of written revelation, we do not have a text that states that slavery is morally unacceptable. This is not because slavery was unknown then or because today we can say that then slavery was valued. Rather, in the same Pauline letters we have texts that seem to recognize clearly the fact of slavery as legitimate. At least they do not consider it to be an important problem[8].

Here, too, the question (present in the texts) is about how to live that type of relationship, of dependence or ownership, as believers. When it is said that there is neither slave nor free person (*Gal* 3:28; *Col* 3:11), it is not simply saying that these things are irrelevant for eternal life. It is saying, certainly, that these differences are not decisive for salvation, and that therefore they must not assume for believers the importance they have for others. But this also means specifically

8 Cfr. *Eph* 6:5-9; *Col* 3:22-25; *1Cor* 7:20-24.

that you who are a Christian master must not think of being worth more than your brother who is a Christian slave; your being master is not a title of merit and it does not release you from true fraternity; it does not enable you to legitimize ways of relating that have a foundation different from that of charity. Of course, what is said goes to the heart of ways of thinking today. It is a criterion that calls for a re-examination of one's own framework and hierarchy of values. But slavery as a legitimate social institution is not condemned.

This means there is a historicity, an inevitable cultural conditioning about the moral understanding of social problems; there is a historicity already present within the important texts, also from the point of view of the limit of the indication and possible formulation of values; but such historicity is at the same time the place in which the effectiveness of faith is expressed, in that it is entrusted to the responsibility of believers, in its animating and stimulating moral understanding toward further development and fullness.

3
Theology and social morality

Theological reflection on ethical problems important to social life must consciously assume the implications of the necessary correlation with other fields of knowledge. Such implications also concern the character dependent on objective phenomena on which it is necessary to reflect in order to discern the morally important human values that are implicated therein. The *traditio* of faith, rooted in revelation, offers its specific assistance, recalling the meaning and goal of social life itself understood in faith, offering therefore interpretive criteria to the actual exercise of discerning the present historical reality.

In a similar way to what happened concerning moral understanding of social problems within the biblical traditions, so also the reflection that matures in the church will have the opportunities and restrictions of history. From this point of view, there are also some problems that result from the fact that the indication of a morally important human value does not arise from history as an indication already complete and perfect from the outset. Someone will begin to understand and to develop a morally important value, beginning with his/her culturally determined and personally assumed pre-comprehension. Often the identification of a value, or its peculiar emphasis within a framework of recognized values, happens in a problematic context and needs to pass the sifting of further clarification. The «newness» is often suggested in a conflictual way and calls for discernment. The problem then is to see, as it is suggested, if it may effectively be the indication of a value perhaps to be *better* understood, or to *understand* and *assume*.

3.1. HELP IN TODAY'S STORY

The understanding of the real data, and of the attempts at positive moral realization in social issues, is what enables the identification of the restrictions and therefore prompts further understanding. The explicit reference to faith and revelation, as the proper interpretive element of specifically Christian reflection, sets itself as a requirement of integration of the scientific data proposed. There must be a passage from the scientific result to its interpretation regarding the significance of human life (anthropological interpretation, we could say), with the need to integrate this level of reflected understanding not simply on the basis of reason, but on the basis of a *ratio* that lets itself be enlightened and guided (not replaced) by faith. The resulting image is that of a necessarily complex process, even in the sense of implying a development in time, with successive clarifications.

The Church's Magisterium intervenes with its social teaching during the course of history and while moral theological reflection continues in the Church. Each time they have been issued, the major social encyclicals have proposed «the accurate formulation of the results of a careful reflection on the complex realities of human existence, in society and in the international order, in the light of faith and of the Church's tradition»[9]. The Church's proposal has stimulated and accompanied further careful reflection in the context of changing historical, cultural and social conditions, and in the interaction between the various disciplines committed to understanding the social reality. Further elaboration in moral theology in the social sphere has made possible further expressions of the Magisterium itself, which has not simply «repeated» preceding interventions.

The Magisterium which expresses itself on social issues will find itself addressing questions which, as is already a priori known, cannot be defined once and for all; thus, the task of the Magisterium *in re morali* is that of offering assistance today, as far as is possible. The fact that it might not be possible, on specific

9 *Sollicitudo rei socialis*, 41.

questions, to make an ultimate and definitive pronouncement, does not take away the opportunity and duty of authoritative and prudent interventions, capable of helping to integrate the understanding of human problems about social life within the understanding of faith and capable therefore of correctly guiding Christians' responsible participation in social life.

Part Two

Morality in social life

Chapter 5

The relationship between charity and politics

BASTIANEL S., «Rapporto caritá e politica. Aspetto etico», in MARINELLI F., BARONIO L., EDD., *Carità e politica. La dimensione politica della carità e la solidarietà nella politica*, (Fede e annuncio, 21), Edizioni Dehoniane, Bologna 1990, 223-241. There is a shorter article «Carità e politica: problema etico», in *La Civilità Cattolica* 3341 140/3 (1989) 345-358. Under the fourth point are inserted two paragraphs taken from the article «Moralità e politica», in CANANZI A., ED., *Politica come servizio*, Piemme, Casale Monferrato 1994, 43-60.

The term charity, in normal use and in theological language, has various levels of meaning, which it is appropriate to recall in order to be able to clarify the meaning of the relationship between charity and politics, in view of the demands that it makes on Christian life and the expectations that can be placed on the political value of the witness of charity.

There are *charitable works* such as concrete gestures of neighborliness, help given to a needy person, concrete fraternal behavior. In this sense, every action that establishes a relationship of closeness is «charity». In attempting to define the «works» of charity, even in simply describing them, we must make reference to something that is not a work, but that defines the very personal inner self of someone who carries out an «act of charity»: it is the *virtue* of charity. This is sometimes understood in very general terms, such as an attitude of kindness and helpfulness, an openness to welcoming requests from others, a certain generosity and gratuitousness. Even when one adds the adjective «Christian» often it is in fact a generic reference to Christian teaching about love of neighbor.

This way of understanding things should not be undervalued; in it can be recognized one of the ways in which the Christian faith has made itself present in current culture, consciousness and thinking; however, there is a degree in which this cultural understanding is insufficient for the mature faith; it is not the «specific» Christian way of understanding the virtue of charity, and thus seen, in fact, it would be just *one* among the various virtues (de facto a «moral» virtue).

In *theology*, even though the explanations are not always the same, and above all there are different emphases, one speaks about charity as a *theological virtue*. It is a *gift* from God, belonging to the reality of grace, of communion with God. Together with faith and hope, it is a constituent part of our *receiving* salvation in Jesus Christ. Naturally, that does not exonerate us from the *exercise* of virtue; but rather it urges us to it, precisely because it is a gift of communion with God. Our responsibility is to accept the grace and care for it.

Even for someone who knows the catechism well and for whom knowledge of Christian theology about the virtue of charity is not an unknown, there nevertheless remains the possibility of still understanding it in a reductionist way. Sometimes, in fact, even considering it as a theological virtue, it is nevertheless seen at the same level as the others—more excellent, but *one* among the virtues. It is possible not only to distinguish it from the others, but also to separate it into a different field. For example, the Christian must have the moral virtue of temperance, and must also have that of charity; but charity does not necessarily come into play in determining what «temperance» might mean and how it should be lived.

Even in order to bring out the meaning and importance of charity as concrete gestures of closeness, the question of charity as a Christian virtue must be clarified. It is a matter of understanding how charity can be the «fulfillment of the law». St Thomas Aquinas speaks of charity as «forma virtutum», since «through charity the acts of all the other virtues are ordained to the ultimate end»[1].

To demonstrate the excellence of charity, or to show how it can be the «form» of the other virtues and fulfillment of all moral needs, there is a clear need to maintain the distinction between it and the other virtues, for example the distinction between charity and justice. Sometimes, however, one argues not just about distinction, but in fact separation, as if it were a matter of two different levels or planes: first justice with its need and its rationale, and then beyond this, charity with its needs and its rationale. In this way, on the plane of justice charity is not «regulatory». If necessary, it is remembered that there is not simply justice, but also a need to «go further»; however, in this way of thinking, charity is not crucial for understanding what is just and carrying out works of justice. At the level of the current mindset and sensitivity, this viewpoint is expressed in the widespread conviction that justice can be demanded and charity cannot. This is true at the level of juridical needs, but is it also true on the level of ethical needs? And on the level of morality lived in faith in Jesus Christ? In fact, today just as yesterday, it seems possible to assert the excellence of charity and at the same time to declare it to be irrelevant on a practical level.

1
Christian charity

Rooted in the gift of the theological virtue, in communion with God, Christian charity is a love «like that of Christ»: recognized in him, made possible through him, learned from him. The believer who has thus truly met Jesus Christ in his/her own life so as to be able to be called Christian (because everything is defined by that encounter), is the person who has «known» God's love for him/her, has welcomed it and makes it the *raison d'être* of one's own life. Accepting the gift

1 «*Per caritatem ordinantur actus omnium aliarum virtutum ad ultimum finem*» (*S.Th.* II-II, q.24, a.8, c).

of communion with God is to live it. Familiarity with him (with his word, in the awareness of his active presence) is the maturing of a personal inner self that allows itself to be formed by his Spirit, which gradually assumes in free responsibility *the very intentionality* of God's action and assumes for life on earth the same criteria to which the person of Jesus has given historical visibility. Thus one sees the passage from *knowledge of God's love* for us to *being with him* in our outlook on our brother or sister.

From the point of view of the dynamic of Christian conscience, knowing and accepting God as father is the same as knowing and accepting the other person as brother/sister (cfr. *Luke* 15:11-32; *1 John* 4:7-8). To recognize and accept the saving love of God in Jesus Christ is to give one's life as mediation of this saving love; it is to live in him, to walk as he walked (*1 John* 2:6). To recognize in Jesus the closeness of God who loves and saves is to become a neighbor (cfr. *Luke* 10:29-37). God's love for humanity achieves its goal in fraternal love (cfr. *1 John* 4:12)[2].

Charity is not fulfillment of the law in the sense of adding to the observance of the law other still more noble observances. It is not added to perfect extrinsically a construction that at any rate remains what it is. The sense of «fulfillment», or gospel radicalness, demands that every moral need (every «law» or «moral norm») be understood and lived within a significance and fundamental decision, which is charity. Therefore the perfect execution of the law is not its fulfillment, and therefore what is necessary is a «greater justice» (*Matt* 5:20). And the path of this fulfillment is shown to us *in the person of Jesus*, in the manner of *his* disciples, in a journey of conversion in which familiarity with the Lord gradually «converted» them to him[3].

To place charity at the foundation of one's own moral life, as that which defines in a Christian way the very demand of conscience (to «do good») does not mean carrying out extraordinary gestures of heroic unselfishness. Rather, it means making charity the *ordinary* dimension of every gesture (including those that are «heroic» if necessary), making it the interpretive criterion of life itself in all that concerns personal free responsibility. It is charity as *governing criterion*,

2 Cfr. MALATESTA E., *Interiority and Covenant. A Study of «einai» and «menein en» in the First Letter of Saint John*, (An Bib 69), Biblical Institute Press, Rome 1978.

3 For a more detailed examination of the connection between conversion and discipleship, BASTIANEL S., «Conversione», in COMPAGNONI F., PIANA G., PRIVITERA S., EDD., *Nuovo Dizionario di Teologia Morale*, Paoline, Rome 1990; cfr. MONGILLO D., «Conversione», in *Dizionario Teologico Interdisciplinare* I, Marietti, Turin 1977, 576-590; RAHNER K., «Conversion», in *Sacramentum Mundi* II, Burns & Oates, London 1968, 4-8.

what moves and guides all personal understanding and decision-making. It is the soul of Christian morality, the form of every virtue. Concrete action (not just doing, but also thinking, evaluating, feeling) will be an expression of the «measure» of our conversion, our discipleship in Christ, our charity.

2
The common good

Having noted the role of charity for a Christian's morality (for his/her honest, that is, virtuous life), we can at least illustrate this same role with respect to some ethical problems concerning the political life. The centrality of the theme of the «common good» is due to the fact that it constitutes the very *raison d'être* of the various forms of social structuring in life. This does not mean that the way of understanding and pursuing the common good is averse to misunderstandings and temptations. We will look at it in the actual context of pluralism, attempting to see what perspectives might be indicated, if the common good and pluralism are interpreted within the rationale of charity.

2.1. POLITICAL LIFE

We are thinking in this context about politics in the first instance as «life of the *polis*». In this sense all that contributes to building up human life together in a «city», in a structured society is politics. Of course, to that sphere belong legislative and administrative activities, but not only these (which, moreover, on their own would not be able to construct anything). Above all we have in mind that de facto unity which binds between them the various aspects and spheres of social interaction, making people who live side by side interdependent in their attempt to realize their own existence and even to understand and plan it.

The activity of professional politicians is possible and can be effective only inasmuch as it is rooted in the political life of the non-professionals and succeeds in influencing it. Political structures, in their very being and functionality, depend, from the most profound depths of their organization, on the relationships that express, in the visibility of daily life, people's ways of understanding and feeling. Thus, political activity is everything that impinges on this understanding and feeling, everything that contributes to forming the underlying mindsets of every organization of political life; we could easily say everything that contributes to forming consciences.

In this sense, a person's free and responsible action always has a political dimension and therefore implies a political responsibility[4]. In this sense, politics is a task common to everyone and one that cannot be delegated, even if specific tasks and roles can and must be delegated.

2.2. PLURALISM

In recent years much has been said and written about the crisis in western democracies[5]. Among the problems indicated, one that especially seems to us today to be of great importance in an ethical reflection is the difficulty, if not actually the incapacity (which seems to happen continually and in a substantial way) to propose/assume directions, options and unifying aims, in order to be able to establish goals sufficiently shared to be pursued with a unity of purpose and stability such that results might be achieved. Here at the various levels of co-existence we are faced with a reality extremely fragmented into social projects and different policies with, at the base, a great diversification with regard to hierarchies of values pursued and consequent prospects.

This seems to be a problem that goes beyond the level of political praxis in its legislative and administrative moments. It is a question that at heart touches the manner of living side by side and the ability to integrate diversity. For this—in addition to the practical questions about possible solutions—there is also a question about meaning, which involves the ethical dimension and questions the free responsibility of consciences that are involved.

Our era is characterized by a *de facto pluralism*. This is not simply a plurality of voices, like various harmonious shapes[6]. In our reality, it is about a pluralism that constantly generates conflicts, because it concerns the way of understanding

4 In this regard one often hears talk of «social» responsibility. By calling it «political» we mean to emphasize clearly the fact that it is a responsibility directly relating to political life, since this is what politics lives on, what makes possible and effective, or even nullifies, laws and administrative decisions. Here one could spell out the sense of personal responsibility with regard to the structures: cfr.. BASTIANEL S., «"Strutture di peccato". Una riflessione teologico-morale», in *La Civiltà Cattolica* 140 (1989), I 325-338.

5 Cfr. ARDIGO A., *Crisi di governabilità e mondi vitali*, Cappelli, Bologna 1980: AAVV., «Possibilità e limiti della partecipazione politica», in *Fenomenologia e Società* I (1978) 231-355; SASSON D., «La crisi del Welfare State», in *Quaderni di Azione Sociale* 30 (1981) 14/15, 23-45.

6 Cfr. NARDONE G., «Il pluralismo come esigenza di distinzione: il privato e il pubblico nel pensiero di Locke», in *Fenomenologia e Società* I (1978) 111-157.

and planning life. At issue are convictions, mindsets, and ways of understanding fundamental values. It is not a superficial pluralism, but a profound one, which expresses and tends to create fragmentations and oppositions in people's lives. It would be naïve to think of this pluralism as a goal, an ideal, and an achievement of civilization. The fact that people cannot succeed in living side by side is not an achievement.

What one sees in political life, with its consequences that always end up weighing down on the weakest, is true as well on the cultural and moral level: not just variety, but divergence and opposition in recognizing and appreciating morally important values.

If, on the one hand, there is the temptation to value naïvely the de facto pluralism as positive in itself, there is also the temptation to experience pluralism with impatience, which translates itself into various forms of impatience (even if hidden in «polite» forms) toward those who do not have the same convictions and do not pursue the same objectives. The seriousness of this temptation is revealed in the fact that the attempts to overcome conflicts with this attitude would be guided by methods and means internally consistent with the conflict itself and its causes: «overcoming» would be understood in the rationale of exerting one's own point of view as much as possible because it is one's own (of course, one would say «because it is true»).

Between the two temptations (of naïveté and actual non-acceptance), the correct *path* will be—as often happens in questions concerning conscience—the *assumption of the fact* (acceptance of it, without pretense of exorcizing its limits) and the *actual attempt to overcome it*, inasmuch as it implies the negative, adopting a rationale that is contrary to one that disrupts. The Christian will also find here the interpretive strength of charity; it is a matter of living a *rationale of communion*. Pluralism will be understood as the true historic place, or the path along which each person is called to the *human task of communion*, the human task of morality and faith lived on the earth.

The believer should have a degree of «more» hope in reading the conflict situation; some «more» utopian ability in planning paths of communion, by virtue of his/her *knowing* that the word «salvation» has already been pronounced, and that from the point of view of human co-existence, the *last word* will be *communion*, not by virtue of our abilities or a favorable situation, but by virtue of the salvific interventions of God (that are not only future, and neither only in the past).

2.3. COMMUNION (THE COMMON GOOD) AS GOAL

There is a way of understanding the common good that is difficult to be interpreted in terms of charity. When one thinks of the common good as sum of the goods possessed by many and directed toward the utility of individuals, it is meant as something functional for the *private good* of individuals (which therefore remain fundamentally *privately realizable*)[7].

But the human significance of social life, understood in faith, interpreted from the perspective of Christian charity, instead indicates moving toward a genuine communion of life. Thus, fundamentally, part of the «common good» will be the *common reaching out* to realize a way of living together that can be accurately called *communion*. The common good as reaching out toward the communion of goods, or even better as reaching out toward communion of/in the good, suggests the ideal on the basis of which to understand the human significance and human value of the even limited achievements of the common good that can be realized at the various levels of social interaction.

It is important to avoid a basic confusion, capable of working within every expectation or tension to realize the common good; a confusion present in the idea that it is a matter first of all of seeking one's own good, and—as a means to this end—of realizing a common heritage of goods (submitting also to specific rules of co-existence in order to guarantee it). In actual fact, to validate this signifies validating (declaring morally correct, morally sensible) a rationale of living together in which—even in seeking the common good—each person sees the other profoundly as basically a rival, an adversary, an enemy.

That approach, however, means legitimating even theoretically the fact of *generalized conflict and unavoidable competition*. In some way it is assuming an understanding of humanity on the premise that, *homo homini lupus*, the mutual confrontational relationship (and not of marginal unrest, but rather radical and constituent unrest) is the nature of the life of people on this earth, nor will it be different.

7 On close examination it is an idea linked to a history of sin that already characterizes human self-understanding in which society is understood as constituted by virtue of a contract, according to a rationale in which each person seeks his/her private personal good and, in order to be better able to pursue it, puts him/herself together with others. In such a way there is a mutual guarantee about the effectiveness of this privately seeking one's own good. With a mutual agreement, the other is, for each person, a tool for his/her own ends. On this basis it is «logical» to understand the common good by the same standard as a «common wealth», to which all contribute (the least possible) and from which all seek to profit (as much as possible).

If we look at political life in our countries, with the average intelligence we can have about what happens, we see that the understanding experienced about life together is often of this type. The assertion of rights and the search for guarantees for them are perhaps usually understood from the perspective of a private good in which recourse to the public dimension seems to be the attempt to make a radical conflict livable on the basis of some rules of compromise. So, we will have individuals and individual groups who will try to impose their weight as much as possible in order to incur the least cost possible—stated in economic terms—and have the greatest benefit. This becomes the rationale that structures relationships. But, if this is the rationale that structures relationships, it will be fairly difficult for it to come about on the chance that there would be a sufficiently stable fellowship over a political plan.

Therefore, what we must address from this point of view is something profound: the capacity, or incapacity, for *free responsibility*. On a moral level, freedom is the capability of responsibility when the goal is defined and choices motivated not just by one's own idea, one's own good, or one's own political plan (or those of the group to which one belongs, or one's «side»). Until in fact the *proper good*, as such and because it is such, constitutes the *object* and the *ratio* of choices and direction, it is impossible to see how the results can be anything but disruptive. What's more, a result will not just be constant disruption, but will mean *non-morality*, the pretense of building an ethic focused on self-seeking.

If we take into account the relationship between the institution and what animates the institution, between the structuring of co-existence and the formation of consciences, the conception/experience of the common good poses a crucial question about the morality-social interaction, the morality-politics relationship.

From a biblical-theological perspective, we must highlight the most profound reality of the «common good» in the common reaching out toward communion. In the biblical traditions this is indicated by the very intentionality of the creator, the very intentionality of God's salvific interventions, from the Exodus to Jesus' Passover: interventions that create unity of the «people», that create and demand communion, because the adherence of faith translates into mutual care, in true solidarity, in humanity in the full sense of the word, indicated and made possible in *agape*-gift of God and moral responsibility of the believer.

3

Dialogue as a Christian virtue

In an historical situation of pluralism, the way to communion can only be through dialogue. Here, too, we can be precise: dialogue as Christian virtue. That does not mean to claim it to be an exclusive or privileged prerogative of Christians. It is simply meant to recall that it too must be interpreted in a Christian way, that is, as a virtue animated by charity.

The emphasis «as a virtue» is meant to indicate a fundamental and constant attitude in dialogue. It is not a question of precise individual acts; it is a matter of *understanding one's own life as necessarily one of dialogue*, so that it can be morally positive.

3.1. MISUNDERSTANDINGS

The term «dialogue» has in fact assumed various meanings. Sometimes it is used to ennoble—with a more civil, refined, modern word— something that would be better described with terms such as clash, desire to prevail, or rationale of the strongest.

Thus, dialogue can be a confusing term, both at the level of social and political debate and at the level of discussion. Without wishing to reduce everything to the same level and give everything the same value, one can note, however, in the duel between the sword and «civil confrontation» that is «astute» dialogue, what generally changes is simply the type of weapon, while the meaning of the relationship between people is unchanging. It is always a matter of having an aim, wanting to achieve it and doing so in such a way that the other person would be left out if he/she is seen only as being functional to my aim. If his/her presence is an obstacle, I will in every way possible (or in the most «appropriate» way) remove him/her from the equation. This can be done either with the sword, or with the weapon of intelligence (making the other persons see their ignorance, lack of understanding, and so on), the weapon of politics (excluding them from the ability to influence matters), the weapon of economics, or the weapon of elegant and diplomatic dialogue.

Dialogue can also be instrumental in affirming and communicating important values. This, in fact, can be sought in two radically different ways. The first is that of placing one's own existence, experience, knowledge, in effect one's own person, alongside the person of the other as he/she is; in doing so, it shows the significance of what one lives and understands to be of value, and it indicates as well —by the way in which one opens up one's own conscience to that of someone else— the «why» of the desire for which he/she takes on that value. This is called *dialogue*: this placing of one's own word alongside that of someone else so that the *logos* proceeds through the two «words», the two subjects who understand and dialogue.

The same aim could nevertheless also be pursued in another way (neither purely hypothetical nor completely unheard of). It is that of the one who, at all costs and by all means, tries to obtain the desired result. So one tries cross-talk, a discourse and relationship that forces one to be on the defensive, always in such a way as to leave as little room as possible for freedom, in such a way as to make the adversary capitulate by using weapons of discourse, psychological mechanisms, and weapons less noble than these (as if these were noble!), such as ties of a social and political order, pressure, actual coercion, and so on. The skill of the persuasive discourse can be «instrumental astuteness». In the situation just described, this dialogue is called «violence». In this sense the term «dialogue» is used as an excuse and its use is clearly confusing.

Good intentions focused on reaching the material outcome are not enough. Good intentions that initiate correct relationships are what is needed, while at the same time leaning toward the result. The means are not justified simply by a good end, if this is attempted by *morally* evil means. In fact, where relationships are improper, we are in the realm of a moral, not just *physicum*, disvalue.

3.2. DIALOGICAL RELATIONS

The search for truth requires truthful discourse, internally *dialogical* in meaning; it is not enough to speak with a person at length, because words, too, are a tool, destined at the same time to communicate and to communicate what the person has to communicate, namely, the content and the person who communicates it, with his/her universe of values. The relationship between the content of truth or of lies that I communicate through the words and the reality of the relationships I establish —through communication of content— are two realities interdependent in their meaning and human value. If my word is uncommunicative or deceitful, then I am uncommunicative or deceitful, that is, falsely related to the other; this is the *primum* I communicate. If then my uncommunicative or deceitful word manages to convince the other (this is the art of rhetoric, the persuasive discourse) without there being a corresponding truth worthy of being accepted as such, if there is a desire to persuade because that is *my* truth and I wish to get it accepted, thereby I am not communicating only the content of the truth entrusted in the word, but at the same time I am communicating the conviction that the rationale of the word as well, is the *rationale of the strongest* and that one can be *master* of the word also, and through the word one can be *master of the other*. I am communicating the lived understanding that truth is a tool; that truth is that which the strongest communicates; and that truth is of no use in terms of shared humanity. When it is a matter of communicating a morally important value, in such a way one is also communicating one's own distrust in the objectivity and human reasonableness of the value itself[8].

Dialogue entails an *ability to speak and listen*. «Ability to listen», in its positive ethical value, does not mean just any state of listening, nor simply having the patience to listen to someone else speaking. Sometimes, even though this listening may not be so easy, it is still not the virtue of which we are speaking, since listening, too, can be done in a manipulative manner. One thinks of the case in which someone wishes to gain somebody else's support for his/her own ends and for this reason listens, is patient, shows him/herself to be understanding, interested and attentive —and at the right moment gets his/her results. Such a «dialogue» is a weapon, or rather it is skill in the use of the most appropriate and effective weapons. Instead, a true ability to listen means *giving over one self, one's time and ability to understand the other person*. It is not just hearing what the other says, but «listening»; it means *wanting to be in communion with him/her* through the word, to fully accept him/her as he/she is, not as one would wish that person to be, or in the way in which he/she is as one wishes.

The ability to listen is not the same as «knowing how to respond». One can be facing the other person like someone in a duel, attentive to the adversary's movements and moves, in order to parry the strikes and intervene effectively, exploiting his/her weaknesses. This in fact would be like listening to oneself, scrutinizing the other in order to know what to say to him/her, with a view toward achieving one's goals. This too is a rationale of an abuse of power.

The genuine ability to listen has all the signs of *giving oneself over*. It is the attempt to draw near in order to understand, to search for an understanding that is capable of shaping one's own word on the basis of how much will be understood

8 From this point of view, too, L. Wittgenstein's statement comes to mind: «the dominant morality is the morality of the dominant».

and with the aim of proceeding to the understanding of the truth through mutual understanding. Every human word, in order to be truly humanly meaningful, must be placed in an authentic context of relationship. It must be pronounced in «proximity». A theoretically human, valid and meaningful word, but expressed in an inhuman context—as would be the case in the absence of a true ability to listen— would, in fact, in the concrete reality of communication no longer be a human word (would not *speak* of humanity). One has only to think of how many words, discourses, ideas, testimonies, even concrete gestures of testimony, placed in such a manner as to be incomprehensible, remain unaccepted.

One might be quick to conclude: «Well, the other person didn't listen». In truth, we can see that often we ourselves, if we were in the other person's place, would not have understood; and this is not through any malicious intent. Often, the *defensive word* (self-defense) has all the ambiguity of a *war of defense*: the other is the one who probably does not want to listen, does not want to understand, does not want to accept; the other is the one from whom one can expect behavior, attitudes, responses, but the prior judgment is that he/she probably does not want to give them. Here is the substantial difference between «being a neighbor» and the demand that «the other become a neighbor».

Why can we call dialogue a *virtue*? Because in the midst of the difficulties of making oneself understood, it is a matter of maintaining without defensiveness—that is, with a real desire for communion— that communion is possible, that understanding is possible, that truth is not a good for one person and an evil for the other. A dialogical attitude, then, as expression of humanity in the manner of behavior and discourse, in the concrete human ways of entering into and remaining in relation with others, is the assertion—experienced and perhaps suffered, too, in both the internal and external aspects of relations— of the very meaning of personal morality. It is a virtue, because it is about the *way of relating oneself*, needing to find expression in all the different and many relational situations that present themselves. Virtue indicates a *personal unity*, that is, a prospective unity and continuity of attitude, which guides the concrete ways of expression. In this sense, the dialogical attitude is creator of personal unity; in this sense it encourages gradual growth in moral personal maturity.

3.3. TEMPTATIONS

There are *temptations*, variously but often present, which express themselves as *objections* to the prospect of a *dialogue as a virtue*, as a morally demanding and binding attitude. There are temptations that claim to be based on the experience of failure and the impossibility of dialogue, such as saying that I tried, we tried, but it did not succeed; I want to, but the other person doesn't, even though he/she benefits from it. It should be noted that similar arguments express a fundamental negative judgment about the other person, linked to the *presumption* of one's own truth and correctness. To assert —perhaps even on the basis of an actual experience of setbacks and failure— that therefore dialogue is impossible in its deepest reality, means dividing the world between the good (which is us) and the bad (which are the others).

When one feels and evaluates living together in a fraternal manner as being impossible, that is, the failure to live in full communion through the realization of concretely feasible levels of communion (attributing this failure to others «who don't want it», who «can't be changed»), one thereby expresses a radical rejection of dialogue, with the presumption of not needing to learn from the other, of already being converted. With this premise, even in the most courteous forms of behavior, what remains of dialogue does not go beyond a sort of magnanimous goodness, which concedes to others because one is tolerant and «superior», and therefore well-disposed. In fact, what is affirmed is that one does not need the presence of someone else and his/her word in order to better understand one's own words and the manner of one's own possible presence.

Another way of avoiding, and justifying in so doing, the effort and objective difficulties of establishing dialogical relations, seems to be that which is linked to the need for results, or the need to obtain consensus. In this case dialogue can also be verbally appreciated, but in fact, this also is seen as a tool, as if to say, if it were the most «appropriate» tool it would be used, but unfortunately that requires a long time and its effectiveness is not always guaranteed, and above all, the outcome must be guaranteed. This can be a matter of important human values, or vital truths, but to renounce dialogue in order to realize a human value is to profess to assert the value of the person by exploiting the person. To renounce dialogue in order to assert the value of truth is to declare that truth is a child of deceit. On the level of human authenticity, morality, and faith, it must be remembered that no value can be *truly* asserted or pursued by means that are internally contradictory to it.

In the light of the discourse elaborated here, it should be fairly obvious that in the manner of our relating to the other, depending on whether that is truly dialogical or not, beyond explicit intention and declaration, we inevitably communicate our freedom or reliance on the work of our hands, the hope or desire to possess one's own life. The term «dialogue», therefore, can clearly indicate a way of relationship or communion that, at all levels, expresses the truth —greater or lesser truth— of our faith and our hope. Here, too, one recalls the extremely close connection between life-moral testimony and life-testimony of faith: the unity of personal experience and personal communication, for which existence as a believer and the testimony of faith are accomplished in the *medium* of lived morality, in the life and manner of inter-personality.

4
The witness of charity

122 Having illustrated the meaning of charity as the «soul» of Christian morality[9] in reference to the two great themes of social life (the common good and dialogue), we can better appreciate also the witness value of the individual gestures of charity and fraternal charity experienced in the ecclesial community, particularly if we take into account some element of the crisis in democratic life today.

4.1. THE CRISIS OF DEMOCRACIES

One aspect of the so-called «crisis in values» today seems to impact particularly upon our human society (now evidently not only on the western world): the great plurality of options and values pursued manifests itself also as a lack of shared aims and an inability to form sufficiently stable fellowships around demanding projects, to the point of seriously burdening social life and contributing to rendering us incapable of operating effectively at various levels within the institutional bodies themselves[10].

Obviously, the problem is not just at the level of the functionality of the political and social structures, but also at the level of social conscience, mindset and ways of co-existence. A human society in which non-sharing, the multiplic-

9 Cfr. BASTIANEL S., «La carità anima della morale Cristiana», in DONI P., ED., *Diaconia della carità nella pastorale della Chiesa locale*, Lib. Gregoriana Ed., Padua 1986, 293-305.

10 Cfr. ARDIGO A., *Crisi di governabilità e mondi vitali*, Cappelli, Bologna 1980; AAVV., «Possibilità e limiti della partecipazione politica», in *Fenomenologia e Società* 1 (1978) 231-355; OFFE C., «Ingovernabilità. Lineamenti di una teoria conservatrice della crisi», in *Fenomenologia e Società* 2 (1979) 5, 54-65; SASSON D., «La crisi del Welfare State», in *Quaderni di Azione Sociale* 30 (1981) 14/15, 23-45.

ity and fragmentation of plans, and the episodic and limited character of proposals or attempts at consensus seem to prevail as givens, is a reality that tends to form consciences in its image and likeness. Sometimes in an explicit manner, more often in a hidden way—but nonetheless still substantial and harmful—a temptation of «resignation» easily advances, assuming different guises and justifications. In various ways, it is always a *tendency to justify the fact as inevitable*, thus justifying a whole world of evaluations and consequent behavior. At worst, the proposal is to share as a civil value and goal the opportunity to provide the greatest space possible to the private sphere; that is, the common good would consist in guaranteeing only the necessary (minimal) conditions for itself so that the private good can be privately pursued.

It would seem that one can read into this tendency a type of resignation in the face of the setbacks of hopes previously nourished, a unilaterally negative interpretation of recent historical social process. Along with this is a similarly naïve trust in a kind of instinctive goodness of humanity, which would keep individuals in the position where they were hardly defended in their existence.

In fact, recent history and contemporary events seem to reveal this trust to be of little foundation, indicating instead the risk potential (already not simply hypothetical) in which disruption with respect to the pursued ends is capable of intensifying. In reality, the figure of conscience implied in such a tendency, which I call «resignation», is that of someone who radically trusts only oneself and that which is within one's own hands. Once again it could be a rationalization of *generalized mistrust*, in which the other person is seen as a rival or at least prospective enemy, and the pursuit of common ends is feared as limiting the potential of personal expansion and is therefore humiliating.

It must be emphasized that a similar form of conscience, wherever it is widespread, can only be paralyzing for civil growth, tending to create «spontaneously» a structuring of social relations that entrusts the necessary minimum to social interaction, and moreover has a fundamental attitude of defense and suspicion. The problem has direct ethical impact.

4.2. SERVICE AND GRATUITOUSNESS

When the subject understands him/herself simply in relation to a complex of values judged as such on the basis of the possibility of «realizing oneself», in his/her eyes everything is fundamentally available. The ultimate criterion of evaluation is self-assertion and one's own personal free development. A similar attitude is also possible within the structure of a complex and sophisticated society, as well as in people who actively participate in social life, accepting its rules and contributing to creating and transforming them.

In such a scenario, therefore, when looking at the individual person one must say that unrecognizable in it is the figure of a genuinely ethical conscience. Looking at the results of human co-existence, one would say that convergence about discernment of values and aims remains entrusted to chance, while the possibility of the genuine sharing of values and aims remains fundamentally contradicted.

With respect to political activity in the specific sense, the ethical requirement is more than just a recalling to the correctness of behavior that is respectful of lawfulness and inspired by faithfulness toward institutions. This aspect, which is also fundamental and would perhaps be a great achievement for constructive political praxis, still represents only the necessary minimum. The positive requirement, which must animate political life in general and specific political activity, is the search for the common good *because it is good*, without secondary aims, and therefore without privileging oneself or the group to which one belongs, and without conditioning one's own commitment to that benefit.

To introduce (or strengthen) a soul of morality in politics means allowing the dimension of gratuitousness to mature in it. It is a question of ethical conscience, of conscious and free responsibility in the search for the objective good, according to what is concretely possible. Only thus can the diversity of roles and the multiplicity of competences be organized and become an actual convergence of aims. It is not a matter of «adjusting» something or modifying some strategy. At question is the mindset, the way of thinking and feeling, evaluating and choosing. For the renewal of political life as well, if it is to be understood in terms of humanity, the necessary path is that of the formation of consciences; and formation often means conversion.

4.3. THE WORKS OF CHARITY

The concrete gesture, an expression of charity as Christian morality, has manifold value from the point of view of its effectiveness. It is the realization of a positive human value (for example, a life saved); it is the realization of correct human relations and therefore the realization of a positive morality that assumes historical visibility; it is a concrete indication of the moral good as «humanly effective», as true human realization. In terms of faith that means that the Christian witness of the believer is pointing toward the kingdom of God by making it present. It is «making the earth fruitful» by making it become the kingdom of communion. It is making a contribution so that culture and politics may truly become the place and opportunity for genuine humanity, according to the intentionality of the creator and redeemer.

The newness that is Christ and that makes us be in Christ is not a purely spiritual-intimate reality (to be experienced only in the intimacy of conscience), nor only individual (confined to an individual relationship with God). Instead, it is such as to produce a dynamic of historic effectiveness in the concurrence of relationality and its structuring within social life[11]. That is, if I carry out a gesture of justice, it is something that lasts longer than I. Its effects are also entrusted to the relational life of someone else and can thus also grow independently of me (and even of my possible successive sin). These effects contribute to form the rationale on which social life is structured, encouraging positive opportunities in this life.

Care for the objective value of the «charitable» responses to situations of need, in the context of a moral life in which «charitable» tends to be every response to the appeal to human values that engage personal freedom and responsibility, therefore unites the effectiveness of the concrete gesture with the communication of meaning. The charitable response is a «good» for the individual and a«good» for the morality of social life; it interests the external appearance and the innermost being of the people directly involved, reaching through them the same dynamic of political life.

In saying that the morally good and correct concrete gestures have *historical effectiveness*, we must also remember that the outlook we bring to the world, to the social situation, to society, must be a look internally, deeply animated by the experience of faith[12]. This means to live the experience of faith as a relationship with the present Christ, as an experience of a salvation present and active, that is, the salvation of which the Christian life is called to be a witness, a «sacrament».

11 Cfr. the reflection on the «structures of sin» in the Encyclical *Sollicitudo rei socialis*.

12 We wish to allude to the fact that the Christian cannot presume to have an effective witness of charity without caring for his/her foundation of lived faith. In particular, here the importance of personal adult prayer must be emphasized, precisely in its relationship to the capacity for Christian morality: cfr. BASTIANEL S., *Vita morale nella fede in Gesù Cristo*, San Paolo, Cinisello Balsamo 2005, 69-175.

4.4. CHRISTIAN COMMUNITY AND POLITICAL COMMUNITY

Christians are called to live in the manner just discussed in order to indicate —through their way of behavior, along with their explicit word— the newness in which they are constituted, the kingdom of God on earth, a present and possible authentic humanity.

The two terms —present and possible— aim to recall the fundamental reality (which is the work of salvation already decisive and active), its partial visibility, and the fact that it is also entrusted to our free responsibility. At the same time we are both children and parents of our history. This fact comes to us as responsibility. It is a task that is more precise, and therefore binding, the more one has the gift of being able to recognize it clearly. That is, the believer, having by virtue of his/her faith a further possibility of hope regarding the positive interpretation of history, has therefore a more precise and clear task of manifesting and making present this reality. It is the responsibility of incarnating a «rationale of communion» (the opposite of the rationale of possession and opposition, in which sin is expressed).

A rationale of communion is achieved through the realization of free and liberating relationships. Fraternal charity is the name of a gifted freedom that makes the freedom of the other person possible, of a gifted life that makes possible the life of the other, of an existence shared in the mutual witness of faith.

Of course, trust in the effectiveness of making oneself a neighbor needs a previous experience. For the believer in Christ such previous experience is the very meeting with him. The believer's trust is rooted in the resurrection of the Lord, the foundation of his/her belief that his/her own life is definitively under the sign of salvation. This means that the possible «risk of freedom» is not experienced like the risk of one's own annihilation. It means being able to carry out gestures in true freedom, not conditioned by previous evaluation about effectiveness in terms of one's own benefit, but determined by free and objective evaluation of that which is good.

The experience of being saved is the experience of the one who has not merited salvation; it is the experience of one who has been saved being a sinner, not that of someone who is rewarded because he/she is just, with a gesture of salvation because it is due to him/her. It is the experience of a love received gratuitously, as *love that gives life* and as love completely free from nuances of possession, while the experience of human love, at different levels, always bears the mark of a desire to possess. The fact of having, as terminus of our understanding of relationality, God's gratuitous love —*analogatum princeps* of experience, not just of idea— liberates the understanding of love from that withdrawal for which it is always exposed in our experience.

Thus, we must have an interpretation of the human, and therefore of history, which does not escape into idealism (almost as if evil did not exist), but neither is it resigned to evil (almost as if it were inevitable). This fact supposes and witnesses to the awareness that the active intentionality of God is always newly present and victorious and that the believer becomes part of this intentionality, appropriating it as his/her own. To make themselves people of the kingdom means assuming as one's own perspective on life, action and decisions, the meaning that God's work has in history.

At its various levels, to live charity is *moral witness*: it points out the way of living in free responsibility, in the face of the challenge of human values and disvalues that present themselves. It is a witness of humanity —assertion and incarnation of humanity— that is always making possible further humanity. Such a moral witness belongs to the Christian vocation. When expressing the reality of being saved, one expresses the reality of a true humanity that is concretely possible and not simply ideal. A church that lives and is structured, in its visible expression also, according to a transparent rationale of charity/communion, is a church that in a significantly visible manner points to what the human story is called to be.

Just as the individual's witness, so also that of the believing community is born and develops in communion with God and by virtue of it. At the same time, it is a reality that is incarnated in history and has its historic effectiveness. The believing community, inasmuch as it truly is such, can indicate, by making it present, a more human «earth», in which the humanity of individuals is made possible and promoted also by the institutional forms and human structures of life together.

Chapter 6

Human values, moral values and economic structures

BASTIANEL S., «Valori umani, valori morali e strutture economiche», in CIPRIANI S., ED., *Nuove frontiere dell'etica economica*, AVE, Rome 1990, 71-92.

1

An ethics of the economy?

To a certain extent it is common knowledge today that certain major economic problems are not just economic problems, at least in the sense that the economy alone cannot solve them. It is easy to see that politics plays a significant role in them. With politics one can see how social and cultural problems are present. By looking at social and cultural problems in particular, one is perhaps forced to recognize that the ethical question, the question about free responsibility, cannot be avoided in the role that it plays at the cultural and social level, at the level of politics and the economy.

1.1. ECONOMY AND MORALS

The economic reality —especially if we are speaking about economic structures— presents itself today as something highly complex. Inevitably, in order to be able to understand a complex problem, we must distinguish its various aspects. Doubtless, however, the «distinct» consideration of one aspect is not enough to understand a complex human phenomenon; for example, North-South relations cannot be understood simply by considering the monetary issues involved.

Regarding moral reflection, the necessity that it should take into account the economy, politics, and so on, must be recognized. At issue is the objective reality of morality in its concrete historical dimension; the aspects on which to reflect and assess cannot be obtained unless it draws from appropriate sources.

It should also be said that, even in economic matters, the moral dimension cannot be introduced in a way that is extrinsic to the end, after the operative «economic» conclusions have been treated. Morality concerns the economy (like politics) in the objective reality of its concrete historical dimension; however, often it is perhaps something one tries to avoid, arguing from the fact that the economy has its internal laws, which are not *moral* laws, but simply *economic* laws.

In no way can moral reflection substitute for economic reflection, nor can it by itself reach technical conclusions of an economic nature. However, moral reflection does show how even the «technical» questions about economic institutions and structures are never *just* technical questions. They always involve some hidden options of meaning and imply certain aims, with their ethical value, and there is also always involvement in structures of human relations, which have an impact on people's lives. No structure is historically «neutral», since at work in the structure is the intentionality of the person who sets it in motion and who makes it live by living in it. The critical aspiration of morality is made clear in the question about the *authentically human* that a particular structure in fact expresses, facilitates, prevents or denies.

Perhaps the crucial point of the matter is to recognize that the economy has its specific «autonomy» (its «laws» are not deducible from other fields), while at the same time recognizing how this autonomy can only be relative, not just relative like all human things, which are not absolute; not just relative to other social and political factors, because it is connected to them; but relative also on the level of values, on the ethical level, in the sense of a normativity that on this level derives from the values, from which it cannot escape, and in respect to which it cannot pretend to be neutral[1].

The Encyclical *Sollicitudo rei socialis* met with approval and objections precisely because of its presumption to interpret political and economic processes from an ethical standpoint, stating that they are never ethically neutral and calling for interdependency among the various factors to be assumed in a perspective of solidarity. The question is, then, in what sense, at what level, with what dynamics do economy and morals interact between them?

1.2. A PERSONAL AND CULTURAL PROBLEM

In personal life all that belongs to the freedom of choice belongs to the responsibility of conscience. Even at the level of economic activity the ethical dimension occurs: in personal life, at all levels of interpersonal relations, from the simplest and direct, to those more complex and involved. Responsibility of conscience is at issue in the personal choices of individuals and in participation in collective choices. It lies at the basis of the process of formation of a cultural ethos, of moral thinking that develops in the sharing of evaluations and hierarchies of values,

1 For the ethical problem of the economy cfr.. AUBERT J.M., *Per una teologia dell'epoca industriale*, Cittadella, Assisi 1973; CHIAVACCI E., *Teologia morale*, III, *Teologia morale e vita economica*, Cittadella, Assisi 1985; GATTI G., *Morale cristiana e realtà economica*, LDC, Turin 1981; MATTAI G., «Problemi etici di vita economica», in GOFFI T., PIANA G., EDD. *Corso di Morale, 3, Koinonia*, Queriniana, Brescia 1984, 331-451; MOSSO S., «Etica ed economia nell'insegnamento degli Episcopati Cattolici dei Paesi industrializzati», in *La Civiltà Cattolica* 3313 139 (1988) 52-59; VIDAL M., *L'atteggiamento morale*, III, *Morale sociale*, Cittadella, Assisi 1981, 260-316.

which are the usual criteria of behavior. On it lie the structures of human life, in their organization and consolidation, as well as in their variations; moral responsibility cannot be eluded in the reflection and in the theoretical justification of models and criteria that are posited and proposed as morally valid.

Thus, when faced with serious social problems caused by the economy, the individual is not capable of solutions that can morally cure the whole relational system of our world. It would also be futile to try to point out the guilty, isolating responsibilities and making a self-declaration of innocence. Political and economic systems, even the most robust and stable, do not stand without a genuine and widespread basis of consensus; at least the known or presumed advantages must be preferable, despite the also known evils or injustices.

Serious and lasting injustices are not possible without extensive connivance. They cannot be resolved by individual interventions. They require correct mentalities, ways of thinking and acting, habitual appropriate behavior. For moral problems connected with the economy, what is at issue is a recognized and shared sound morality, an *extensive ethical culture*, which makes possible and favors the recognition and realization of more human ways.

2
Personal morality

To clarify first of all the terms of the problem about the relationship between morality and the economy, we must consider the dynamic of the personal moral life inasmuch as it is expressed in the sphere of social interaction, taking into account the structure of social life. This concerns the morality of people and their responsibility for the human values to be realized; at the same time, it concerns the relationship between the inner level of morality and the establishment of structured relations in the visibility and concreteness of social institutions.

2.1. HUMAN VALUES

We recall some of the constitutive elements of the moral life, remembering the necessary relationship between the objectivity of the value terms, to which personal action is addressed, and the intentionality of the subject who assesses, decides and acts[2]. By «human values» we mean all that is «of value» for the person,

2 Cfr. BASTIANEL S., *Autonomia morale del credente*, Morcelliana, Brescia 1980, 24-66.

for his/her effective life, at the various levels and in the various spheres of existence, that is, that which satisfies a need, which expands the opportunities for growth and authentically human self-realization, in a word, that which is objectively «good» for a person. In this general sense, values and disvalues, good and evil, indicate what objectively is useful or not to the life of human beings.

Determining what is properly of value, or what is instead an evil for the person, is not done on the basis of the human person him/herself and of his/her arbitrary will. Rather, the person finds him/herself in an objective context of reality that is not his/hers to give. In this context, he/she finds him/herself confronted by needs, opportunities and restrictions, and is called to assume, understand and assess. Proper to the human being is the ability to recognize values and make decisions with reference to them. He/she can and must do so, on the basis of his/her experience, in his/her ability to understand him/herself and understand the implications. With such recognition and decision-making, he/she transcends the pure factuality of existence and creates further opportunities or further restrictions with respect to the conditions of good and evil in which he/she finds him/herself.

It must be remembered that the exercise of the human capacities for understanding and decision-making about values is always situated in a cultural context, that is, that understood personal experience is related and relational, the fruit of history and the creation of history. In this, too, historical and cultural conditions are at the same time the locus of opportunities as well as restrictions. In concrete terms they constitute the actual space of freedom and therefore of personal responsibility. The impossibility of realizing a good or avoiding an evil cannot be attributed to a person (as long as that person is not the cause of the impossibility itself). On the other hand, if today there are opportunities for good that were not there yesterday, that means as well, that today there are also responsibilities that were not there yesterday.

2.2. MORALITY

In the search for and realization of human values, we recognize a «modality» of human worth that we describe as «moral», or «ethical». By this we recognize the fact that, in the relationship to what is good or evil for someone, we assert or deny the personal value of the other person. It is not simply a matter of «doing» things, but rather of accepting or rejecting the presence of the other as person. A realized human value is a «good» for someone (a person's hunger is satisfied, people are healed, educated, consoled; have work, can provide for their own life, have a family, defend themselves in court, and so on). To realize a human value without secondary intentions, but because it is a human value, that is, because one wishes for the good of the other person, makes the one who achieves it «good». Such «being good» is also a human value for the person; it expresses and realizes his/her humanity and even positively defines the whole person in his/her personal authenticity. Not only is it *a* good, but it is *the* good that he/she is called to live, what the classical moral principle refers to in the phrase «do good and avoid evil». While other human goods can justly be sacrificed for a more important or more urgent value, the moral value (what defines the person in his/her being or not being «good») can never be sacrificed. Precisely because individual human values as such are «values» for the human person in that they make the person «human», they cannot be truthfully asserted while denying or contradicting the goodness of the person him/herself.

The moral value is not identified with any of the other human values. It consists in the quality of the personal relation to human values. It is about the personal liberty in assuming or not assuming in one's own responsibility the search for and achievement of human values as such, that is, inasmuch as they are a good for someone. In relation to the concrete value as a good for someone, at issue is the relation to the other person (to others), whose ethical requirement demands precisely «a response»[3]. It is a matter of responding to the other person by assuming objective reality as it regards actual opportunities for the realization of human values. If I avoid such responsibility, I deny the «human» worth of value, I deny the personal value of the essence of the other person, and I deny that moral goodness is the value of my person.

It should be remembered here that to accept the other person in a conditional way (if that person benefits me or does not damage my interests too much) in fact is not actually acceptance of the other, nor is it doing a good because of the value recognized, but rather it is self-seeking and exploitation of the other person: the criterion is the jealous possession of one's own life.

3 For example, in signing a contract, while on the ethical level I am not called to respond «in the eyes of the law», I must respond to the other people involved in the contract, and not because of what they might be in a position to demand, but rather because of what they are as persons. Beginning with and by virtue of that, the law too commits me in conscience, through and beyond the letter of the law.

The ethical requirement of personal life is that of being a *morally good* person in the search for what is *morally correct*, or to be precise in attempting to understand and achieve what is objectively good in the actual opportunities. The contingent choices, with the restricted opportunities for action that belong to human life, entail the necessity of a comparative assessment between the good and the evil they offer for personal decision. This assessment cannot be taken on the basis of objective criteria of hierarchy and urgency if one wants the choice to be a choice of the good and not of subjective will. It entails the objective requirement to sacrifice goods or accept evils, but with the genuine personal intentionality linked to the good to be achieved, that is, the good practically possible and understood as good and possible.

2.3. CHRISTIAN INTERPRETATION

In revelation and Christian theology, the connection between relationship with God and relationship with the other person gives the meaning and value of fraternal love to the positive moral value[4]. This is then specifically interpreted in the very person of Jesus Christ, and that implies a radicalization (not in the sense of demanding extraordinary gestures, but in the sense of requiring complete transparency) of the theme of personal «free responsibility», assumed in its most profound human significance. Any type of behavior is morally defined as «good» only on the basis of the fact that it is guided by the logic of love, the assumption of the other person's responsibility, life, freedom and good.

The interpretive horizon is history itself interpreted as salvation history. The intentionality of God's interventions, from creation to resurrection in Jesus Christ, is a love that creates communion and makes us capable of creating communion[5]. In this light the believer is called to understand and assume in his/her own life the meaning of that which is authentically human, the perspective in which to interpret the opportunities and difficulties of action, and the utopia toward which to direct planning in the various spheres of existence.

4 On charity in the unity of its two dimensions cfr. RAHNER K., «Reflections on the unity of the love of neighbour and the love of God», in ID., *Theological Investigations*, VI, Darton, Longman & Todd, London 1974, 231-249; with specific reference to the theme cfr. BASTIANEL S. «La carità anima della morale cristiana», in DONI P., ED. *Diaconia della carità nella pastorale della Chiesa locale*, Lib. Gregoriana Ed., Padua 1986, 293-305; ID., «Carità e politica: problema etico», in *La Civiltà Cattolica* 3341 140/3 (1989) 345-358; ABIGNENTE D., *Decisione morale del credente. Il pensiero di Josef Fuchs*, Piemme, Casale Monferrato 1987, 13-37, 85-104.

5 Cfr. *Gaudium et Spes*, 32.

In this sense we may say that fraternal love is the rule and soul of Christian behavior. Charity is not fulfillment of the law in the sense of adding something to the observance of the law. It does not extrinsically perfect moral behavior. The meaning of «fulfillment», or evangelical radicality, calls for the understanding and living out of every moral requirement (every law or moral norm) within a meaning and fundamental decision which constitutes charity. Therefore the perfect fulfillment of the law is not its completion, and thus «a greater justice» (*Matt* 5:20) is necessary; the means for this fulfillment is shown to us in the person of Jesus, in the manner of his fulfillment, in the manner of his love. If fraternal love is the rule of every relationship, the ethical aspiration always proposes the search for what is good for the people with whom one is involved, with respect to their objective conditions and according to one's own possibilities.

Charity is the soul of Christian morality inasmuch as it confers on each understanding of values, each assessment, decision, and conduct, a profound meaning of fraternity rooted in communion and inclined toward fuller communion. This is valid for every sphere of behavior, including economic activity. In the gospels we find the answer to concrete questions about the values implied in economics; but we are told that each value is judged beginning with love of neighbor, which humanly corresponds to what makes the other person live. This concrete action must express and realize the meaning of making oneself the neighbor (*Luke* 10:29-37).

In a specific situation, when determining what constitutes concrete behavior consistent with justice, we are aided by laws, institutions, customs, and so forth. These, however, do not exhaust justice. By observing them, one is «justified» in the eyes of the law, the institution, and the custom, but that does not necessarily mean one is justified in terms of conscience[6]. The Christian, faced with his/her conscience, is addressed by the meaning and requirement of charity. Charity will justify his/her behavior «in keeping with justice», precisely in his/her being or not being in keeping with justice, based on the fact that there may be or not be a true intentionality of love in trying to understand, assess and decide on behavior.

6 The distinction is well known beyond the Christian environment as well. The law can also be a weapon that kills («*summum ius summa iniuria*») and can be deliberately used as such. But, without addressing extreme cases, it can also be a pretext for self-justification, with the aim of avoiding demands one doesn't wish to recognize.

3

Structured moral and social life

One now moves on to consider the relationship between personal morality and the social dimension of our lives. This consideration raises the issue of personal responsibility in regard to the values of life in society and asks the question about the basic criteria for understanding the meaning of social life from the moral point of view; however, there is also a question about the influence of social life (culture, structures and institutions) on personal morality. The mutual dependency between morality and social interaction must be understood coherently from the point of view of ethical understanding and living.

3.1. MORALITY AND SOCIAL INTERACTION

Morality is the experience of freedom that is called to be responsible before the other person, accepted or rejected in his/her personal value, through decisions that directly or indirectly concern that person in what is good or evil for him/her. The relationship with the other person is the place of moral experience, which thus is involved at the root of the social dimension of our lives. Human co-existence is structured, in fact, in relationality.

The interpersonal relationship between two people tends to «structure itself» in time. Regarding its effects, free responsibility exercised in relationships never ends at the precise moment of the relationship. It creates the liberating or constraining conditions of future relations, pre-guiding them in one way rather than another, since it creates expectations and manners of reacting, modeling previous understandings, assessments and decisions that contribute to building up a person's actual existence. If, for example, the criterion that sustains and structures an interpersonal relationship is that of the individual usefulness of two people, this will be evidenced in both by a series of choices and preferences, attitudes and sentiments, reactions and plans. Individual benefit will tend to qualify how one usually looks at another person, or another thing. In the exercise of subsequent and continued concrete choices thus «motivated», there develops a personal interiority qualified by self-seeking and possession, which tends to subdue everything and everyone to one's own ends, attempting to make them an instrument for one's own life. If people thus «formed» live together, they can only bring these same criteria to giving structured and institutional shape to their social life. If this happens, the individual finds him/herself confirmed in those criteria by the fact that they are common, utilitarian to society thus established, corresponding to the expectations of others, bound by laws and institutions and protected by them[7].

Therefore, an individual relationship always fits into a context of relationships and depends on others and influences others. It always belongs to a more complex phenomenon, the structuring of personal existence within the structuring of human society; individual action depends on it (not necessarily in a passive manner) and has a precise influence on it, consolidating or trying to modify what is already given.

3.2. MORALITY AND STRUCTURES

Personal moral goodness is realized in the search for and realization of objective human values. The more genuine the moral goodness is, the more, *coeteris paribus*, is the person able to recognize what is authentic human value and to be able to plan the most suitable ways for achieving it. The reason for this more favorable condition lies in greater inner freedom. Here there is a genuine objective historical strength, that is, goodness belongs to history and builds up the history of recognizing and achieving good.

Personal moral goodness is the realization of relations in the presence of a liberating freedom. In social life the structuring of relations puts into effect the logic of de facto active relations. Thus, the structures that people create for their social life provide visibility, consistency, strength and stability to the rationale of the relations on the basis of which they are constructed[8]. The structures, therefore, the work of human beings, in their effectiveness will bear the mark of the moral quality of those who construct them and those who assume them, both positively and negatively. It is in this sense that one speaks about «structures of sin», and likewise in parallel one could talk about structures of conversion.

When within a relationship the other person is seen as a prospective rival, as a possible enemy, as someone from whom one must above all defend oneself, human society tends to structure itself according to a rationale of possession and

7 It is what is rightly said about so many problems, such as abortion, divorce, matters of sexuality or genetics. But that concerns no less the sphere of laws relating to wealth, salaries, financial policies, and the various problems that involve economic relations.

8 For further treatment of this, BASTIANEL S., «Strutture di peccato. Riflessione teologico-morale», in ID., ED. *Strutture di peccato. Una sfida teologica e pastorale*, Piemme (Moralia Christiana 3), Casale Monferrato 1989, 15-38.

defense, which will be quick to sanction conflict and domination as necessary. The result is a fundamentally violent society, even if sometimes in a refined way and usually under the protection (for the strongest) of the law. People's justice will be inclined to this rationale. Personal morality will find difficulty with the restrictions on human life that are the historic result of sin and that have the strong foundation of what inwardly structures mentalities and what socially structures institutional mechanisms.

Of course, that does not mean that there is no longer room for responsible freedom in our world. Rather, it means that sin and its strength (not something marginal and not something in some way external to our being and our life) present themselves with the seduction of being a benefit or even a necessity and of being rational. They are realities so rooted in and structuring of personal and social existence as to define, not just good will, but also even sound judgment, basically solicited by self-justifying «reasons».

A specific culture, to the extent of its relative stability, expresses what de facto within its sphere is shared concerning the understanding of human beings and human values, concerning the planning of human life according to a hierarchy of values, and concerning the practical rules of behavior assumed as normative. Culture is the result of exercised and shared rationality. It is the mediation of such rationality, and as such it suggests assistance and restrictions to the further exercise of the same rationality of human beings. In the sphere of moral experience that means a plethora of pre-assessments and pre-judgments, which are offered to be assumed, with the claim of already tried and verified validity.

Structures and institutions express themselves mostly in terms of the strength of a cultural moment. They live out of the culture that they express, but the culture cannot live on them. A culture's rationality and ethical principles are alive when they are exercised; they cannot live on past exercise, and they cannot simply be repetitive (this is the illusion of «preservation»).

The morality of social life, amid the institutions and structures already given, is a requirement of one's personal assumption of the transmitted ethical principles and rationality[9]. That which is «already-given», however important, in

9 The Apostolic Exhortation *Reconciliatio et paenitentia* noted: «At the heart of every situation of sin are always to be found sinful people. So true is this that even when such a situation can be changed in its structural and institutional aspects by the force of law or —as unfortunately more often happens by the law of force— the change in fact proves to be incomplete, of short duration and ultimately vain and ineffective, not to say counterproductive if the people directly or indirectly responsible for that situation are not converted» (16).

itself does not have guarantees of truth, nor normative force. It belongs to the offered possibilities (help and restrictions) for the actual exercise of a rationality that guides the exercise of free personal responsibility.

3.3. SOLIDARITY

The Encyclical *Sollicitudo rei socialis*, which proposes solidarity as the interpretive criterion for the values of social life, defines it as «a firm and persevering determination to commit oneself to the common good; that is to say, to the good of all and of each individual, because we are all really responsible for all» (n. 38).

The Second Vatican Council spoke about solidarity particularly in connection with the relationship between the church and the world (*Gaudium et spes*) and about the presence and witness of the laity in the social and political spheres (*Apostolicam actuositatem*), in reference to the themes of the common good and the co-responsibility in it: progress, peace and universal brotherhood[10].

In regard to the foundation of solidarity, the Council recalled that, from creation to redemption in Jesus Christ, God's action is aimed at fraternal communion between human beings, and he calls on believers to assume the same intentionality as he in their action. This concerns that love which has in Christ himself the model and pledge of its possibility on earth. One remembers that he identified himself with the needy (*Matt* 25:40) and that, in assuming human nature, he has united to himself all humanity in a supernatural solidarity that makes of it one single family. He has made charity the distinguishing mark of his disciples, in the words: «By this will everyone know you for my disciples, by your love for one another» (*John* 13:35)[11].

In a similar fashion, John Paul II's Encyclical indicates solidarity as Christian interpretation, founded on charity, of the virtuous moral attitude about the values of social life. The theme is linked to analysis of social phenomena in which politics and economics are closely entwined, and on a global scale and in successive generations, they bring to light the historic datum of the fundamental unity and interdependence that links between them human beings and peoples, in good and evil, in progress and catastrophes wrought about by man. Solidarity[12]

10 Cfr. *Gaudium et Spes*, 1, 31, 32, 38; *Apostolicam actuositatem*, 8, 14.

11 *Apostolicam actuositatem*, 8.

12 Cfr. GIORDANO M. CARD, «Il fondamento cristiano della solidarietà», in *RdT* 30 (1989) 399-412; CODINA V., *De la modernidad a la solidaridad. Seguir a Jesús hoy*, CEP, Lima 1984; SORGE B., «Solidarietà e sviluppo», in BASTIANEL S., ED. *Strutture di peccato. Una sfida teologica e pastorale*, Piemme (Moralia Christiana 3), Casale Monferrato 1989, 57-63.

translates charity in the sphere of socially structured relations. By it one recalls that the meaning of political and economic structures lies in their being at the service of the common good. The moral legitimacy of institutions depends on this, as does the morally correct way of living and working in institutions. If the Encyclical speaks about «structures of sin», it is not in order to demonize institutions[13], but rather to remind us of the roots of the evil caused by the structures of human life: people's free responsibility[14].

4
Morality and economic activity

By way of illustration, we will examine some of the themes relevant to economic issues in relation to moral responsibility. They are very common, general themes, in which perhaps there are also some serious misunderstandings, somewhat rooted in current thinking, in which there is a tendency to take as obvious and morally legitimate, things that are neither obvious nor morally legitimate. In these themes, what is at issue is the current moral custom and its influence in forming and preserving mentalities, opinions, and the guidelines for personal decisions.

4.1. THE COMPLEXITY OF THE PROBLEMS

Economic structures and their interconnections with political structures often present extremely complex and sophisticated mechanisms. Taking into account the complexity of the problems is certainly a requirement of objectivity. In concrete judgments, under the moral profile, prudence is strictly necessary. In fact it is not easy to discern what is actually possible and what consequences are actually predictable. The personal responsibility of individuals and groups depends

13 «A situation —or likewise an institution, a structure, society itself— is not in itself the subject of moral acts. Hence a situation cannot in itself be good or bad» (*Reconciliatio et paenitentia*, 16). Cfr. *Sollicitudo rei socialis*, 36.

14 «If certain forms of modern «imperialism» were considered in the light of these moral criteria, we would see that behind certain decisions, apparently inspired only by economics or politics, are real forms of idolatry: of money, ideology, class, technology. I have wished to introduce this type of analysis above all in order to point out the true nature of the evil that faces us with respect to the development of peoples: it is a question of a moral evil, the fruit of many sins that lead to "structures of sin". To diagnose the evil in this way is to identify precisely, on the level of human conduct, the path to be followed in order to overcome it» (*Sollicitudo rei socialis*, 37).

on people's genuine awareness and freedom, which can only be appreciated by consideration of the complex of internal and external circumstances in which each person finds him/herself having to act. The objective complexity of interacting factors translates into an objective difficulty about choice, both in regard to the correct assessment of what is to be done, and the capacity for completely free choices, that is, the difficulty to understand what is morally good and the difficulty to genuinely want it, with no reservations.

One can appeal to the actual fact of the complexity in order to legitimize the refusal to accept ethically important requirements, in particular if these are such as to question things that one would prefer not to be questioned. Likewise, in this way, responsibility can be avoided, relegating to «inner conscience» (or more precisely: to the so-called good intentions and pious desires) the moral requirements, while economic reasons would belong to a completely different order of problems. It would be tantamount to saying that morality is extremely important, but it must not cost too much. Thus, from the fact that things are not all clear and not everything can be resolved, it is quite easy to conclude that therefore one solution is worth the same as another (and that therefore one's own is the best).

Certainly it is necessary to recognize that the responsibility of individuals is restricted, corresponding to the actual space for freedom they have and their understanding of the good that might be feasible. It should also be said, however, that each person is strictly responsible for the actual space for freedom that is his/her own. The good that is concretely possible and understood as such is not arbitrary, but binds conscience. If custom and current mentality are at issue, if well-established structures are at issue, that outweighs the opportunities for individual consciences in regard to global solutions, but no solution can come about if not *through consciences* and deliberate *sharing* of understanding and behavior, that is, through that historic process which constitutes (and preserves or modifies) a common ethos, a culture, the structures of human society.

4.2. OWNERSHIP AND USE OF THE GOODS OF THE EARTH

The moral legitimacy of private ownership is usually recognized in Christian tradition (and not just in that tradition), as an appropriate way to peacefully regulate social relations with regard to the availability of resources. That does not exempt us from the question, which seems well motivated by the facts of anything but sporadic custom, of whether the institution of private ownership is in reality defended and used according to its true meaning.

a) The common destination of goods

For all the questions concerning the relationship to what one needs in order to live, the foundational principle is that recognition of the equal dignity of all people implies their equal right to the necessary means to life. In the Sacred Scriptures and in the church, the theological traditions interpret this right on the basis of the will of God the creator. He created the human family and gave to it the earth with its resources, entrusting to the industry of human beings the «cultivation» of the earth itself, so that in history it responds to a human being's needs for life, a life in which people perceive each other and love each other as brothers and sisters. If this is the creator's intentionality, then free personal responsibility is asked to assume as its own this same intentionality; the believer is the one who adheres to God's plan, who makes it his/her own.

Therefore, in determining the content of justice («give to each their own») it appears that a «right» on the basis only of de facto possession or self-attribution has never been theologically justified[15]. And yet the principle of the common destination of the earth's resources does not seem to inspire the rules of behavior. With various justifications, it seems that in the field of economics an almost permanent regime of «exceptions» has been established, and not just where secondary matters are concerned.

In fact, even the tension toward communion, referred to above as the goal of human life understood in a Christian way, would be completely nullified if its realization were to be understood apart from the sharing of the means necessary for life. The division of goods, therefore, can only have a functional meaning to life together in an «ordered» way. If we ask ourselves what this «order» means, we must actually remember the meaning and the goal. It must be ordered to the aim indicated by the common destination of goods, and it cannot distort this without becoming «disorder» and losing its value and legitimacy. When practical rules are established, or defended in the economic sphere, we cannot avoid the fundamentally significant question: practical rules for what?

15 Here one could note that St Thomas Aquinas and with him a considerable stream of Christian theological tradition interpreted the right to private property as a *secondary right*. The natural primary right is the common destination of the goods of the earth, common access to them, and equal right of access to what one needs in order to live and which has been given to the human family. Private property, on the other hand, is a secondary natural right and is interpreted in relation to the primary right, that of the common access to goods, which is therefore to be verified historically, a matter of seeing which is the most suitable way to achieve the goal. If St Thomas defended private property as the most suitable course, he also denied the right to private property if it is understood as the right to the exclusive use of the goods, because the common destination of goods demands that they are «*de facili*» shared with the needy (II-II, q. 66. a.2).

b) Access to the goods

The object of the common destination of resources (not just those found «in nature», but also those «cultivated» by human industry and the fruit of it) is verified or disproved by the fact that all have true access to the resources themselves. Therefore, with the right of ownership legitimized, there remains the question about the use one makes of that right. It is not just a matter of respecting the property of others; instead, it is a matter of not seeing and not making ownership a right for exclusive or privileged use. When economic assistance is given to those in precarious or disastrous conditions, there is no basis in the idea that this is an unnecessary gesture of kindness. Large and small economic institutions usually appear to be structured in such a way that the principle of legitimate ownership remains the unique and independent criterion of that which legitimizes them morally. This does not mean that there cannot be any rules and that ownership cannot be protected; otherwise the institution would not be able to carry out its role nor even survive. It means, however, that the rules that defend ownership of the goods must be inspired by the foundational principle of ownership itself and cannot be contradictory to its meaning.

With various emphases, certainly due to the variety of situations and the cultural climate present in the analyses used in the different documents, the Church's Magisterium presents an unambiguous line in linking the right of ownership to the universal destination of goods. The Second Vatican Council took up this perspective with some fervor[16]; the papal encyclicals have repeatedly drawn attention to the «social function» of the right to ownership of goods[17]. «Christian tradition has never upheld this right as absolute and untouchable. On the contrary, it has always understood this right within the broader context of the right common to all to use the goods of the whole of creation: the right to private property is subordinated to the right to common use, to the fact that goods are meant for everyone»[18].

As recalled, in *Sollicitudo rei socialis*, solidarity is decisively proposed as a criterion for economic institutions and structures as well, at all levels. The reference is always about the purpose and therefore about the meaning and ethical foun-

16 Cfr. *Gaudium et Spes*, 69, 71.

17 Cfr., for example, *Mater et magistra*, 20, 28, 109-110, 116, 120; *Pacem in terris*, 8; *Populorum progressio*, 22-24, 26, 49, 56ff, 87; *Octogesima adveniens*, 43, 45-46; *Laborem exercens*, 14.

18 *Laborem exercens*, 14. Here the phrase «*ius privati dominii*» is used, with a deliberately different nuance compared with «*ius privatae possessionis*».

dation of the structures in question, for which the necessity that derives from them cannot be simply that of some «adjustment» that one can try to achieve, leaving undisturbed the rationale by which the structures live. Resistance in the face of such unambiguous and continuous indications is explained by the strength of structures not easily modifiable and by the fact that they have strongly established ways of thinking and assessing that are internally coherent to them, and which in turn come back to strengthen the structures themselves by approval.

Therefore, it is not just a question of good will; it is also a question of understanding and assessing. We can recognize as present, and it is not new, a widespread tendency to expand the rationale of legitimate possession, separating it from what makes it morally based and applying it indiscriminately. Possession seems to become, perhaps not rarely, more an end than a means, so that possession of goods becomes an expression of the possession of one's own life, while this is assumed as criterion and purpose of life itself. In the moral thinking that is widespread today, with the socially dominating models, it seems that precisely the «rules» of the economic sphere have their own particular importance. Economic activity assumes de facto the purpose of possession and tends to justify itself on the basis of this aim, accepted as obvious and unquestioned[19]. Other aims are admitted «alongside» this, but not in such a way that this may in any way be subordinated and directed toward them (also leaving aside the problem about the actual value that one gives to other aims, compared with the value attributed to possession).

4.3. PROFIT AND MORALITY

The Encyclical *Sollicitudo rei socialis* states: «Among the actions and attitudes opposed to the will of God, the good of neighbor, and the «structures» created by them, two are very typical: on the one hand, the all-consuming desire for profit, and on the other, the thirst for power, with the intention of imposing one's will upon others» (37). We ask ourselves what moral disorder is indicated by the «all-consuming desire for profit».

It is appropriate to recognize that the desire for profit is in some way necessary in economic activity as one of its particular aims. But it is necessary to clarify in what sense and under what conditions, if it is to be interpreted morally.

19 One can note here what is said in *Laborem exercens*, 13, about the perspective of «economism».

At the various levels of economic activity, there is always human activity. What is at issue, however, is the personal decision to pursue a specific aim. There are then operative decisions about the means to be used for pursuing the aim. The «all-consuming» desire for profit is that search for profit that sees it as an end not directed to other superior ends and not conditioned by the correctness of the means to be employed.

The very goal that a person sets, individually or with others, must be understood and desired in a morally «ordered» way, remembering that it is not the only goal in life. In our case it is not even the highest and most urgent; in itself it has no meaning and ultimate end. Translated in Christian terms, it means that profit, as a goal of economic activity, must be harmonized with the other goals of human activity and needs to be understood and desired in the order of communion in God with one's brothers and sisters.

With regard to the chosen means, it must be remembered that it is always a matter of activity that, in a more or less direct but always very real way, implies relations with people, involved or excluded, who benefit or suffer from the choices. But relations with people must always be an expression of charity, the realization of the reaching out to communion.

The moral dilemma, therefore, is not that of approval or disapproval of profit, but rather that of «ordering it» in a rationale of human solidarity. It is the rationale of possession that makes it disordered, because it tends not to recognize restrictions on the basis of higher or more urgent values. What is denied is that profit, in the way in which it is pursued, can be regulated only by economic reasoning or, worse still, only by the economic reasoning of the one pursuing it.

4.4. ECONOMIC RULES AND MORALITY

It is clear that the economy cannot endure unless it is on the basis of its own internal reasoning, which produces its increasingly complex functional rules within structures that link between them the various factors in interdependence on a global scale. Ethical reasoning is not in competition with economic reasoning; it only asks that the latter be «human», that its aims and logic be verified within the order of united human life. Faced with the rules of the economy, morality asks that its results be assessed by what they produce in terms of good and evil for the lives of the people involved in it. In an economy that consciously plays an expanding role on the world stage, the question is about its human results on the world stage, taking into account precisely the actual consequences with respect to the actual opportunities.

From the moral point of view, the rules of the economy are like those that concern other spheres of human activity in that they do not have value simply because they exist or because someone is able to impose them; instead, they must be maintained and strengthened, or changed, on the basis of the fact that they correspond or do not correspond to the human values to be promoted, in order that social life may be a true promotion of people, without giving privileges to anyone to the detriment of others.

Economic rules can also be protected by law. This involves a «presumption» of justice (that is, the rules are valid until the contrary is proved), but that does not exonerate one's conscience; the rules should not only be respected to the letter, but rather must be «used» responsibly (at issue is the actual intentionality of the one using them), which can also involve the need to cede the advantages that the law would allow. There remains, then, the fact that economic rules might also need to be relinquished or modified for reasons of justice, on the basis of new situations and opportunities. A connected and rather delicate question, but one that cannot be ignored, also concerns the subjects who establish the rules: from whom and for whom, on the basis of what relationships and aims, with what freedom and genuine participation of the interested parties are the rules determined? We are thinking, in particular, about problems in North-South relations and development.

One can rightly say that it is the task of politics to socially regulate economics. That should not, however, be a diversionary maneuver to forestall the ethical problem. Economic politics, in fact, usually assumes the internal criteria within the current economic structure, which it proposes to administer prudently in relation to social forces. Theoretically, politics governs the economy, but politics does not usually dominate it. Economic structures possess their strength, not secondarily, from the fact that they are tied to coherent political structures. This appears even more evident if one thinks that the structure of social relations tends to give shape to the same rationale of relations in the various spheres.

Personal individual responsibilities, likewise, entail the responsibility for concrete action and its direct consequences. At the same time, there is also co-responsibility in the concrete action, which is also assessed and assumed, with respect to the structures and their logic. Faced with the serious human problems dependent on the economic systems in force, the fact that they are not within the bounds of the good will of individuals or groups highlights the cultural dimension of the ethical question, which concerns the formation of a moral mentality in which the economic aspect frankly has a human face. However, the economic dimension is only one of the dimensions of our social life; from a rational standpoint it will continue to be basically coherent with the other dimensions. Therefore, the reference to what constitutes personal morality seems essential as a way of understanding the common good. Solidarity is also essential as a criterion for living out morality (charity) in the social sphere. Personal morality involves a matter of conscience as well as dialogue between consciences, as is the case with all the ethical problems that have cultural and social importance, specifically when it is a matter of establishing a shared ethos capable of translating itself into the social structuring of life, from the level of directly verifiable relationships to those of national and international institutions.

Part Three

Morality and development

Chapter 7

Hunger, a challenge to united development

For a briefer treatment BASTIANEL S., «La fame, una sfida allo sviluppo solidale», in *La Civiltà Cattolica* 3520/1 (1997) 330-343.

1

The problem

Let us consider the reality of hunger in the world from the ethical-theological point of view. We will endeavor to define and clarify the specific points of view, attempting an in-depth study of the foundational meanings and value that lie at the basis of the problem, in that they address personal conscience and the veracity of our profession of Christian faith.

We recall some essential elements of the problem of «hunger in the world»: one part of humanity does not have at its disposal sufficient food, while others have it, and others still in even greater abundance; the potential of the earth's resources has not been exhausted; much energy and resources go into aims that are not as urgent as the need for sufficient food; this happens in a structured society, with institutions and laws at regional and world level; and at various levels, decisions about resources (the production and distribution of goods) are taken by those who do not suffer from hunger.

We ask ourselves about the meaning and values implied in the relationship between human beings and the goods of the earth, about the meaning and causes of hunger in relation to personal free responsibility. There is, in fact, an ethical problem in which a person's free decision, directly or indirectly, involves the relationship with other people, with their lives and personal values. In our case, there is for us an ethical problem if and to what extent our decisions influence in some way the fact that there are people in the world who are hungry.

We also ask ourselves if Christian revelation has some exhortation in this regard, or if it points to some fundamental implications about meaning. For believers the exercise of free personal decision implies that responsibility for the other person is consciously assumed within their own relationship with God. The moral life understood and desired as discipleship of Christ is specifically Christian, by virtue of the gifted encounter with him, in the living relationship with him.

2
Faced with the starving

Before considering the reality of hunger as a world problem, it is worthwhile considering the situation of the personal individual relationship with the person who is starving. This simpler relationship should enable us to identify more easily some morally defining or problematic elements, which then return with greater complexity in social relations.

2.1. IF YOU ARE ABLE, YOU MUST GIVE HIM SOMETHING TO EAT

We begin with the simplest question: what must you do when faced with a starving person? The answer seems to be obvious and clear: you give him/her something to eat, if you are able to do so. This statement is not just ethically correct from a theoretical point of view, but —at first glance— would also seem to be commonly shared in current morality. Perhaps there is not much coherence in living it, but in general the validity of the statement is not contested (if need be, there may be an attempt to justify different behavior). In order to clarify somewhat the import of the statement, we can suppose circumstances, not purely imaginary, that illustrate its two parts: «give something to eat» and «if you are able to».

2.1.1. *GIVING SOMETHING TO EAT*

Let us imagine that yesterday I gave someone the food that person needed. If today I meet the same person, still hungry, and likewise tomorrow and the day after tomorrow, what must I do? Some might say that after the first or second time that person should look elsewhere. If I reason like this, perhaps I would find myself «justified» by the opinion of many others. Leaving aside the question about the possibility that the person in question «look elsewhere» to seek help, does the phrase used above mean that «someone should» provide something to eat, or that «you must do it»? In itself, it has one unique condition: if one is able to do it. Is there some foundation in being able to state precisely, for example, «once or twice»?

In a case in which I already know today that the hungry person will be in need tomorrow as well, am I free in conscience if I give something to feed him/her and then hope not to meet the person again (or proactively try to avoid him/her)?

Does that «give something to eat» indicate a precise act, the fact of providing a quantity of food on average sufficient to satisfy someone's hunger, and that's enough? Or, does giving food «to him/her» imply solicitude for his/her real condition as person? Let us suppose that, at the precise moment when I encounter the hungry person, I am not personally able to give that person what he/she needs. Does this free me from any obligation toward the person?

2.1.2. *THE RELATIONSHIP*

The encounter with someone who is hungry involves a relationship. It is about accepting a person, responding to his/her concrete condition of need. To take bread and give it to someone is not a gesture that —on its own and in itself— makes someone good. It can be done for a thousand reasons, even self-interest, or simply with a cunning or even nasty spirit. That gesture is morally good only when it expresses acceptance of the person. With this premise, of wanting to bring about a personal relationship of acceptance, the gesture that responds positively to a real need is «that which must be done». The intentionality of the gesture unifies care for the person in his/her conditions with the search/realization of the good that is practically possible.

2.1.3. *THE CONCRETE GESTURE*

Such a gesture is responding to a concrete need; it accepts the person. To deny the (possible) concrete gesture is to deny oneself to the person in his/her present reality. Personal morality is inner reality, but in no way is it at the subject's will. Rather, it is measured by the objectivity of the reality to which one must «respond». The intentionality of acceptance (and with it the sincerity of conscience) is verified or proved false by the choice of means capable of fulfilling it.

2.1.4. *«IF YOU ARE ABLE TO DO IT»*

Even the significance and demands of this hypothetical phrase, logically necessary so that the statement may be true, can be reduced, so that it becomes a pretense for self-justification. The hungry person could meet someone who is even hungrier. Since he/she is unable to satisfy that person's hunger, and therefore is not bound to do so, is that person «without any moral obligation» with regard to the other person's hunger? Could he/she, for example, try to be «more cunning» as soon as he/she sees any opportunity to satisfy his/her own needs, trying to do the best one can, no matter what that might mean to the other? In a case in which there is actually little that one can do, is one therefore excused from doing it, because it would not be a «decisive» intervention?

When there is a genuine possibility of intervening with assistance, but in a way that is extremely «costly» with respect to one's own conditions, what must one do? To be able to do it does not mean to be able to do it without any personal inconvenience. On the other hand, nor can it mean that «whatever cost» is acceptable. Without any arbitrariness, how should one evaluate «up to what point» one is bound?

Even with respect to personal opportunities, the phrase we have used calls for objective comparisons, that is, comparing the actual conditions of the subject (his/her opportunities to intervene and the personal values that would be involved) with the value of that personal good that the need of the other person proposes to realize.

2.2. HIERARCHY AND URGENCY OF VALUES

The need for objectivity, in the case of personal costs for whoever wants to assist the hungry, demands that the goods in conflict be assessed comparatively, in terms of a hierarchy of values. Is what I do not want to lose a higher value (in itself, not «for me») than the survival of the other person? On this level, conflict is real (in the objective sense) only when the two values have the same degree of importance. If they do not, and yet the subject feels in conflict, the cause could be purely subjective, such as a lack of psychological or moral maturity, an error in the assessment due to insufficient formation, or insufficient inclination or willingness to achieve the good.

Conflict, however, even in the case of inequality in value on a hierarchical level, might not be a subjective issue. In the reality of existence every individual value is in fact linked to other values, in a network of conditions determining the true opportunities for achieving the values themselves. Circumstances, including foreseeable consequences, belong to the tangible to which we are called to respond and as such cannot be disregarded at the evaluative moment. Thus it can also happen that a value in itself less important than another might be more urgent than the other, either because it is foundational for other more important values, or even because it is a necessary condition for realization of that same value (for example, the proclamation of the gospel is a higher value than food, but there can be conditions in which it is necessary first to ensure the survival of the person to whom one wants to make the proclamation, precisely so that it might be possible for the person to receive it).

2.3. JUDGMENTS AND PRE-JUDGMENTS

Judgments based on criteria of hierarchy and urgency, therefore, can be highly complex. Our evaluating and decision-making in daily life is normally guided by general evaluations and previous decisions, supported by the common consensus that expresses itself in the shared ethos of our environment, strengthened by formation and one's personal story. Without such previous evaluations and decisions, it would be impossible for us to live, both because many decisions present themselves with immediacy, and because we cannot begin from nothing to understand and evaluate only on the basis of our experience and intelligence about things. In fact, we attribute a *praesumptio* of validity to what is suggested to us by the ethos of our environment. But the need for formation of one's own conscience —a fundamental ethical task— requires that the cultural ethos be gradually understood, evaluated and assumed in proper free responsibility, by virtue of a conscious discernment. The appearance of a conflict between different and important values clearly obliges conscience in a concrete case to verify that *praesumptio*[1].

2.3.1. *SELF-PRIVILEGE*

We are protected by the previous judgments of our cultural ethos, protected, for example, in terms of everything that we «spontaneously» believe we cannot do without, or is necessarily linked to our state of life, profession, and so on. This may provide us with «certainty» in our decision-making, but it does not guarantee us truth in making assessments. It is true that *if* some good in particular is necessary for the fundamental tasks in our life, such necessity must become the determining criterion for real choices, even when faced with the hungry person. But this is a hypothetical proposition. What often happens is that we take the hypothesis as proven, simply on the basis of the fact that it corresponds to common judgment. Now, precisely at this level it is not difficult to realize how the evaluations of hierarchy and urgency can be easily characterized by a criterion that tends to privilege oneself and the group to which one belongs. Think, for instance, of what is considered necessary for life, what is considered inalienable. Naturally, we have different criteria, depending on whether we are thinking about our life or that of others (even in the same environment). On what foundations can such discrimination be morally justified?

1 The legitimacy of «presumptive» trusting in the competency of others or in tradition, precisely because it is linked to the responsibility of conscience, is always conditional, unless proven otherwise. When there is a reasonable doubt, then it is a matter of verifying the *nisi aliter constet*.

2.3.2. *DIRECT AND INDIRECT OPPORTUNITIES*

On the level of the genuine possibilities for positive intervention for the hungry, I would like to highlight the importance of not restricting the moral task to the possibility —or impossibility— of an immediate and conclusive direct response. The fact of not considering partial or indirect possibilities raises a question about the sincerity of responding to the effective need; it could reflect an attempt at hurried self-justification and avoiding the genuine requests on the pretext of the impossibility of responding to *one* of them (even the most immediate and obvious).

2.4. SOCIAL RESPONSIBILITY

In this context, the discourse inevitably comes around to an unavoidable implication, which necessarily broadens the point of view of the relationship between one individual and another. If it were limited to this point of view, the same estimative consideration about the existence of the hungry person and the opportunities to respond to the need would be disproved, because they would not be objective. Thus, at issue are the social context and social responsibility. By that it is not meant simply that society is responsible for the fate of the hungry. It is interesting here to remember clearly the social dimension of the individual's responsibility, his/her responsibility in contributing to ensure that society responsibly assumes the condition of the needy person. This responsibility has an immediate and concrete dimension in doing what is possible for the immediate resolution of the problem as well as a mediated and longer range dimension, that of contributing to the formation of a common moral sensitivity in which such problems are not disregarded or delegated.

2.5. QUESTIONS ABOUT FOUNDATIONS AND MORAL FORMATION

The plea to conscience made by the presence of a hungry person is not simply a matter of «sensitivity of soul». At issue are not charitable gestures in the sense of «good works» that would not be binding in conscience, but which would be suitable for «embellishing» a person's moral and spiritual image.

What is at issue is the veracity of fundamental moral attitudes. It is a question of understanding and living out moral responsibility as a freedom that «responds» to the known objective good and to the other person, accepting his/her presence and the needs for good that the presence suggests. One cannot see how one can find hope in an authentic humanity if one consents to a way of understanding morality that legitimizes at its root an attitude of self-seeking, rather than the fundamental claim of the gratuity of the good.

For the Christian this means not thwarting the meaning and import of charity as fulfillment of the moral law. A love like that of Christ is the aspiration within which the believer is called to understand and assume what is of value and what commits conscience.

To live a Christian morality in the world implies taking care to interpret in a Christian way the values to be assumed, searching for the ways suitable for promoting and making them humanly understandable and meaningful, for greater human truth in the historically given opportunities. It is about offering help and moving toward a «true» humanity, as it is understood in faith. That calls for a responsible, creative freedom (in faith, in love, in hope) with respect to the current cultural ethos: capable of assuming the positive, but interpreting it and re-proposing it interpreted in faith.

3
Faced with hunger in the world

The reality of hunger in our world is one of those problems that make the negative strength of the evil present sharply felt, like an evil greater than us, and in the face of which our efforts do not seem to measure up. Despite the evidence of the needs, despite wide agreement in affirming the right to the necessary means to live as being among the fundamental human rights, despite the commitment of many to find a remedy, the solution to this problem has not been found. There is division in interpreting the causes and diagnosing the path toward a solution. There are obstacles from ways of thinking and cultures, from economic politics as well as from major interests involved. A common inclination seems to persist of not wishing to recognize that realities such as hunger in the world can pose a radical ethical need, along with a question about the (*human*) validity of our structures and life styles.

3.1. THE GOODS OF THE EARTH

The ethical question about the use of the resources and their distribution is a question about the significance the earth's resources have for human beings, that is, for human beings properly considered as persons in relation with others. In fact, implied in the relation with things is the relation with people. Theologically understood, drawn directly from the very beginning of the biblical traditions that come together in the book of Genesis, the ethical value of the relationship to the goods of the earth is connected with God's will, not in an extrinsic manner, but rather as seen from within the very intentionality of the creator. At issue is the meaning of the creation of humanity and the meaning of the world created for humanity.

God created the human family and gave it the earth and its resources, entrusting to the industry of human beings the «cultivation» of the earth itself, so that it can respond in history to the needs of a human life in which people recognize themselves and enjoy each other as brothers and sisters. Personal free responsibility is called to assume as its own the same intentionality as that of the creator; the believer is the one who adheres to God's plan and makes it his/her own. In communion with him and by virtue of it, communion between people constitutes the goal of their life on earth.

The account from *Gen* 2:4b-3:24 can assist us in this reflection. The text presents a theological interpretation of the story that has its origins in the already lengthy experience of Israel as «people» of God: human life established in the knowledge of the foundational presence of a God who saves, but a co-existence in which, however, injustice is present. The account of original sin and its consequences is placed in relation to the «before» of the creative intentionality (and then with the «after» of redemptive intentionality). Thus it responds to the need to explain the reality of a «hostile land» (of injustice and violence).

In developing a theology of creation, it is understood that one cannot attribute to God that same hostility of the land. There is a need to understand, in faith and in the discernment between good and evil, the true reality of sin, not as something inescapable, almost as being the fruit of evil divinities or superior forces; not as something «natural», almost as being a consequence of the creative will of God. In the Genesis account, one can see how sin is not just an individual reality: the «land» has become «hostile», that is, humanity, which is realized in it, is marked by habitual and consistently hostile relationships.

The image of the human couple placed in the garden is the image of a harmony that had its origins in the relationship with God, who out of nothing brings being and creates man and woman, making them dialogue with him as well as between themselves. God establishes these human creatures in a condition of possible and proper dialogue.

The images of the «garden» reveal a land fit for humans' serene and harmonious life (*Gen* 2:8-15). God the creator not only provides for that, but is present himself and speaks to the man and makes him able to understand the meaning of reality (*Gen* 2:16ff), so as to be able to rule according to the intentionality of the creator himself (*Gen* 3:18). Man's relationship with woman, different from his relationship with the rest of creation, is a relationship of communion, something that is also recognized by the man, who is therefore placed in a position of being able to look after her (*Gen* 2:21-23). This condition, which speaks of the «nature» of the interpersonal reciprocity of human life, means the earth can be made «human»; it is the gifted opportunity of sharing existence by virtue of the foundational relationship with God, assuming in one's own free responsibility the realization of his creative intentionality.

It is clear what happens, then, when that relationship is broken: sin constitutes an historic condition of relationships that are no longer in communion. At first, Adam and Eve seem to be united in wanting to build their own lives without depending on God (*Gen* 3:1-6). But when the discord with God is expressed in their attempt to avoid his presence by hiding themselves, even the apparent communion between them is revealed as deceptive. As soon as Adam has to respond, he attempts to defend himself, and in order to excuse himself, he has no hesitation in blaming Eve. The hostility of the land itself derives from this fabricated relationship, and thus, human beings no longer live in the «garden». Relations between them are now based on possession and defense, resulting in the fruits of death that immediately afterward begin to appear (cfr. *Gen* 4:1-16).

The theology of the covenant present in this text explains creation in the same way that God's various interventions throughout the course of history are explained. Each of God's interventions is a gift of the relationship with him, and thereby he is creator of humanity, sustaining and calling for the establishment of a fraternal people. And the responsibility of replying always has the sign of responsibility for establishing relations of liberated and liberating reciprocity.

In this profound sense, then, the *collaboration* of human beings with God's activity is like a person created to be capable of working in communion with Him. To establish in our history a *rationale of communion* means making this hostile land become a «garden». It is the rationale of «making oneself neighbor», which the believer can learn and assume, having recognized God's gratuitous making himself a neighbor. To do so means having an interpretation of the human, and therefore of history, that does not escape into idealism (as if evil did not exist), but neither is it resignation to evil (as if it were almost inevitable).

3.2. THE COMMON DESTINATION OF GOODS

When we are considering the relationship to that which one needs in order to live, the foundational principle is that the recognition of the equal dignity of all people implies their equal right to the necessary or useful means for life. In the Sacred Scriptures and in the church, such a right is understood as based not on a human agreement, but rather on the very nature of the human being, according to God's creative intentionality, as previously noted.

In fact, every act of striving toward communion would be completely nullified if its realization were to be understood apart from the sharing of the means necessary for life. If we live in a social system that involves the division of goods, this can only have a functional meaning as it relates to living together in an «ordered» way. If we ask ourselves what this «order» means, we must seriously remember the goal, that is, the way in which we socially structure the relationship with the goods must lead toward the aim of genuine sharing those goods. This aim cannot be distorted without becoming «disorder» and thus losing its value and legitimacy.

A fundamental lie, an expression of the sinful logic of self-privilege, tends to suggest one's own good as opposed to the common good. At the level of economic justice, this understanding tends to expand the field of «legitimate ownership». «Do not steal» comes to be understood as a restriction on free self-development and, even when this command is recognized as a valid and reasonable indication, it will tend to be interpreted in a minimalist manner, that is, «in one's own favor». The obligation to help the needy and to contribute to common needs will be understood in the same way.

Within this same line of lies is also the temptation of the various forms of partial solidarity, such as the (alleged, but in fact false) solidarity limited to the group to which one belongs or with which one shares interests. However, a genuine understanding of universality (in the sense of searching for the good of all, without previous discriminatory preferences) reveals, in fact, the fundamental criterion exhibited in partial solidarity: it is self-seeking and the search for one's own individual good in the most effective way possible. What should be an exercise of honestly judging reason, on the basis of the objectivity of values and their possible realization, thus easily becomes an exercise in astutely self-justifying reason. This is what appears obvious from all the ways of legally interpreting one's own «duties», in the economic field as well.

4
The responsibilities of Christians and the church

Since the problem of hunger in the world calls into question elements related to meaning and value, believers must effectively understand these values and live them in faith in Jesus Christ, sharing them in the believing community, and proclaiming them in a significant way. The first requirement that suggests itself to us is that of a more profound life of faith, therefore, a more profound personal and communitarian conversion.

4.1. INTERPRETING HISTORY THROUGH FAITH

At the origins of faith and theological reflection witnessed in the Old Testament is the reality of the encounter with God signified by the concept of «covenant»: the experience of God who comes to meet us, calls, reveals himself, offers communion with him, and thereby saves. The whole of history has been understood beginning with this covenantal act. Moral responsibility involves living on the earth within this foundational relationship with God, recognizing ourselves as established by God in a community of brothers and sisters and wishing to be in this relationship. It is not only individual relations from person to person that are interpreted in this framework of faithfulness to God's work, but also relationships structured socially: institutions, laws, and the administration of justice[2].

In the New Testament, God's gift is the «new covenant» in Jesus Christ, which is once again a gift of communion through communion. Made participants in his life, guided by the Spirit, we are given the possibility of consciously living in this reality of salvation that is active in history by virtue of the Father's salvific decision. We as believers are asked to learn from Jesus the way of living on this earth in faithfulness to the Father's work, allowing ourselves to conform to him, according to the Spirit given to us, in order to assume his own perspective on other people and the world, as well as to assume his criteria of evaluation and

2 For a summary treatment of these themes and an appropriate bibliography, see BASTIANEL S., DI PINTO L., «Per una fondazione biblica dell'etica», in GOFFI T., PIANA G., EDD., *Corso di Morale*, 1, *Vita nuova in Cristo. Morale fondamentale e generale*, Queriniana, Brescia 1983, 77-174.

behavior. The believer assumes the role of a love like his, a task made possible by the fact that his love for us is a present and effective reality, a role that calls for our free responsibility in accepting the communion with him that he has given to us.

The radical nature of the gospel calls for learning in such a way from the Lord Jesus; it calls for our discipleship on the basis of a full and unconditional decision. Adherence to the gospel does not destroy anything that is of authentic human value, but calls for, beginning with the relationship with the Lord, a complete redefinition of all that is understood as authentic human value. In itself, this does not upset the picture of moral values and the rules of hierarchy and urgency between human values, but in fact it can upset our constructs of hierarchy and urgency, which are the fruit of a past history and a present in which sin is still at work[3].

Conversion means, above all, identifying and overcoming the «reservations» that in a more or less conscious manner accompany our journey of discipleship of the Lord. They will be, in our own way, the difficulties the first disciples encountered in knowing the Lord and following him. The believing community was born when the disciples began to live their own lives «given over» like Jesus' own life, when they had no other criteria to interpret situations and events apart from those they had learned from him, and when communion with him became the place of their discerning and acting.

4.2. LIVING THE EUCHARIST

The bread and wine are the reality-symbol of that which sustains our lives, what we need to live. As such, in the history of humanity they have been and are the cause of division and dispute, a motive for struggle and death. We can say that *for bread* people become enemies in order to possess and guarantee themselves the goods of the earth. The bread is not shared among us; rather, it divides us.

In the Eucharist it is exactly the bread and wine, with all that they signify in the complex system of interhuman relations, which are assumed and are handed to us as the reality-symbol of communion. What is suggested here is an interpretation of life and history, a significance that implicates the conscience of the one who makes this symbolic gesture of sharing the bread. The symbolic gesture, in fact, will be verified or disproved by the life of the one who makes it; its capacity for true significance is entrusted to people's free responsibility.

3 Suffice, for example, to measure ourselves against texts such as *Matt* 5 and *Luke* 6:17-38.

The gesture of breaking and sharing bread is not the same as a possible gesture of «giving away» the bread. Sharing speaks about a relationship between people, with the overcoming of boundaries between «mine» and «yours». Bread can be given away with a disdainful and even murderous heart, with aims of calculated benefit, but that would not be shared bread. Real sharing of the means necessary for life is an expression of the real will to share life.

The interpretive words of Jesus make of this bread and wine his body given and his blood poured out, the historic concrete existence of Jesus in his redemptive self-giving. It is his life handed over that becomes the place of communion: communion *with* him and communion *in* him. By virtue of this presence we are saved. By virtue of this salvation we are established as brothers and sisters. By virtue of this fraternity life can be shared on earth. By virtue of this sharing of life, bread can truly be shared and become the cause of life.

Jesus' gesture and words at the institution of the Eucharist (*Luke* 22:19-20 and parallels) are an interpretation of the whole of his life. They speak about the meaning and manner of his making himself a neighbor to men and women in order to save them, of his total faithfulness to the Father in total faithfulness to men and women, and of his sharing in the whole human condition without ceding anything to the rationale of sin, right up to the moment of his final giving over of himself as redeemer and giver of life. From the incarnation to the resurrection, his surrendering of himself is a gift without reservation, not previously measured on the basis of being accepted, but rather, sustained by the sole intentionality of love and communion.

To recognize one's own life as founded in the communion of the very life of the Lord (as we do in the Christian profession of faith and celebration of the Eucharist) means affirming as one's own, freely and responsibly assumed, the same «rationale» as his giving over of himself. To live in communion with him is to live in communion with his body and blood; it is to live in him an existence guided and sustained by an intentionality of communion that places no qualifications on the giving over of self to one's brother or sister. The Eucharistic celebration, therefore, interprets the life of the believing community and involves it, because it recognizes its foundation in Christ and because it makes it a living being, so that the common participation in his life may become mutually the instrumentality of salvation.

The emerging church community in Jerusalem included the sharing of goods among the aspects that constituted it as a believing community of Jesus

Christ[4]. The account of the institution of the Eucharist in *1Cor* 11:17-34 arose as a response to a division about «bread». It is not possible to celebrate the Eucharist, assuming its significance and letting oneself be guided by the Spirit of Christ, while at the same time avoiding recognition that the communion of life on earth is necessarily experienced through the sharing of what is needed in order to live. Revelation does not provide us with an answer to the question about the ways of achieving such sharing. However, we are reminded that every form of «self-privilege» in relation to the goods of the earth expresses some reservation about accepting the other person, and in that reservation is also implied some reservation about adherence to the gospel and discipleship of the Lord.

4.3. PARTICIPATING IN TODAY'S EFFORTS

There are currently in progress attempts and projects of various proportions to respond to the situation of need of those who suffer from hunger. The moral need to be involved in such efforts receives a specific confirmation and urgency from Christian faith. If the Christian utopia on earth is communion as an end to be pursued, it must be an interpretive criterion for today, for discerning from among the practical possibilities those realizations that best express a true path of communion, that is, those that best realize it in the current conditions. Thus, attention will necessarily focus on creating further conditions for genuine opportunities to respond to hunger.

To be concerned about the problem of hunger also means striving for consistency between the ultimate and the immediate ends, as well as between these ends and the choice of means suitable for achieving them. «Charitable» realization, at its various levels, must have and communicate a soul of deep charity. In this, the perspective of meaning and hope that Christian faith reveals can help non-believers, too, in purifying and deepening the human values pursued, as a sign of gratuity and non-partial solidarity.

4 This is stated explicitly in *Acts* 2:42-48 and 4:32-35. We know from the very context of Acts that these two passages idealize somewhat the life of the community in presenting it. But this says precisely how the community itself understands its being as a believing community. Communion in concrete life, with the mutual care for the needs of others, must be the counterpart to communion in faith, in prayer, and in the breaking of bread. The second passage, which directly highlights fraternity of life in the sharing of goods, interprets the emerging community as a realization of the community of the covenant promised in *Deut* 15:4: «there will be no one in need among you».

4.4. FORMATION OF CONSCIENCE

The reflections here seem to confirm the priority of formation of conscience as a specific ecclesial task, both within the Church itself, and as a contribution to true humanity in our world. *Signifying the meaning* of what is human according to the design of creation and redemption *by making it present* belongs, in fact, to the sacramentality of the Church.

4.4.1. *EDUCATING THE INNER SELF*

To bring the human person back to him/herself means above all leading him/her back to the capacity for personal free responsibility and sincerity of conscience. If this is not achieved, then recalling values or suggesting problems, important though they may be, will in some sense be an «extrinsic» allusion that will be interpreted as a requirement that is to be «added» to already numerous usual commitments. It would seem that a requirement proposed in this way does not have much chance of countering the culturally dominant ways of thinking, of overcoming objectively and personally costly difficulties, and of resisting the wear and tear of time. In addition to the question of foreseeable effectiveness, this approach would not even be morally correct. The proposal itself would be internally contradictory, avoiding the fundamental problem: at issue is not a thing to be done, but you, your humanity, the meaning and possible fulfillment of your life.

For the Christian, internal formation means, above all, formation to living one's own truth in conscience within an explicit relationship with the Lord. It is about being educated in personal knowledge of the Lord, in familiarity with him and his word, in the gradual assumption of his «sentiments» (*Phil* 2:5ff), so as to understand and live with and in him all that is intended within one's free responsibility.

Both in Christian moral formation, and in the contribution to the formation of an increasingly authentic human morality, one cannot ignore the fact of prospective personal unity, which binds together the various aspects and dimensions of life, as much from the point of view of understanding (and subsequent evaluating and deciding), as from the point of view of possible witness. Therefore, the problem of hunger in the world will not find adequate responses if they are sought only or largely at the level of «technical» possibilities. If something is done on the basis of a rationale of opportunity, the objective good realized will bear with it the trace of that rationale, spreading and confirming it, that is, helping the other person, *if it benefits you.* Fraternal humanity requires that fraternity be the fundamental criterion in evaluating and decision-making.

4.4.2. EDUCATING TOWARD THE COMMON GOOD

As has been discussed earlier, a basic misunderstanding in the manner of living out personal responsibility toward the common good results from interpreting it as functional to the private good (of individuals and the groups to which one belongs). Broadly speaking, this interpretation seems to reflect the current mentality in today's more widespread cultures and constitutes a fundamental obstacle to the interpretation of life and of social life in terms of charity-communion. On this basis, emphasizing the ethical need to search for the common good can only seem to be an additional obligation.

It is necessary to form an understanding of self and an evaluation of what is fulfillment of one's own life on bases that are not radically egocentric. The reaching out toward a shared humanity must be understood and desired as belonging to the meaning and fulfillment of one's own personal humanity. The search for the common good, then, even in its partial realizations, simply qualifies the search for the good. It is not expressed merely at some specific occasions or in some area of life, but rather, it belongs to the criteria for discerning what is good and for making evaluations among the possible positive realizations in terms of the hierarchy of importance and the degree of urgency.

If there is a difficulty of culture and custom in understanding the fundamental human value of gratuity, in this is presented a specific challenge for the Christian; at issue is his/her assuming charity as a fundamental criterion of the moral life and his/her knowing how to translate it in terms humanly meaningful for the life of the world.

Chapter 8

Toward an ethic of development

There is a continuous circularity between reflection on general ethical principles and reflection on particular or circumscribed questions. I will now present a general ethical reflection, stimulated by a reading of questions about business ethics and its relationship to the development of the South. If we speak about the «development of the South», it is because we recognize a difference between the North and the South, interpreting the relations that this difference highlights, indicating possible solutions to the problems posed by difference and relationship. As a starting point I am offering some reflections on ethical questions related to development, bearing in mind the relationship between morality and economic relations, between personal morality and moral custom.

1
Development

To speak of development and to be alert to the ethical dimension of the issue requires above all that we ask questions about *the meaning* of development itself, about its human meaning, on the basis of which to understand and evaluate which *global goals* must be suggested. Clearly at issue are many scientific skills, with their analyses and proposals, necessary for the most objective and exact understanding possible of the real conditions from which one begins and the actual opportunities that such conditions present. Philosophy and moral theology have no possibility of replacing such skills. Instead, they have the role of reflecting on the different contributions in order to mediate a global perspective of meaning that might be capable of basically integrating them into a *humanly rational coherent aim.*

In a reflection on the meaning of development, which is obviously linked to the meaning of human existence, at issue is the question about who we wish to be as people who live together. To speak in a humanly rational way about development means to have a global perspective on the aims, rather than just a partial one. The ethical dimension gives precise attention to this coordination between the particular and the global perspective of meaning for the existence of the individual. Likewise, in addressing social issues, it is essential to have a global perspective of shared existence in organized structures, in socially structured relations.

Today, for example, it is easy to see that an exclusively economic perspective would not be able, on its own, even to guarantee economic progress. At the same time, however, the answer does not lie in simply searching for an ethic as a function of the economy. It must also be recognized that, if genuine economic progress were achieved exclusively (or almost so) on the basis of economic criteria, with significant indifference to other factors (which would only be considered if and inasmuch as they are economically important), there would not be true progress in terms of humanity. In fact, it would suggest economic progress not as *an* end, but as *the* end to pursue, with all of the consequences that this would have on moral thinking and conduct.

There is always the risk of subjugating ethics (and personal morality) to other objectives, for example, by first addressing scientific research and then, consistent with that, giving attention to the different morally important values that can be at issue. Instead, the order should be first, to address personal honesty and subsequently, within the framework of honesty, to address scientific research. The same is true for the relation between economic efficiency and morality. But personal morality is not a value-mean; it is a value-end, and as such, a regulator of choices.

To interpret progress with a specific and explicit *human* aim entails the need to *order* the different choices on the basis of a hierarchy of values, with criteria for prioritizing, so that the different circumscribed aims may be truly directed toward a global aim and correctly ordered by it. This *ordering* is an ethical requirement. On a personal individual level it responds to the question of what meaning you assume for your existence. On the personal social level it responds to the question of what meaning you (plural) assume for your living side by side.

2 *Development of the South*

The need for objectivity, on the cognitive (in the order of the truth of understanding), operative (in the order of the possible effectiveness of the interventions), and moral levels (in the order of correct behavior), calls for consideration of the problem of a region's development not just on regional bases, because the reality of a region is properly considered only when it is understood as a reality of *this* part of a *whole*, therefore, in its relation to other regions[1].

1 Cfr. AAVV., «Etica cristiana e economia: il conflitto Nord-Sud», in *Concilium* 16 (1980) 1627-1824; CIPRIANI S., ED., *Nuove frontiere dell'etica economica*, AVE, Rome 1990.

The South is not the South if it is not in relation to the North. This is not simply a geographical observation. With reference to development, too, the question about the inter-relationship existing between the «being south» of the South and the «being north» of the North is inevitable. The question is rightly posed as to whether it is prudent and respectful of the identity of a region to think of its development in terms of importing the development model of another region. It must also be asked if the development in a region is also the cause of non-development of another region, or if perhaps it even perpetuates it.

On the ethical level that means asking whether or not the North can think of the need to develop the South without asking whether its own development model should be reconsidered and redefined, specifically on the basis of the fact there exists (sadly, for some time) a South in need of development. More specifically, why and how, in what conditions, does the North want the development of the South?

On the level of personal morality it is precisely the presence of the other person, with his/her dignity as person and in his/her concrete conditions, which demands that freedom not be exercised in an arbitrary manner, but rather, by assuming the responsibility for the personal existence of someone else, and in this way defining one's own plan on the basis of the presence of another person. On the level of the morality of social life, at issue in a similar way is the mutual responsibility of various groups or social «regions», according to respective levels of opportunity[2]. Perhaps it is a sensitive problem, but it is not resolved by denying or ignoring it.

3
Ethical problems in North-South relations

One of the issues we must address concerns the meaning and values implied in the relationship between humanity and the earth's resources, in relation to the difficulties of the development of the South. We will confront the questions that

2 Cfr. BASTIANEL S., *Autonomia morale del credente. Senso e motivazioni di un'attuale tendenza teologica*, Morcelliana, Brescia 1980; LÉVINAS E., *Totality and Infinity. An Essay on Exteriority*, Duquesne University Press, Pittsburgh PA 1969; PINTO DE OLIVEIRA C.-J., *La dimensione mondiale dell'etica, Situazione e futuro del mondo umano*, Edizioni Dehoniane, Bologna 1986; ID., *La crisi della scelta morale nella civiltà tecnica*, Borla, Rome 1978.

arise in our conscience when we ask ourselves about the very essence of this problem, about its causes and our own possible co-responsibility in it.

When a person's free decision directly or indirectly involves relations with other people (their lives and personal values) an ethical problem is involved. In our case it relates to when personal decisions and cooperation in collective decisions impact in some way on the difficulties of the development in question.

The ethical issue is always a matter of human relations, even if complex and indirect. To understand and evaluate a relationship, or a complex of relationships, in this perspective means to consider carefully the objective conditions of the two «ends» of the relationship (between the North and the South, and the individual and the context of his/her relations), the objective relationship of dependency between these conditions, and the objective opportunities for modifying such a relationship. Furthermore, it requires consideration of the meaning of all these elements, evaluating it on the basis of the meaning of human life on earth and what makes a person's existence and conduct morally good.

A constant theological thread (from the Old Testament to the Church's current reflection) interprets the fact of the differences in social and economic conditions in relation to the meaning of human life and in terms of justice and responsibility, proposing aims and fundamental criteria. This thread refers to the various forms of «poverty», which are interpreted as the result of moral evil, as expressions of objective injustice. In this situation is raised the need for a clear link between attention to the *objective values* (objectively correct behavior) and attention to *personal morality*, against the various temptations of a heteronomous ethic. Attention must be paid to the motivations behind morality, rather than just to the specific motivation for a specific type of behavior.

When there are major problems at issue such as those linked to non-development or hindered or difficult development, we cannot launch into an ethical reflection, while leaving to one side questions about fundamental meaning. With respect to development opportunities, which historically are always what they are, one cannot propose ethical responsibility for non-existent possibilities. One must take into account what is actually possible, that is, how important in personal individual behavior in each case is the link to the good that is genuinely possible here and now. In a social perspective as well, it obviously will be necessary to be aware that it is a matter of verifying the genuine possibilities, recognizing that in this case, common responsibility is important.

A crucial question, which also is not primarily technical, but rather ethical, could be phrased in this manner: is it reasonable to think about a positive overcoming of the problem of North-South relations, therefore of true development, while keeping intact the current social «systems», with the dominant thinking that sustains them and the justifications that legitimize them on the level of the current mentality? In fact, there appears to be a need not just for greater sensitivity to social problems; it is not just that sensitivity to social problems must be deepened, but that it must move well beyond the affirmation of principle, demands and protest. What appears necessary is a conversion of that very social sensitivity, toward a truer and more transparent morality at its foundations, which seeps into animate cultures, social processes, and the structuring of relations in human life.

In this context it is appropriate to take note again of the fact that the Encyclical *Sollicitudo rei socialis* refers to the evils that confront us with respect to the development of peoples, especially when decisions, economic or otherwise, are in reality based on forms of idolatry: money, ideology, class, technology.

4
The possibility of development and ethical responsibility

In the face of objective possibilities for development, the responsibility of consciences must be involved in order to realize the possibilities in a rational manner and to create further possibilities.

4.1. THE COMPLEXITY OF THE PROBLEMS

We often are undeniably faced with extremely complex and sophisticated mechanisms and structures. Moral judgment must of necessity take into account the complexity of the problems in order to be objective, and therefore it will necessarily be prudent. The personal responsibility of individuals and groups depends on people's genuine awareness and freedom, which can only be evaluated through consideration of the complex of internal and external circumstances in which each one finds him/herself and in which each one operates. The complexity of interacting factors translates into an objective difficulty of choice, both with respect to the difficulty of understanding what is morally good, and the difficulty of actually wanting it, with no reservations.

Faced with questions that involve ways of thinking and well-established structures, the possibility of direct global solutions overwhelms the ability of individual consciences and even those of large groups, but no solution to such questions can come about unless through *consciences* and the *deliberate sharing* of understanding and behavior, that is, through the historic process that constitutes (and preserves or modifies) a common ethos, a culture, the structures of human society.

4.2. PEOPLE AND SOCIETY

Each of us is born and grows within a specific culture and works in a specific society. The mentality and exercise of the human capacities in understanding, assessing, and choosing are inevitably marked by the cultural and social environment in which one lives. Everyone is a child of his/her time and culture. We come into the world, or more precisely, we come into *a* world, receiving from it an influence of all that belongs to the human essence of our existence. This means that at one and the same time we are faced with both opportunity and restriction: it offers the possibility of developing one's own uniqueness, and yet it is our conditioning that affects this very possibility. From the moral point of view it is important to discern how the space open to freedom is both *limited* and is a space *open* to freedom.

In assuming one's own freedom, each person contributes to the formation of the culture and society to which he/she belongs. Social responsibilities are not responsibilities of an anonymous society; they are responsibilities of the people who constitute that society. The network of relations, and the way in which these structure themselves, create the conditions (opportunities and restrictions) within which one continues to live and into which others come to live. In this context, the freedom of each person becomes liberating or constraining on the freedom of others. There is a personal responsibility involved here, because culture, and the ethos it mediates, can either become a locus of gratuity and the acceptance of relations, or a locus of manipulation and violence.

4.3. PERSONAL MORALITY, MORAL CUSTOMS, STRUCTURES

The consideration of personal morality in the perspective of social relations encounters the difficulty of sorting out the relationship between people and structures. Sometimes these structures seem to be imperative, in that they can hold personal morality in check. This is what needs to be considered carefully.

Personal moral goodness is expressed in the search for and realization of objective human values. All things being equal, the more genuine the moral goodness is, in fact, the more a person is able to recognize what an authentic human value is and to plan the most suitable ways for achieving it. The motive for the most favorable situation lies in achieving greater inner freedom. This speaks to the opportunity for authentic objective historic effectiveness: goodness belongs to history and shapes the history of recognizing and achieving good.

Authentic consensus on ethical questions is based simultaneously on a sharing of the values in question and a sharing of the basic value of honesty. This sharing at the level of conscience is at the basis of possible «rules»; it makes possible a shared moral custom or the changing of a present moral custom, as well as making possible the effective transmission of the moral knowledge reached.

There is therefore a relationship between the morality of an individual and the moral custom of a group. In the thread that runs from ethos to morality one can recognize the cultural understanding that a person receives for his/her own understanding of and living out of morality. From morality to ethos one can perceive the personal contribution to the stability or the transformation of the current moral custom.

The expression of personal morality always makes a contribution to the historic effectiveness of the convictions and ethical praxis that have already become culture, either through assumption or confirmation, or through discord or potential change.

Usually the assumption of the current mentality is easier, because there is no need to make a great impression, while the visibility of the models and the actual sharing about values and behavior facilitate adaptation, if not even conscious assumption. However, the result is also more fragile, more exposed to manipulation and variations due to various circumstances. Compromise is also easier in the face of significant costs that may be involved. However, the assumption of responsibility in contrast with the current way of thinking is more difficult. There is a need for strong motivation and conviction, but at the same time, the capacity for morality (free and conscious responsibility) is more rooted, and any possible influence on others by communication is more effective and more lasting.

5
Human values and moral value

If considered from an ethical point of view, the theme of development is not a question that interests just a few individuals or groups of people. It is at the root of a question about thinking, a widespread way of thinking and evaluating, which concerns anyone who directly takes decisions and agrees to them, in an explicit and direct way or even in terms of «not wanting to create any problems». In this sense it is a question of formation, personal formation of conscience and sharing about values, urgencies and priorities, and perspectives of common choices.

We speak of human values regarding everything that, at various levels and in the different spheres of experience, responds to a genuine need for the human person or constitutes his/her greatest accomplishment. A human value is that which assists in the authentic fulfillment of human existence as human.

Where important human values are concerned, one sometimes takes a short cut and calls them moral values. Such an inappropriate identification between human value and moral value is made easier by the fact that one rightly notices how personal morality is engaged when faced with human values, above all if they are extremely important. However, when we attempt to explain the relationship between human value and moral value, we must recognize that it is not possible to equate them. When we speak of moral values we intend to allude to the personal unity of knowledge, freedom and responsibility. This unity is not always at issue when faced with a value, and when it is, it is not always seen in the same way.

The human value «physical life» does not always, nor necessarily, have something to do with someone's conscious free responsibility. For instance, if someone dies of old age, the value «human life» that is lost is not attributable to someone's knowledge, freedom and responsibility. Someone's morality is at issue, however, *in the relationship* between the subject and the human values, asking the subject to make oneself responsible within the bounds of one's conscience and the genuine possibilities for intervention.

What is morally qualifying as a value is not just any objective human value, even though it might be extremely important, but a person's relationship to an objective human value. What is morally qualifiable is my relationship to the human value «a person's life» at the moment when I decide to accept or reject that value. However, at the objective level, that value is not in itself a moral value, inasmuch as, by itself, it does not necessarily involve my conscience, freedom and responsibility.

This distinction between human and moral values is important in order to avoid possible serious misunderstandings. If we convince ourselves that certain values are intrinsically moral, conscience feels guilty for not assimilating or accepting the values as moral, while in fact it was not morally bound. If, for example, I was not in a position to save a human life in danger, I would rightly feel saddened by the death, but I should not feel guilty. That human life is highly important, but my morality is not at issue in that death; in fact, precisely because I was unable to do anything to save that life, the loss is not due to my free responsibility.

If, faced with that same human life in danger, I am able to save it and I do so, if necessary even with great sacrifice or at personal risk, but not because I perceive the value and I want to do what I can to save it, but rather, because I see greater benefit for me with that person alive, my gesture is not an act of moral goodness. Instead, it is an egotistical gesture; I have not assumed responsibility for that life in danger, but sought my own benefit.

Therefore, moral value indicates the moral quality of the person in relation to objective good and evil. Traditionally, this distinction was indicated by the terms *bonum physicum* and *bonum morale*. The *bonum physicum* concerns the human value in its objectivity, that is, that which can be recognized as a value suitable for enabling someone to accomplish something. The distinction aimed at connoting the specificity of the *morality* is that when faced with the *bonum physicum*, personal free responsibility is at issue. The person is involved in a relationship that calls that person to assume responsibility for realizing that value within the bounds of his/her capabilities. For example, the fact that someone might hear the call of the gospel, or offer spiritual assistance, is a *bonum physicum*. But when I decide to offer or not to offer that help, when a person decides whether to permit him/herself to be helped or not, here the *bonum morale* comes into play.

This distinction, traditional in Christian moral theology, tends to stipulate the proper locus of moral experience as the experience of free and conscious responsibility. From the fact of being responsible when faced with someone, stems the fact that everything which involves responsibility (intrinsically qualified as conscious and free) assumes a moral connotation.

Contemporary sensitivity about the necessary freedom of every individual, even though it concerns a fundamental human reality that continues to be contradicted in many ways, in its current emphases is a somewhat recent affirmation. It was once believed legitimate that someone could decide about someone else's life. (One thinks of legalized slavery, but also about the ways in which authority was understood and exercised). Today slavery is no longer recognized and great emphasis is placed on democracy and co-responsibility, but the question still needs to be asked if in the various spheres of social life the value of personal liberty is genuinely recognized. Perhaps it is generally true that our institutions tend to ensure the possibility of effectively deciding one's own life. Yet in fact, precisely the «free» associations, also through public legitimization and institutional manipulations, often represent what are actually conditioning forces, from which some or many (even entire social classes or populations) are constrained by conditions that do not allow them to decide about their own lives, even at basic levels.

The question, then, is not only that of understanding and affirming specific human values in themselves, but also, and not secondarily, of recognizing the values and interpreting them in different historic situations. We have no other way of becoming acquainted with the values, if not by looking at objective reality with the help of all the tools that can help us to understand it. Moral reflection must interpret the results of the knowledge of the sciences from the point of view of the meaning of human existence. By interpreting reality on the basis of the human, one attempts to identify the criteria for establishing a hierarchy between the recognized values and the criteria for evaluating the urgency of the realization of recognized and compared values in the concrete circumstances.

With regard to known human values, the person's responsibility comes into play as a person called to respect and to implement them. Moral experience and reflection also come into play here. Reflection cannot forget the relationship between the *morally correct* and the *morally good;* between what is objectively recognizable as value and personal moral goodness. Objectively, just behavior is important, but it is equally important that this should not only be the realization of socially important expectations for those who benefit from them. There also must be a personal assumption of responsibility in the face of the good made possible by virtue of an inner conviction that expresses personal morality. It is about being *good* people attempting to recognize and bring about *good.* It is about being able to share the search for the good that is possible, sharing a journey of personal goodness.

5.1. THE CONTRIBUTION OF CHRISTIAN FAITH

Let us briefly recall a statement about the relationship between faith and morality. When, as it relates to the theme being examined here, it is a matter of recognizing values and clarifying concepts that are human (not specifically Christian), the believer cannot manifest his/her faith, but neither can he/she proceed as if not believing in his/her attempt to discern the human.

In pointing out the meaning of the relationship to the other person, placing the emphasis on the gratuity of the relationships in connoting the specificity of moral responsibility, and in putting in first place a perspective of shared existence, the believer sets in motion a way of understanding the *human*, which is deeply marked by how much he/she understands by virtue of his/her faith, which goes well beyond quotations and possible explicit references to the Bible and the church's tradition. We cannot (and must not) divest ourselves of the understanding we have of the meaning of the human person by virtue of listening to the Scriptures.

Faith has an explicit influence on the very horizon of understanding that we have as believers. Faith has an influence on understanding things in an objective and ordered manner within a horizon of understanding that has its reference point and that necessarily influences the possibility of recognizing and stating meanings. When we speak of a horizon of knowledge we think of a spatial image of a subject situated in a reality that lies before us in an ordered way, so that we can say where one thing is and where another, indicating the relations by which they are linked. This can be said not only because we are in the midst of the world, but also because we are looking from our point of view, from where we are consciously situated in the midst of the world. Thus the believer can look at the world, at objective reality, at human values, as if looking at a rational reality ordered toward an end: the fact of knowing that the meaning of the world, its origins and end, is not indifferent to the understanding of its individual elements and what is of value in it. This, however, does not mean that where the non-believer perceives a value the believer perceives an evil and vice versa. The horizon of prior understanding certainly concerns the interpretation of what is real, but does not imply arbitrariness or external attribution of meaning, and does not make verification impossible or excuse one from the possible task of verification.

Of primary importance in this sense, particularly with regard to dialogue and communication (connected to the responsibility of verifying one's own understandings in terms of objectivity), is the awareness of one's own presuppositions with openness to objective knowledge. The believer must not forget that what comes to him/her from faith comes within a history, with the assistance and limitation of culture.

Interpretation means to perceive a significance and at the same time to understand that significance within the meaning system within which it is located. Faith's specific contribution to morality is then also that of helping to correctly raise questions about the meaning of the reality in view of action, inasmuch as such questions about significance are raised having in mind a *telos* to which meanings are directed.

5.2. NORMS, CODICES, AND MORALITY

Of course, «codified» moral custom has its specific role, by virtue of the proper effectiveness of explicit social control, with the relevant «sanctions» (not just those of a penal code). It also, however, has its weakness, through possible misunderstandings of a heteronomous morality and behavior led from outside, with all the attendant risks for morally weak and easily manipulated people. One can be «honest» because it is convenient. But one cannot set great store by this supposed honesty. Authentic honesty calls for attention both to the content of the value proposed for sharing and to people's moral status, to the content of the choices and the rationale with which they are examined and affirmed.

Personal responsibility and social co-responsibility for possible development are also, of course, both a question of good will and a question of understanding, evaluation, and judgment. In the correct evaluation of what is possible, at issue is the rationality of our judging and a question of our ethical principles and morals, which already call for liberty and responsibility in the search for a precise understanding, even before deciding in the correct way.

There are issues that arise almost immediately as problems having to do with ways of thinking, shared moral behavior, and shared motivation. It is important to be attentive to the relationship between ethos (moral custom de facto shared in a certain place and time) and morality as personal, free assumption of responsibility in one's own context. This means that it will be extremely difficult to work only on the level of personal individual moral conviction, because the strength of persuasion of what is commonly shared, of what is also declared as a just praxis, can be very strong. But at the same time it will be illusory to think of working only on the level of ethos, at the institutional level, at the level of norms and rules, including rules of self-regulation. These rules in themselves cannot have any *ethical* effectiveness without being viewed through the lens of personal assumption and the value and values that the rules propose. A norm or rule could also be assumed for extrinsic motives, perhaps because there is social pressure, because others want it thus, because otherwise costs would be incurred, penalties caused by the fact that others do not share specific types of behavior and that, at least in the long run, one cannot avoid paying the consequences. A good rule, however, achieves its ethical aim when its value is recognized by people who take on in free responsibility the value indications it proposes.

Such personal assumption makes possible a genuine sharing of values even beyond the immediate. It recalls the general problem of the transmission of moral values and norms, that is, whether it is a matter of not repeating what has been learned from others, or rather a matter of mediating the possibility of someone else's experience understood through the communication of one's own personal perception and personal assumption of the values in question.

Part Four

The story of evil, the story of good

Chapter 9

Moral evil

When we think about the great evils that afflict humanity and are caused by human beings, even when we can ascertain specifically who is responsible, we have a perception of the seriousness of evil that is not «explained» simply by assigning blame. As we examine our position in the history of humanity we can see that evil does not pass us by: not just because we suffer the consequences, but also because we are not innocent. In some way we are also the cause. In every case, we perceive the universality of evil as a reality that hangs over us. We are not able to resolve it, not even with the greatest good will possible.

In a certain sense, we know this *Mysterium iniquitatis* very well. It is the reality of our daily experience; and yet we succeed neither in explaining it, nor in dominating it. In recent times much emphasis has been placed on co-responsibility, speaking about «social sin» or «structures of sin»[1]. But in what sense is it properly called «sin»?

We propose a reflection on moral evil, therefore, as it relates to the personal unity of consciousness, freedom and responsibility. We will ask ourselves how this evil becomes ingrained in history and how it assumes a dynamic of historical strength with outcomes that go far beyond the individual and that have a lasting impact on individuals.

From this standpoint one can also raise questions about the relationship between human nature and human nature in history, about the possible good and unavoidable evil, as well as about the conditionings of freedom and the corresponding responsibility.

With this type of questioning, theology interrogates its specific main sources, that is, the biblical traditions. In fact, biblical hermeneutics enables one to find similar questions in historical contexts very different from ours, with a reflection not just present, but central to the ethical and religious traditions of the Scriptures, in a fundamental continuity that extends across the entire span of revelation.

We will examine in particular one of the more significant documents in this regard, that of the Yahwist (especially the text of *Genesis* 2-3) and one of the prominent figures at about the time that an important part of the Yahwist's reflection was developing: the figure of David, who is described in his sinfulness and his conversion (a specific reference to the text of *2 Samuel* 11-12). An overview of the New Testament will focus attention on the humanity of Jesus and his disciples.

1 Cfr. Sollicitudo rei socialis, 36.

1

Evil as an ethical and theological problem

With respect to the universality of the problem, or *mysterium*, that evil constitutes for us, to assume an *ethical* consideration implies a fundamental distinction, the boundaries of which are not easily recognizable in individual concrete cases, but which must necessarily be defined and clarified in terms of what constitutes the actual objective of the specific reflection.

Within the sphere of ethical experience belongs per se all that constitutes the life of a human being (including therefore, every type of «evil» that limits, thwarts, or represses), but the only aspect that is called into question here is the internal unity of personal moral conscience, expressed in conscious and free responsibility. If an unexpected thunderbolt kills a person walking in the forest, we are of course faced with an evil: the death of that person. There are questions about this evil, but that death and its cause do not constitute a moral evil. Of course, there could be, for example, someone who rejoices in that death and *in this* there would be an ethical issue, about the free responsibility in rejoicing at an evil[2].

What concerns our reflection, however, is the evil caused by people through conscious free decision. This brings to the foreground the evil in which people themselves are the doers of evil. How does one explain the existence of a murderer, an exploiter, a cheat? How does one evaluate the existence of such people from the point of view of the human meaning of life? Furthermore, there are not just the obvious figures of iniquity, but also those who construct their lives without murdering but not without humiliating others if it benefits them. There are those who seem to exploit no one, but every day play a crafty game to their own advantage and the disadvantage of others.

The network between the evil person and the evil he/she carries out, united together with the network between the evil of many people in the continuity of history, raises further questions about the historical effect of a human life that generates evil and produces evil-doers. In this story how is one to understand the dynamic of freedom and responsibility?

2 On the classical difference between *malum physicum* and *malum morale* and the precisely ethical connotation of evil, linked to sin and people's guilt, cfr. BASTIANEL S., «Strutture di peccato. Riflessione teologico-morale», in ID., ED., *Strutture di peccato. Una sfida teologica e pastorale*, Piemme, Casale Monferrato 1989, 15-38; SCHOONENBERG P., *Man and Sin*, Sheed & Ward Stagbooks,

Whoever lives an existence consciously qualified by the experience of Christian faith will have specific theological questions linked to ethical questions about evil. At issue is one's own understanding of God in perceiving his will and action in relation to free human responsibility. At issue as well, is the understanding of the human person in his/her relationship with God, the meaning and value of freedom, the meaning and value of personal responsibility in concrete existence, and the meaning and value of the history of humanity. What interpretive help does faith in Jesus Christ offer in the face of the scandal of moral evil and the consistency of its historical effectiveness[3]?

As is the case with every authentic ethical question, questions about evil also have their specific theological implications for the believer. And this is not something new, as we will see in interpreting some elements of the biblical traditions. Nor is it something incidental, because it belongs to the claims of faith: in its being made manifest in speech, in enlightening the understanding of life in its fundamental aspects of meaning and value, in its aims, in its *eschaton*. The experience of evil, particularly in its dimension of sin, continues to raise radical questions to which our own image of God is linked[4], in God's intentionality of good and salvation as affirmed by faith.

2 *The evil that comes from the human person: Genesis* 2-3

The text of *Genesis* 2-3 (from 2:4b onward) belongs to what is known as the «Yahwistic» document[5]. The Old Testament traditions that converge therein also suggest a reflection that seems intent on responding to questions very similar to our questions about evil.

London 1972, 78-108; SIEVERNICH M., *Schuld und Sünde in der Theologie der Gegenwart*, Knecht, Frankfurt 1982.

3 Cfr. BÖCKLE F., *Fundamental Moral Theology*, Gill and Macmillan, Dublin 1980, 77-138; GÖRRES A., RAHNER K., *Male. Le risposte della psicoterapia e del cristianesimo*, Edizioni Paoline, Cinisello Balsamo 1986.

4 Cfr. FUCHS J., «Our Image of God and the Morality of Innerworldly Behaviour», in ID., *Christian Morality. The Word Becomes Flesh*, Georgetown University Press, Washington DC 1987, 47-78.

5 For the interpretation of the book of *Genesis* cfr. J.B. BAUER, «Israele guarda nella preistoria (Gn 1-11)», in SCHREINER J., ED., *Introduzione letteraria e teologica all'Antico Testamento*, Edizioni Paoline, Rome 1982, 150-171. WESTERMANN C., *Genesis*, William B. Eerdmans Publishing Company, Grand Rapids Michigan, 1987. On the literary character and theology of the Yahwist tradition, see WOLFF H.W., «Das Kerygma des Jahwisten», in *Evangelische Theologie* 24 (1964)

In all likelihood this interpretation of history began its formation in the Davidic-Solomonic era at a time of Israel's great expansion. A unity was being consolidated among these people, who increasingly recognized themselves in the foundational traditions of Exodus and Sinai. With the strengthening of the state's internal structure, relations with the neighboring peoples, likewise, were in a phase of positive expansion, along with cultural and economic life. Israel was becoming a united, great, strong, and respected people. This people interpreted the whole of its history as a result of that *covenant* in which it saw itself as chosen, accompanied, and protected by God. It claimed to be, and wished to be, Yahweh's people.

In this context of expansion, progress, and recognized development, there remained, however, a jarring internal contradiction. Actually, Yahweh's people were not living in accordance with the covenant. Rivalry, privilege, and conflict bore their fruits of injustice, and not in a sporadic manner. The very structures of social and political life, which should have helped to realize a unity among a fraternal people, became arenas of injustice and marginalization, the privilege of the strong and the affirmation of self-sufficiency and independence from God.

The historic experience raised a question about an explanation for the evil present that continued to provide its fruit of deprivation, suffering and death. A people that declared itself to be inspired by the covenant with God and ready to assume God's will as the rule for one's life at all levels, this people is still, and not incidentally, sinful. There are not just individual sinners, but something of a shared, even concerted sinfulness; there is an evil that pervaded the concrete structuring of social and political life.

The tradition that takes form and expression in the Yahwist's document is aware of explanations about its own evils that are present in other peoples and religions. Among these, there is often present the temptation to explain the consistency and force of evil by stating that it is inevitable or that it is part of human

73-98; RAD G. VON, *Old Testament Theology*, vol. 1, *The Theology of Israel's Historical Traditions*, Oliver and Boyd, Edinburgh 1968, 129-164. On the formation and dates of the document, exegetes are divided in their opinions. For some 20 years the «documentary» theory (Cfr. Wellhausen), based on the history of the formation of the text, has been challenged. At any rate there is a degree of consensus among experts in considering the Yahwist as the great theologian of Judah linked, by religious-political interest and by the era of composition of an important part of the material, to the monarchy of Solomon (not before the IX-VIII centuries B.C.). On this matter cfr. BONORA A., «Pentateuco», in ROSSANO P., RAVASI G., GIRLANDA A., EDD., *Nuovo Dizionario di Teologia Biblica*, Edizioni Paoline, Cinisello Balsamo 1988, 1141-1151, with the bibliography indicated there.

nature or it is provoked by some evil divinity which makes the heart of the human person inevitably evil. There are interpretations that, in different ways, end by excusing the human person from the reality of the evil that he/she commits. But the experience of Israel's faith cannot accept such forms of self-justification. Reflection on the founding events of the liberation from Egypt and the covenant has led to the development of the theology of creation in harmony with the theology of history: God's faithfulness coincides with his working on behalf of the human person, with his will for communion forever[6].

In the literary genre of the account, the text distinguishes in time the creation of humans and the origin of sin. It thereby differentiates the human reality as it derives from God's creative plan, that is, human nature, from that which humans become through sin.

The second chapter of the book of Genesis, from v. 2b onward, presents the creation of humans in a language and in images that speak about a harmonious reality. God creates man placing him in a «garden», a place suitable for him and in which he finds what he needs in abundance. The garden itself is entrusted to his hands so that he might cultivate it as a place for possible existence. God creates, placing before himself the man to whom he gives being, breathing within him a breath of life. To him God speaks; he creates man capable of listening to him and responding to him. In relationship with God, man can recognize the garden and what populates it; he can understand reality and can care for the garden, can understand and plan, can live. Man's life at that point, however, is not defined by infrahuman relations, and it is not enough for him to know and plan; the garden is not yet his home. God knows he has given him a life that is not fulfilled without relating to a «you» similar to him.

In vv. 21-26 the text presents a new beginning. Woman is created. Adam *recognizes* her and knows himself in being *recognized*. His existence on earth is qualified by this personal reality. He can communicate and share his life, because he is addressed by and sharing in the life of Eve. What does Adam's presence mean for her? Through the strength of the nuptial image, the gift of a shared existence is declared. The creative plan for human existence is fulfilled in mutual recognition and acceptance.

6 Cfr. BONORA A., «Male/Dolore», in ROSSANO P., RAVASI G., GIRLANDA A., EDD., *Nuovo Dizionario di Teologia Biblica*, 870-887; WOLFF H.W., *Anthropology of the Old Testament*, Fortress Press, Minneapolis, MN 1974, 123-130; 205-212.

Thus are man and woman created. Within the relationship with God the relationship with the other person is the place of their humanity, their opportunity for self-understanding and living as human persons. The otherness, from which they receive the gift of personal quality, of their own human life, is entrusted to them so that they make of it the essence of personal human existence[7].

Out of communion with God arises communion with the other person. The garden is a place in which it is possible to establish existence through sharing life, sharing precisely what is necessary to live. The human significance of the earth and the cultivation of it stems from this aim of communion. A triple harmony, therefore, characterizes the meaning and opportunities for existence carried out by human beings according to the creator's plan. In the sign of communion with God, who creates in communion with him people capable of communion between themselves, he entrusts to them the task of building that communion in a land suitable to be the place of their humanity. This is creation.

The following chapter of the book of Genesis presents what we could call the entrance of sin into the world (*Gen* 3:1-24). The fact that the human person is a sinner does not belong to the realm of the creative word; the human person is not a sinner by nature. There are no divinities or forces at the level of divine power contrary to God's creative plan, his creative word. Furthermore, the text seems to suggest that we can also recognize how humans became sinners. Through the literary genre of the account of the first sin, an explanation is given of the way in which contradicting the creative word became the human story. With the affirmation that sin comes from the human heart there is also an awareness of how this happened[8]. It is suggested to Eve that perhaps God doesn't really have good will toward the human person. Is it true that God has put you in this garden and forbidden you to eat the fruit of these trees? The suspicion is introduced that God's will is contrary to the good of people and their legitimate desires; that he imposes prohibitions for no reason, basically against them. The manner in which this temptation is expressed is obviously too deceitful to have been accepted. It is not true that he forbids eating the fruit from the trees in the garden, but if one thinks about it carefully, why is there a tree from which they cannot take the fruit however and whenever they want? The seeds of suspicion

7 Cfr. BASTIANEL S., *Autonomia morale del credente. Senso e motivazioni di un'attuale tendenza teologica*, Morcelliana, Brescia 1980, 34-44; BUBER M., «Io e Tu», in ID., *Il principio dialogico e altri saggi*, San Paolo, Cinisello Balsamo 1993, 59-146.

8 Cfr. DUBARLE A.M., *Il peccato originale nella Scrittura*, AVE, Rome 1968; FUCHS J., «Il problema del peccato mortale», in ID., *Ricercando la verità morale*, San Paolo, Cinisello Balsamo 1996, 183-198.

are sown and internally the personal relationship with God seems to be clouded with the thought that perhaps it is not true that God desires our good.

This cloud of suspicion centers on the tree of good and evil. The foundation of good and evil is something that God declares to be not at our discretion. Why? Why should it not be up to us to declare what is good and what is evil, according to what pleases us? Why shouldn't what I say to be good *be* good, and what I say to be evil *be* evil? Why should I have to wrestle with God about good and evil? Why is my freedom not completely in my power, so that I can state its meaning and value? Why must I take God into account about the truth and goodness of what I decide and not be able to do it according to my own will? In other words, why can't I withdraw from this foundational relationship with God? Why must I respond to him and listen to his word, and why can't I instead build my own life as I choose?

Constructed along the lines of «etiology», in the search for the causes of an historic human reality in order to understand its significance, the account of *Gen* 3 returns to the «origins» of a reality that is also ours, in which the image of God is disproved and the meaning of the relationship with him, which is a gift of communion, life, future, and fullness, is distorted. Communion with God is seen as restrictive. As far as the good of humans is concerned, God assumes the face of a rival. Thus the fruits of this tree seem desirable. It seems beautiful and desirable to be able to live according to one's own will, to be able to state what is good without having to answer to anyone. I want what I say to be good because I say it to be so.

The lie suggested by the temptation is actually accepted in its most profound intentionality. It achieves the result of ruining and corrupting the very reality of the personal relationship with God in which the human person had been constructed, that is, his/her life. Thus Adam and Eve, man and woman, decide to be the arbiters of their own destiny, their own lives. They seem to be in agreement over this, they both sin as if in a common understanding.

But God does not break his creative word because of their sin; his intentionality is still for the good of people. He continues to be alongside them and to make them capable of recognizing the truth, continues to speak to them so that they might understand. Their arbitrariness has placed them in their own hands, as if separated from him. They know it and would like to hide themselves, but because he does not abandon them —on the contrary he searches for them— they must respond. Called, Adam tries to justify his hiding. While he justifies himself, it is clear that the reality of his concrete existence is well known to the one who created him. When God makes himself neighbor to him, this situation of the relationship that God continues to have, makes Adam uncomfortable, like someone who cannot maintain the conversation, the dialogue with the other person. In his heart has developed his personal place outside the relationship with God; he has assumed arbitrary freedom, has desired to be arbiter of his own existence.

What appeared to be interpersonal human communion, even in sharing sin, really was not a sharing of life. To defend himself Adam accuses: what happened is because the woman made me do it; it is the woman who accepted the temptation, in fact, «the woman you put with me» (*Gen* 3:12). It is like saying: if someone has to pay, let her pay. The internal reality of a drama of radical division is expressed in this concise phrase. Adam declares himself to be a victim. God and the woman are against him. Through people's free responsibility communion with God is broken, and communion between them is broken. The lie of temptation, concretely expressed in decisions and conduct, becomes the human story in its inner nature, which falsifies relationships.

At this point the resulting picture is in stark contrast to what was described in the preceding chapter. There follows, in the literary genre of the curses, a series of signs that interpret the human story through the consequences of sin (*Gen* 3:14-19). In subsequent chapters the more obvious fruits of sin appear, with the murder of Abel (*Gen* 4:1-16) and the structuring of life on earth through division, boundaries, the impossibility of collaboration, and ecological disasters (*Gen* 4-11). What has happened is that by not accepting communion with God and wishing to be arbiters of their own real existence, communion between people, as well, is fundamentally compromised precisely by the rationale of arbitrariness. To look in a privileged and arbitrary way for one's own presumed good brings division and conflict, even to the extreme form of sanctioning the division that is the physical elimination of the other person, when that person is perceived as an adversary or dangerous rival.

The garden is no longer a garden. The land has become a place of hostility. Possession of the earth, possession and privileged fruition of the fruits of the earth divides us even to the point of division and murder. The earth cultivated by people who do not live in communion with God and the other person is no longer a place of communion; instead, it is cultivated in the image and likeness of divided people and becomes a place of division, conflict, struggle, and murder.

The «curses» interpret the result of sin. They indicate a fruit inherent to sin: a life that is not communion with God and is not communion between people, in a land that is no longer harmonious. People's existence on earth becomes what they wanted: a life that is not built by virtue of the creative word, understood and assumed, but a life that misses its objectives, misses its own ends. This happens precisely because its path was distorted. It does not reach fulfillment through that meaning and value that the creative word of God had declared and entrusted to humanity. The pretense of an arbitrary freedom consigns life itself to arbitrariness rather than to the meaning of life, to truth, or goodness[9].

3
Evil in a story of relations: 2 Sam 11-12

What the Yahwist proposes as universal interpretation of the reality of sin and its resulting evil in people's lives is inserted, with its uniqueness, in a continuity of reflection that spans the various biblical traditions. Again in an illustrative way, we will now consider another text, from a different literary source, probably related to the Deuteronomist tradition, which recounts the sin and conversion of David (2 *Sam* 11-12)[10].

3.1. THE SIN OF DAVID

In this story a series of elements is presented that helps to understand sin in its historic dimension and in the social interaction of human life. Through real figures in a series of relationships highlighted in the story, it relates how decisions mature in the personal inner self, decisions that then express themselves in particularly sinful behavior; how this is possible for someone who has not always been mired in sin but who becomes a sinner; how a person's sinfulness is inserted into the story of his relationships so as to influence the sinfulness of others; and how conversion, even when it is sincere and complete, is not simply a sponge that makes the reality of sin disappear.

9 Cfr. BASTIANEL S., «"Dov'è?": la domanda di responsabilità», in *Servitium* n. 110 ("Dov'è tuo fratello?") 31 (1997) 27-41; SCHOONENBERG P., *Man and Sin*, 109-155.

10 On the well-constructed source and theology of the two texts, cfr. SOGGIN J.A., *Introduction to the Old Testament*, SCM Press Ltd, London 1979, 185-194. On the figure of King David, in connection with the theology of the covenant, the election of David and the theology of sin, cfr. LANGLAMET F., «David fils de Jesse», in *Revue Biblique* 89 (1982) 5-47.

In this context the figure of David is of particular importance. He is described as a holy king and will be remembered as such. His kingdom will remain in Israel's memory as a type of kingdom in conformity with God and in faithfulness to the covenant. In these chapters we have the account of his sinfulness, which even reaches the point of particularly dire decisions. It is not just the sin of adultery; it is also the sin of homicide ordered by him , with the associated slaughter to cover the homicide itself.

The story begins thus: «At the turn of the year, the time when kings go campaigning, David sent Joab and with him his own guards and the whole of Israel. They massacred the Ammonites and laid siege to Rabbah. David however remained in Jerusalem» (*2Sam* 11:1).

This is not simply a news update, since it makes one think about this king of Israel and his way of reigning. It seems normal to go to war; it even seems that there is a time of year that is more suitable for this than other times. David, too, like other kings, scrutinizes the most favorable season for ordering the devastation of the land of the Ammonites. It is not really a war of defense. Of course, the previous year he had been insulted by the new king of the Ammonites, who had badly treated David's messengers (cfr. *2Sam* 10:1-14), and according to a rationale of power, a great king cannot allow an insult against him to go unpunished. However, there was a time when David was not like this. He knew mercy, as exemplified by his relationship with Saul and the house of Saul. One remembers that David had assumed the ideal of a kingship understood through the rationale of the covenant: a king who in the midst of his people assumed in some way the very caring nature of God, who made himself guarantor of justice, a brother in the midst of brothers and sisters in the exercise of his royal role, with the aim of favoring precisely the building up of a fraternal people. Now he has become a great king, a powerful king; he is no longer in the front line in the battles necessary to defend his people. Now he can decide at will to go to war according to a rationale of expansion, in order to strengthen his power. Now he can allow himself to send others into battle and remain at home to enjoy his magnificence, in a house that is not like that of others and surrounded by all those who serve in the king's palace.

Over time he has established this way of living and acting, but certainly he has not done it alone. Obviously, others have made it possible. With a powerful king comes a powerful kingdom. There is the consensus of the people, beginning with those closest to him: those who share his outlook and aid him not just because of ideal motives, those who live in the shadow of the figure of a great and powerful king, those who take advantage of the palace and live there, and those who do not gain any great benefits from it, but feel safer this way. And with consensus like this, David reigns in this manner.

So he remains at home, while Joab and his army go to war. He is not with his forces in battle; he doesn't even seem to be with his people in the exercise of regal tasks. He is simply in the palace, in the indolence of the palace. In this context, getting up late one afternoon and walking on the palace terrace, from on high he sees a woman taking a bath and he becomes infatuated. For the king there is no problem in obtaining more information. He finds out that she is the wife of Uriah, a Hittite who is in battle with his forces. David sends for the woman and she comes to him.

Everything and everyone seem to obey the king's desires and consent to this. Naturally, he knows this and is not even bothered by the adultery. The king's desires and whims can be fulfilled in any fashion, over and above the rules. The rules of nature, however, do not bow to king David, and the woman becomes pregnant. Naturally, the king cannot lose public face, and he still has some resources. He will make it seem as if the child is the child of Uriah. He sends a message to the head of the army so that the husband is sent to his wife. Uriah comes back; David receives news about the siege of the city and then invites him to spend the night at home, sending him also a helping from the royal table.

The Israelites have a rule that enforces sexual abstinence during the time of war. Uriah the Hittite has assumed the rules of this people and keeps them, so he does not go to his wife. David is alerted to this, and does everything to convince him. He makes him stay another day, makes him eat and drink, but not even getting him drunk achieves the aim. Without knowing it, through his faithfulness to the law, this man thwarts the king's designs. But the king is still king, and he cannot allow himself to lose face simply because some Hittite wants to be honest. If Uriah has a scrupulous conscience, that is the worse for him. He returns to the field of battle with a letter from David to Joab, head of the army stating that Joab must see to it that Uriah dies in battle.

Joab, commander of the forces, knows that he owes his position to David. Now he has the opportunity to make himself an even greater friend of king David and a valuable opportunity to bind the king to himself. He will do this favor for David and then the king will be in debt to him. So Joab organizes a military maneuver suitable for the purpose. Many men are killed and among them, naturally, is Uriah the Hittite.

Joab sends a messenger to inform David of what has happened. The king knows something about battles and gets angry at the account of such an imprudent maneuver, but the messenger, duly instructed by the one who sent him, carries on and explains that Uriah the Hittite has been killed as well. So the king is placated; he has achieved his aim. The wife of Uriah the Hittite is a widow. After the fixed days of mourning, David takes her as his wife and everything seems to have fallen under the cloak of custom. The incident has been overcome and the king can be untroubled; he has achieved his aim, despite the unexpected events. Of course someone was murdered, and there was a small slaughter to ensure this death by making it appear as if it were a natural death in battle.

The objectives of the King of Israel should be justice and the fraternal unity of his people, especially the good of the people and particularly for the weak. But these are not the only objectives David pursues. Many passages in the account reveal a life style and a style of governance in which self-seeking and the search for power and prestige are present and well-rooted. The role, structures, and personal position are already regularly used for his own benefit, too. Those who live with him know it, consent to it and, in various ways, pursue their own ends of personal advantage.

The facts narrated occur within this personal and social context, different from daily life only through their particular gravity. Whoever is used to benefitting arbitrarily from the opportunities at their disposal is tempted to do it every time something appears desirable to that person. The fact that a person acts in this way and does not stop even in the face of a serious evil and the fact that there persists in this a continuity of serious negative decisions, are obvious signs of a moral evil that reaches into profound personal intentionality. The person can also carry on and do many objectively good things, perhaps also because to do good serves his/her image well, as long as honesty does not cost a higher price than one wishes to pay.

So it doesn't matter if the king takes a fancy to a married woman. It doesn't matter if premeditated murder, and even a small slaughter is needed. The inner reality of arbitrary freedom produces, in this case, adultery, an illegitimate child, and death by murder. But it also produces something else, something less visible and measurable, but recognizable through its force of evil.

The freedom of others remains entrusted to their own responsibility. This is clearly shown by the case of Uriah who follows his conscience despite the king's persuasive arts. However, through the relationships David has established with others, he exercises some pressure over them, which can contribute greatly to making them also live out of an arbitrary and evil freedom. The woman consents, but has been solicited by the king. The Hittite has not consented, but there has been the craftiness of plotting, the impudence of inviting a subject to transgress the laws. Joab consented and exploited the relationship. Before this event he was probably not very scrupulous, but it is the king who invites him and offers him this opportunity that strengthens him in his wickedness. Then there are all those who live in the court, serving David and benefitting from him, variously called at their different levels to consent and collaborate.

In the dynamic of David's freedom, decision-making and conduct, his evil plan and his way of carrying it out become provocation and persuasion, suggestion and solicitation, which tend to move, facilitate and consolidate the sinfulness of others; his evil will involves the will of others. In this way the force of evil that he puts into operation has the strength of all that constitutes his inner self and image, his role and his relations. Let us not forget that all that is narrated in this story should in reality fall under the cloak of this king's wise governance, thus contributing to the consolidation of a mentality that continues to generate consensus to the profound rationale out of which he lives. Sinfulness thus seems normal.

3.2. DAVID'S CONVERSION

The following chapter of the *Second Book of Samuel* (12:1-4) begins with a parable that the prophet Nathan recounts to David. There are two men, one rich, one poor. The poor man has only a little ewe lamb, which he bought and raised with care. The rich man has a great number of animals, small and large. A guest comes to him, and to celebrate with him over a meal, the rich man, rather than taking an animal from his own plentiful flock, goes to get the poor man's only lamb. Nathan recounts this as if it were something that had actually happened, and David, who immediately perceives that there has been an injustice, is determined to do precisely what is asked of him in his role as king, that is, to provide justice for the weak. David, therefore, because of the fact of having become sinner in such a profound manner as we have seen, has not lost the ability to discern good from evil, the just from the unjust. Herein is expressed what is theologically termed faithfulness to God. God continues to pursue his creative intentionality even in regard to the sinner. He expresses such intentionality precisely in ensuring that the sinful person can still discern good, is still capable of making good, free, and responsible decisions. God does not annihilate the sinner, but continues to make the sinner capable of living in a humanly dignified and reasonable manner, according to his creative plan.

Beginning with this reality we can see how David's conversion develops. A sinner in the strongest sense of that term, a man who has committed a most grave and multiple injustice abusing his power, David knows how to recognize good and can decide to do it in the exercise of his role as king and without considering his own interests. Thus Nathan can remind David that he has acted just like the rich man. The parable achieves its aim of provoking David's understanding and of freeing his capacity to recognize his own sin. That brings him to rebuilding his morally positive decision to search for the good and do it and to avoid evil.

The reality of David's conversion is shown in the decisions he makes. According to the customs of the time, he remedies the condition of the woman he abused. He then continues to live in such a way that, even those who knew of his unscrupulous selfish kingship, including the abuse of power, can now see how he has repented of the evil he has done and by his real conduct shows that he does not want to do it again. Even in difficult situations, he will not misuse his being king, not even against his enemies. He will know how to forgive and be merciful, even when faced with those who from within his own house, like his son Absalom, act against him. He will also be merciful toward those who on the street insult him when he is in difficulties (cfr. *2Sam* 13-24).

The conversion of this man means that in the concrete reality of life and the structuring of his relations, he now establishes methods of decision-making and relationships such as to seek from those who live with him not evil, but good. The reality of his conversion is actualized in the story of his relationships, as it was in the reality of his sin. The force of his conversion will be seen in the fruits of his own decisions, as realization of good, but also in the strength of the relationships he encourages, because his good behavior is now offered for the freedom of those who live with him, and in his good example he challenges them to correct and just behavior.

Just as he did not make Joab a sinner without Joab's free consent, so his conversion does not lead to the conversion of others without their free consent to do good. But, within the dynamic of freedom, his responsible life now establishes a force for good that makes history, through the strength of its internal stature and through the complex concreteness of individual and institutional relations.

4
The humanity of Jesus in a story of sin

Moral evil, as the fruit of shared human arbitrariness, resists God's intentionality of communion and his self-realization on this earth through humanity's free and responsible acceptance. By nature, within a structure of sin, the just cannot die a «natural» death: thus it was, as well, for Jesus of Nazareth. Still focusing attention on the strength of sin as generator of evil in history, we will now turn to the figure of Jesus, looking in particular at the beginning of his public mission and the end of his earthly existence, as the gospels describe them to us.

4.1. THE WAY OF THE INCARNATION

In the dramatic form of the account of the tempter who presents himself to Jesus at the beginning of his public life in order to offer him some suggestions and explain to him how one lives in this world, the gospels of Matthew and Luke provide in summary a profound temptation that comes to Jesus during the entirety of his existence on earth, transmitted through the mentality lived and shared in the environment in which he lives (*Matt* 4:1-11; *Luke* 4:1-13). Even the figure of the Messiah is interpreted in a worldly manner by the Judaism of Jesus' time. From time to time in different ways, Jesus will repeatedly feel the same basic temptation suggested to him by his disciples, by those who question him by putting him to the test, by those who listen to him and do not understand him, including even those who condemn him, even those who insult him from beneath the cross[11].

The texts of Matthew and Luke are almost identical. Jesus has finished his time of fasting and prayer in the desert, and it is suggested to him that since he

11 The Synoptic gospels are in agreement in presenting, immediately after the start of Jesus' public life, a period of time spent by him in the desert, a time in which he experiences temptation (the terms πειρασθῆναι: *Matt* 4:1; πειραζόμενος: *Luke* 4:1; πειρασμόν: *Luke* 4:13, in reference to the verb πειράζω and the substantive πειρασμός, do not indicate just a test, but real and proper temptation). Christian faith believes that the son of God did not know sin, but not that he was spared temptation. In every probability, in fact, the account has an historic basis in the actual experience of Jesus. For Jesus the «first» temptation, that is, that in the desert, is not the only one. Temptation remains throughout the whole of his historical existence, no longer in reference to the choice of a genuine historic-salvific plan, but in reference to the verification of its effectiveness. Cfr. BASTIANEL S., *Vita morale nella fede in Gesù Cristo*, San Paolo, Cinisello Balsamo 2005, 114-120; DUPONT J., *Le tentazioni di Gesù*, Paideia, Brescia 1970; SCHNACKENBURG R., «Der Sinn der Versuchung Jesu bei den Synoptikern», in *Theologische Quartalschrift* 132 (1952) 297-326.

needs some bread and since he is not just any human being, but the son of God, he should simply take a stone and change it into bread. He can do it; he is the son of God. It is then suggested that since he must present himself to the world, he must draw attention to himself (and, as is known, the Messiah will come from on high) by throwing himself from the pinnacle of the temple; his mind can be at rest that he will arrive below upright and in one piece, because God will not allow (it is also written in the Psalm) that he might stumble against a stone; nothing can happen to him and thus people will see that he comes from God. Then Jesus is taken to a high place, as if to admire all the kingdoms of the earth. The devil reminds Jesus that life on earth is organized in a way that he well knows; the earth is practically in his hands. The tempter is prepared to put everything into Jesus' hands, and he explains how this might happen. Jesus obviously wants life on earth to be lived according to God's will. Well, there is a way to do that. The tempter suggests that he take in hand the reins of the world, become the strongest of the strong, more powerful than the powerful, and thus it will be Jesus who decides what others must do. He can impose himself on everyone. In this way the Messiah will defeat enemies, being greater and stronger than they. It will be he who entrusts various administrative tasks on earth; it will be he who lays down the law, and they will have to listen to him. As one sees, Jesus offers different responses, according to the different temptations, but there is a common element that responds to the basic temptation.

His response is that, yes, he is the son of God; he is the promised Messiah, but he is the son of God made flesh, and the path of salvation goes via this entrance of God into the history of humanity by way of humanity. Jesus has assumed the entire condition of humanity except for sin (cfr. *Phil* 2:5-11). So, for example, as far as the miracle about avoiding having to find bread is concerned, he lives on earth as human beings live on earth; when they are hungry, no one can take a stone and make it become bread. Jesus will not use his being son of God to avoid the human condition. Therefore, he, too, when he needs bread he will look for it as other people do. Of course he will perform miracles, but these will be within the rationale of giving signs evoking the proximity of God who loves and saves. There is to be no sign, no miracle allowing Jesus to avoid the real condition of people's lives. There is to be no miracle for his benefit, to extricate him from the human condition, not even when it would seem to be the only way to resist the strength of adversaries. Thus, he will not call upon legions of angels to save himself, not even from those who are putting him to death.

The temptation also reminds Jesus that he must speak to human beings. Therefore, it is necessary that they realize who he is, that they are able to recognize God's presence in him. This is true, but Jesus will speak to people in the manner of people speaking, not descending from on high, but speaking human to human, placing his existence alongside the existence of others. It will be in the human manner of his sinless life on earth; it will be in the human truth of his relationships and in living with others that the loving and saving presence of God will be recognized in him. It is through the human in his truth, in his value, in his goodness, that he will speak about God to people. There will be no miraculous descent from on high, therefore, to call for people's attention.

Finally, a third question is put to Jesus, which concerns the governance of socially and politically structured relations. It is true that life on this earth is structured according to a rationale of power. Many people think this is the only way to live on earth, that it is necessary to counter strength with strength. This thinking is so dominant it seems that in the manner of living relationships and structured relations, in social and political life, there is a prevailing sovereignty which is different from that of God. However, it is precisely in order to overcome this sovereignty, to show that God is the one Lord, to realize on earth the kingdom of God and not other kingdoms, that the Word became flesh. The devil's advice, the advice of so many «devils» Jesus meets, including those closest to him, suggests it is necessary to dominate, to impose oneself, to live this rationale of power even in order to succeed in doing something good. However, this would be to accept that God is not the one Lord, but that there are other lords. This would be to accept the sovereignty of evil, the sovereignty of the devil. This would mean worshipping Satan, as our texts state, indicating the condition placed by the tempter in order that Jesus' work can be effective. On the contrary, the mission of Jesus will be accomplished in his humanity, in his being alongside other men and women on the earth, in a life of total and clear communion with the Father, in the totally transparent gift of himself to humanity. The meaning of human life according to the creating word of God, now the saving word enfleshed in Jesus, will be recognizable in the humanity of his life.

The drama of Jesus of Nazareth's earthly life consists precisely in the fact that he lives on the earth as a human being, like human beings in *everything but sin*. What he does not assume from human beings is that which is not *human*, that which is contrary to the meaning and value of humanity according to God's creating word. But to live in this way within actual history is to live according to a rationale that is not the conquering rationale. It is to live by establishing behavior and words, decisions and ways of relating that seem unable to be victorious, that necessarily seem to have to succumb. At the beginning and throughout the whole of his existence on earth, Jesus does not accept this idea of triumphalism. He does not recognize this way of life and of assuming the mission entrusted to him on these terms. Therefore the strength of the rationale that in fact structures people's lives according to what the tempter suggests, according to what the current mentality suggests to him, is a force that presses on him and against him, to the point of killing him.

4.2. THE KILLING OF A JUST MAN

Considering the contradiction toward Jesus at the end of his life, we can raise questions about those who decided on his fate, those who made it possible, executed it, and allowed it. From the gospel accounts we recognize different levels of involvement, with a complex web of causes, in which often the edges of awareness and responsibility are blurred. The outcome is very clear: a just man is condemned to death by the legitimate authorities who are aware that he does not deserve to die, with the consent of many people and the silence or absence of many others. The sentence is carried out in a public and defamatory way. In this way his cause is declared closed; a disciple has betrayed him, another has denied him, and it seems there is no one to carry forward the mission for which he is killed[12].

If we consider God's plan, it is all «according to the Scriptures». If we consider human plans, it is all according to what had always been said of him. In a certain sense, there is nothing exceptional; it is dramatically normal for a just man to be killed.

Justice, in the person of the foreign ruler, defended this man as far as he could without running any risks. In this, Pilate also defended himself. The soldiers carried out orders. The leaders of the people had tolerated Jesus for a time, but then they became concerned. They had experienced other irrational movements that had gone wrong. They are the guarantors of the traditions of the fathers, and they had to safeguard the difficult political balance with the foreign rulers.

If the leaders, experts, and observers think thus, the people hold carefully to their advice. People who have seen his miracles and listened to his preaching have

12 On the trial and condemnation of Jesus, considered from the viewpoint of the human figures present at the passion and the relationship structures emerging from the gospel accounts, cfr. ALETTI J.N., *L'arte di raccontare Gesù Cristo. La scrittura narrativa del vangelo di Luca*, Queriniana, Brescia 1991, 135-150; SCHWEIZER E., *The Good News According to Mark*, SPCK, London 1971, 315-339.

become enthusiastic, have even followed him, but how could they explain to themselves and the leaders that this is the Messiah, if he does not choose to defeat his enemies and triumph over them?

The disciples, who have closely followed Jesus with sincerity, see their expectations die. For them, too, it is difficult to understand; Jesus does not respond to their own image of the Messiah that they had assumed. If Jesus doesn't even defend himself, what guarantees do they have?

Everyone has learned how to survive on this earth. In some manner they consent, all defending themselves. And yet the evil of that death is not attributable to natural causes.

5
A story of good

Within the symbolic reality of the Eucharist we discover what communion with Jesus of Nazareth gave to the disciples: an opportunity and a responsibility entrusted to them. It is what the disciples were gradually able to understand, what matured in them after the experience of Jesus' resurrection, recognizing him as living beyond death, truly perceiving him as Lord, as *Kyrios*.

From beginning to end, the life of Jesus was a life given. The disciples were able to remember his existence given to them completely, making possible their adherence to him and in him to the Father, making possible that the gift of communion with God in Jesus might become the true story in their existence. In Jesus' humanity, in the human quality of the relationships he established with them, they were able to perceive a continuity of his presence in the sign of freedom and gratuity, in the sign of his giving over of himself to them. Therefore, the life of Jesus liberated them and their capacity for freedom; it enabled them to understand and adhere to the good, thus giving them the ability to live on earth like Jesus of Nazareth.

In Jesus' humanity, communion with God became part of human history, a communion accepted on behalf of humanity. What Jesus gave to the disciples is his concrete existence in its visibility, fragility, and in the truthfulness of his relations. He made himself a neighbor with them and thus made them capable of accepting neighborliness. With them he was creator of neighborliness, creator of possible communion by virtue of his gratuitous love and without previous conditions, just as he demonstrated in the concrete course of his life. This transformed the life of the disciples to the point that, in order to speak of the newness they recognize had come about in their own existence, they speak of rebirth or regeneration. Everything has happened in a story of an encounter, in being met by Jesus and accompanied by him. He gave them time, patience, understanding, closeness, forgiveness, and mercy. In the Eucharist he gave them his flesh, that is, his concrete existence and the meaning of it.

The bread and wine are a symbol-reality of what is needed to live. However, in the history of humanity bread and wine have also become symbol-reality of what divides human beings and causes them to fight and even kill each other. But Jesus uses this bread and this wine as a symbol-reality of responsible freedom, of sharing, of life-giving life given. Jesus' true existence has been this bread and wine, from the beginning until what seemed to many to be the end, and is, instead, the continuity of his presence alongside the disciples as Lord.

The disciples are specifically asked to accept the communion with Jesus and with the Father through him. They are asked to learn to live like him on earth, and it is said of them that they can always continue learning from the presence of Jesus. They are called to be creators of closeness, of neighborliness, of communion. They are called to be people who have the same interpretive outlook on the other person, on historical reality, on what is of value and what is not of value in life, just as Jesus did. In their humanity they are called to be people who live like him on earth.

The path of conversion, for the disciples who have lived with Jesus and for each of the Lord's disciples, proceeds through this son of God made flesh, making himself neighbor, and continues through this rationale of relationships that are structured in time. It is the reality of building relationships in which freedom, nearness, and caring for the life of the other person —all that Jesus experienced— become that by which one lives.

This means living by his presence, living like him. It does not mean, however, the destruction of evil on the earth, but the prospective defeat of sin. What it is possible to recognize in Jesus as reality in the concrete story of humanity is this beginning of a story of relationships in which the rationale that builds and guides them is the rationale of gratuitous love. The building up of humanity and life through freely surrendering oneself, through the search for good simply because it is good, and through ways of relating to the other person that indicate and express fraternal communion and a life that does not die, which is life eternal.

Chapter 10

Structures of sin

The Encyclical *Sollicitudo rei socialis* not only speaks about the social dimension of sin, but uses —for the first time at this level of Magisterium— the phrase «structures of sin»[1]. With respect to expressions such as «social sin», or «unjust structures», which also refer to the same reality, such a phrase is in some ways more precise and succinct. It seems to suggest the existence of «structures» that are historic objectivizations of the social dimension of sin, as «places» for its presence and effectiveness. For moral theology, this Encyclical is an invitation to seek an understanding of how one moves from personal sin to the structure «of sin», how this then influences personal sinfulness, and what specific responsibilities derive from it in terms of personal morality. Thus one must clarify the very concept of «structures of sin», avoiding both a generic meaning and possible misunderstandings[2].

We must attempt, therefore, to understand the reality of human sin in its historic expression in connection with the phenomenon of «structures», suggesting a reflection that can aid in understanding the manner of such a connection.

Our question about the historic effectiveness of sin stems from the historic visibility of the evil caused by people as they live together in society[3], but with the ethical and theological presupposition that sin is simply *an aspect* of the human story. The understanding of human *nature*, as offered by Christian theology, proposes a radically positive sign in the *history* of people, also, by virtue of the creator's intentionality that is nevertheless in action and by virtue of the salvation event already operative in Jesus Christ. This means that the reflection

1 The expression is introduced and justified in n. 36, and is taken up again and used a number of times in successive texts.

2 In the proper sense it is people who are sinners; we do not call structures «sinners». However, it is a matter of understanding how «the result of the accumulation and concentration of many personal sins» comes to constitute a *social sin* (*Reconciliatio et paenitentia*, 16). The phrase «structures of sin», in an ethical and theological context, has certain presuppositions of ethical and theological understanding with regard to the human phenomenon that we call «structures» (a sociologically important and describable phenomenon). At first glance, the phrase has an obvious meaning: there are sinful structures, which cannot be morally justified, to which moral conscience cannot agree. However, problems arise as soon as one asks what this might mean, how such sinfulness might be identified, to what it should be attributed, and how one should behave with respect to it.

3 Even before now, theological reflection on human sin has been faced with the need to explain the existence of an evil that is greater than the sinfulness of an individual: an evil that, on the other hand, cannot be attributed to some evil divinity, nor to human «nature» (which would trace responsibility for the evil itself back to its creator). It is an evil that has its history and its historic effectiveness, that needs to be interpreted as the fruit of people's free responsibility, in its being and the dynamic of its effectiveness. Cfr. the theological reflection of the Yahwist in the account of original sin and the story that follows it (*Gen* 2-3ff).

on sin looks in faith for an understanding of sin that allows not just an understanding of its present reality, but at the same time also its surmountable nature and the possibility of conversion. Knowledge of the salvation that has been given calls for an understanding of the historic effectiveness of redemption as the story of *accepted salvation*, that is, as it becomes operative in history through people's free adherence[4].

In attempting to explain the «structures of sin», attention will focus on the human person in his/her socially structured life and the way in which in his/her life and social structuring shapes his/her sinfulness, knowing that in the same way, he/she lives and structures moral goodness and its effectiveness, historically made possible—despite the force of evil—in Jesus Christ.

1 *The strength of evil and the temptation to avoid responsibility for it*

When one looks at the great evils in our society and the power of what seem to be uncontrollable structures, one gets the impression of an evil that is not only greater than the individual, but that also seems to thwart the possible good will of many people. There are effects of evil that cannot be cancelled out even by the most sincere good will. If there are victims of a person's wickedness, or the iniquity of a political or economic structure, no one can give back life to those victims. Furthermore, no one is in a position to nullify that negative force of sin which, set in motion by personal example or the seductive force of an unjust structure, has already been assumed in the personal sin of others, or has become a sinful structuring of co-existence with others in specific social spheres. In this sense, we cannot nullify evil. As we will see, the purpose of a journey of conversion is

4 The faith traditions of the Old Testament are rooted in the knowledge and remembrance of the salvific intervention of God (Exodus), who creates a covenant relationship and who remains faithful and calls for a response of faithfulness in the relationship with him, expressed in the correctness of the ethical life that creates solidarity (of the «people of God»). In the New Testament it is the newness of the salvific event in Christ, expressed in the preaching of Jesus with the centrality of the proclamation of the Kingdom, which calls for responsible personal adherence in entrusting oneself to the proclaimed gospel and conforming to it one's own way of life. Cfr. BASTIANEL S., DI PINTO L., «Per una fondazione biblica dell'etica», in GOFFI T., PIANA G., EDD., *Corso di Morale*, 1, *Vita nuova in Cristo. Morale fondamentale e generale*, Queriniana, Brescia 1983, 77-174; MERKLEIN H., *Die Gottesherrschaft als Handlungsprinzip. Untersuchung zur Ethik Jesu*, Echter, Würzburg 1978.

not to «cancel» the sin and its fruit, but rather to put into effect positive realities and dynamics that can «overcome» the strength of evil.

In the meantime, however, the negative force of sin also takes shape in some «fundamental» temptations, which aim precisely at avoiding the establishment of an effective story of good. We can note some of these temptations.

a) The tendency to justify an *attitude of resignation*, minimizing the reality of evil itself, or declaring it to be insurmountable. One result of the extensiveness and continuity of negative phenomena is a kind of acclimatization, which leads to «not seeing» the evil present. This is even easier when at the same time there is a tendency to avoid recognition of one's own co-responsibility in it. In that case one will look for those responsible for major incidents; one can point out individual «monsters» or «frenzied mobs», but then cleverly return to the fundamental line of defense: the system is broken, the structure is broken, and *we* are not the culprits. Such a defense seems to be assumed above all when one happens to recognize his/her involvement in an issue of moral responsibility, and one then responds by questioning important and generally legitimized structures or rationales so that one can then say that «unfortunately» there is a cost, that certain negative results are unavoidable. Usually, the «unavoidable» evil weighs down on the shoulders of other people.

b) The tendency to justify *escaping into privacy*, separating the social sphere from the spheres of morality and faith. The fact that morality and faith are inner realities still seems today to find ways to reduce them to the realm of the private. It is possible to recognize the importance of respect for human rights and even to affirm them with some degree of emphasis, and yet at the same time to defend the realms of ethics and faith as belonging to the private sphere because fundamentally these concern the individual and his/her conscience, the individual and his/her relationship with God. Thus, everything else can be extremely important, but not «constitutive» of ethical and religious responsibility. Perhaps precisely because there are often arguments about human rights as being «subjective rights», this reduction to the realm of the private, which misrepresents both the ethical vision and the Christian vision of the person and his/her social life, is not rare.

c) The *escape into the «strategic»*, committing oneself to positive interventions, but without raising questions about systems and structures. The negative outcomes and their seriousness are recognized, as is the need to do something, but only according to a rationale that is internal to the structures themselves; «humanitarian» interventions can or even must be carried out, but in such a way that at the end they strengthen the same structures and reinforce even more their validity and «justice».

At the root of these temptations, in different ways, there seems to us to be an inclination to avoid recognizing the ethical requirement in the question about the (*human*) validity of political and economic structures.

Moral reflection, while not leading in itself to technical solutions, intends to show how even «technical» questions about political and economic institutions and structures are never *just* technical questions. They always involve implicit questions about meaning, and their ethical value[5]. Since it is never a question of structures «in themselves», but rather structures of human relationships, which have good or bad effects on people's lives, no structure is historically «neutral» from the point of view of the responsibility of those who assume and live within the structures. The critical requirement of morality is made explicit in the question about the *authentically human* that a specific structure of relations expresses, facilitates, hinders or denies.

Theological reflection, from the revealed traditions handed down to us in the Sacred Scriptures, interprets and formulates this requirement of humanity beginning with the intentionality that supports the very action of God, creator and savior. People's task is to accept the gifted «land» and make it the place of their humanity. Capable of recognizing in fraternity the meaning of their living together, they are responsible for the manner in which they «cultivate» the earth, responsible for the structures they give themselves and for the way in which they assume them. This «responsibility» is the duty of «responding» to God by responding to others. In the choice and use of the necessary «tools» for co-existence, the question that addresses consciences is not directly about the technical perfection of the tools used, and yet does concern the tools insofar as they are agency of relationships: with these tools what have you done for your brother/sister?

In the case of complex and sophisticated mechanisms, as economic structures and the network between economic and political structures often are, when it is stated that we cannot avoid certain evils, the question is simply this: is it actually true that *we cannot* avoid them, or is it only true that we cannot avoid them *without* questioning things that *we do not want* to question? Faced with the seriousness of the evils caused, their inevitability cannot be presumed.

5 It is through attention to the implied moral values that, in the face of «certain forms of modern "imperialism", one can see that hidden behind certain decisions, apparently inspired only by economics or politics, are real forms of idolatry: of money, ideology, class, technology» (*Sollicitudo rei socialis*, 37).

2
Sin and relationality

In the full and proper sense of the word we speak of sin in reference to the human person in the exercise of his/her *conscious and responsible freedom*[6]. Similarly, the terms «sin» and «sinful», or «of sin», are sometimes also used to indicate realities that *have something to do with sin* or they *facilitate* personal sin, or because they are the *fruit* of it.

So, for example, we speak of situations, conditions, occasions, inclinations, and so forth, which we qualify as «sinful» because experience teaches what may be their negative influence on the capacity of personal responsible freedom[7].

These same realities can also usually be considered sinful from the point of view of their cause, that is, they are the result of personal sin (mostly through a long chain of interventions, of personal sins). Because of this, they spread the effect of sin, in that they express and recall the opportunities of choices that are not good, presenting as «desirable» the content of sinful choices and tending to justify such choices with pseudo-motives and reasonings[8].

In every case, it is in relation to personal free responsibility that the term «sin» can correctly be assumed to have an analogous meaning. This is what must be verified concerning the concept of the «structures of sin».

Remember that the reality of sin in its first and fullest sense is a *personal* reality. This does not mean to affirm, however, that it is substantially an individual

6 *Analogatum princeps* is the *mortal* sin, the personal *status* and *act* by which a person commits and declares him/herself a «sinner»: when in complete consciousness, faced with a responsible choice about the seriousness of «matter», in a free decision the person consents to carry out the evil that is offered as a possibility. Note that, describing it in such a way, as is usually the case (cfr. the Catechism of Saint Pius x), the sin is already understood as placed within a history of sin that precedes and accompanies the individual: the person is «solicited» by evil and «consents» to it. Because of a resemblance to this sin, with respect to the structure of free responsibility in personal choice and the consequences of the evil to which one consents, the term «sin» is commonly used, likewise, when the conditions now noted are not all present, or are but not completely. Then one speaks of *venial* sin, or *mild* sin, according to which one considers the quality of the subject's conditions or the seriousness of the «matter», that is the content of the choices.

7 It would not be a sin to experience the presence, nor even to expose oneself to similar «occasions» for a proportionately serious good cause, but it would be reckless (constituting precisely a «causal responsibility») to act as if those occasions were not occasions «of sin».

8 Aspects of such reality can become assumed as «normal» or positive in the custom of a time and place, thus becoming part of the shared morality: evaluating from that, they will be recognized as expressions of error or ignorance, «hardness of heart» which are the fruit of sin.

and private matter. We must consider relationality, in which the human being is constituted. What expresses or realizes the person in his/her being a person, necessarily expresses or realizes his/her being *in relationship*, or better still, he/she expresses him/herself *through* being in relationship.

Theologically interpreted, the reality of sin is expressed beginning with the relationship with God. Sin is negation of meaning and falsifies the realization of self as a contradiction of God's will, a negation of that meaning of humanity which the creative Word of God brings into being and entrusts to personal liberty: sin is «disobedience», breaking the relationship with God (*ex parte hominis*, as non-accepted relationship)[9].

The reality of sin, therefore, is not exhausted through a pure relationship with God, but rather, it plays itself out in the interplay of human relationships, directly in immediate interpersonal relationships, or indirectly in the interplay of relationships at the infrahuman level, in which the person contradicts the meaning and truth of his/her responsibility toward other people[10].

Precisely because it is personal, because it makes and expresses the reality of the person (his/her «heart»: knowledge, freedom, and responsibility), there is always present in the reality of sin the dimension of interpersonal relationality[11]. Even when it is not externally obvious (for example, in the case of carefully-hidden thoughts of hatred, pride, jealousy, indifference), even then the sin indicates relationality and guides the manner of relations.

a) Sinful relations. One can speak about «sinful relations» at various levels of meaning. Sometimes the relationship itself constitutes a person's sin, as for example when the relationship consists in perceiving the other person as enemy,

9 Cfr. BÖCKLE F., *Fundamental Moral Theology*, Gill and Macmillan, Dublin 1980, 77-125; MONGILLO D., «Peccato», in *Dizionario Enciclopedico di Teologia Morale*, Paoline, Rome 1974, 733-741; ID., «L'esistenza cristiana: peccato e conversione», in GOFFI T., PIANA G., EDD., *Corso di Morale*, 1, *Vita nuova in Cristo. Morale fondamentale e generale*, Queriniana, Brescia 1983, 491-551; PIANA G., «Peccato», in *Dizionario Teologico Interdisciplinare* II, Marietti, Turin 1977, 660-674.

10 The reality and result of sin are presented in *Gen* 3 in terms of separation or the breaking of relationships: no longer the harmony of the familial dialogue with God (faced with God, who continues to speak to him, man tries to hide himself), no longer the harmony of sharing between person and person («the woman you put with me...»; in order to defend himself, Adam accuses, thus establishing at the same time God and the woman as adversaries and enemies), no longer harmony with creation (the earth in which the human person will live will no longer be a «garden»).

11 «...there is no sin, not even the most intimate and secret one, the most strictly individual one, that exclusively concerns the person committing it. With greater or lesser violence, with greater or lesser harm, every sin has repercussions on the entire ecclesial body and the whole human family. According to this first meaning of the term, every sin can undoubtedly be considered as social sin» (*Reconciliatio et paenitentia*, 16).

servant, inferior, marginalized, or when one directly marginalizes or manipulates the other person for one's own ends.

At other times it is a matter of relationships that could be good and correct in themselves, but that in fact are directed toward a malicious end. Such a purpose can be somewhat remote, as when a person creates a network of relationships that give him/her an «honorable» social status, so as to be able to pursue effectively his/her own ends (in this hypothesis, unjust ends).

There are relationships that can be called «sinful» only in that they are the fruit of sin, as for example, unequal and one-sided relationships that the people involved have not created themselves, but in which they de facto find themselves. However, the sin of their forebears cannot be attributed to these people if, however, they are not actually responsible for establishing these unhealthy relationships. Such relationships, in fact, are not in themselves personal sin, but can «easily» be drawn into personal sin.

b) Structuring of sinful relations. Likewise, with respect to the reality of sin it would be naïve to think of interpersonal relationships as isolated or isolable «moments» that come and go in the space of their obvious visibility, and whose results would be the sum of individual results. Human co-existence is de facto structured into relationality. The most profound *result* of a series of relationships is not the «quantity» of accomplishment, but rather the *structured reality of the relationship itself* which is thus established: a reality made up of understandings and expectations, of trust and suspicion, of opportunity and impossibilities. The structuring of relations creates roles and tasks, modifies the interpretation of them and the connected expectations, and guides the modes of accomplishment through consent. If relations are marked by sin, then their structuring in the ways of co-existence will be sinful as well.

3
Sin and the structuring of human co-existence

The interpersonal relationship between two people tends to «be structured» in time. Free responsibility exercised in the various modes of the relationship becomes liberating or constraining with respect to its future exercise, directs in one way rather than another, and shapes previous understandings, assessments, and decisions.

The individual relationship, as «personal», is placed within the complex of relations that constitute a person's concrete existence. The more a relationship is personally qualified and qualifying, the more it will be connected with the world of personal relations, with the exclusion of other possibilities, the orientation of preferences, the formation of sensitivities, and so on. If, for example, the criterion that sustains and structures an interpersonal relationship is that of the individual usefulness of two people, this will be expressed in both through a series of choices and preferences, attitudes and feelings, reactions and plans. Through and beyond what directly constitutes the object of the mutual relationship, that criterion (individual usefulness) will usually tend to qualify the way one looks at the other person, and every other person. In the subsequent and continued exercise of concrete choices «motivated» in this way, there develops a personal «utilitarian» interiority, with all that this involves from the point of view of the exercise of intelligence, freedom and will, that is, with all that this involves in the formation of a moral personality, and additionally, with all that this involves in co-operating in the formation of the personal morality of those with whom one lives (the various levels of influence, facilitation and conditioning of the understanding, assessing and decision-making of others).

The individual relationship, therefore, is always inserted within a context of relations; it depends on others and influences others. It always belongs to a more complex phenomenon, which is the structuring of personal existence *within* the structuring of human society, being dependent on society and having a definite influence on it.

On the one hand, therefore, we cannot speak of «sin» in the proper sense if we are not referring to personal inner life (consciousness, freedom and responsibility in decision-making). On the other hand, personal sin always implies a dimension of relationality, which includes an interpersonal objective result.

In the continuity of the personal subject, the exercise of freedom gradually places positive or negative conditions on the subsequent capacity for responsible freedom. In intersubjective relations, such conditions assume the strength of *mutual interaction*. In such a way, in the experience of relationality, through the cooperating consent of many, and in the structuring of human life, an historical effectiveness of personal sin takes shape.

People «create» their world in their own image and likeness. «Cultivating» the earth, they make it the work of their own hands, fruit of the intentionality of their hearts. Human life on earth is what a «cultivated» earth has made and makes possible; it is the story of humanity. The possibilities of life, humanity, freedom, and morality reach the responsibility of individuals within an historic dynamic of socialized life. This provides assistance and obstacles, opportunities and restrictions to free and conscious personal responsibility. Even before being active in contributing to and shaping co-existence, the person is already in some way pre-formed by structured co-existence (structures and the meanings/values they mediate). Then, when he/she is in a position to exercise his/her own freedom, the real space of this is determined by the actual conditions of his/her living in a context of relations that are structured or are on the way to being so[12].

Thus we can note the dynamic of the force of sin within the concrete story of the structuring of human living: the fruits of sin generate sin, which produces fruits that are producers of sin. But here, too, it is necessary to make distinctions in order to clarify the relationships between the various elements.

The sinful relationship is the work of negative results on two distinct and connected levels. When it provokes a human evil for someone (a person remains offended, or deprived, or hurt, and so on) it is *malum physicum* (not *moral* in the proper sense of the word)[13]. The reality of the evil provoked, simply with the fact of its being, calls relationships into action: the relation to the evil itself with its consequences, and the relationship to who provoked it and to who comes to know about it. Such relations are never morally neutral, whatever may be the actual possibilities of «responding» in the face of evil, which always imply free responsibility. At the same time, in the context of relations, the sinful relationship suggests reason for existence and its presumed meaning, and with that it tends to contribute to the strength and consistency of sin in the structuring of relations of co-existence. It mediates evil's *force of attraction*, the «desirability» of what is sin[14],

12 Perhaps this is the fundamental point of view from which should also be considered the profound inequality existing between people, an inequality that raises more than just a question about the correct distribution of resources.

13 Here we are using the classical distinction between *bonum/malum physicum* and *morale*, implying with the adjective «moral» what deals with the issue of personal free responsibility, positively or negatively, characterizing the person in his/her conscious decision with respect to values or disvalues that are proposed for his/her choice. Cfr. JANSSENS L., «Ontic Evil and moral Evil», in *Louvain Studies* 4 (1972) 115-156; ID., «Norm and Priorities in a Love Ethics», in *Louvain Studies* 9 (1977) 207-238; BÖCKLE F., «Prospettive di valore e fondazione della norma», in *Concilium* 12 (1976) 1607-1612; BASTIANEL S., *Autonomia morale del credente*, Morcelliana, Brescia 1980, 24-42.

14 The strength of temptations lies in suggesting reasons of desirability (cfr. *Gen* 3:6), which make the negative choice desirable, making it appear good. However sin is deceitful, an illusion, shadowy (cfr. the Johannine language in particular). Deceit and its ability at suggestion are stronger the more they are presented as approved by the consent of many people, mediated through the process of shared behavior and judgments in a specific sphere of life.

which tends to be evaluated as «useful», «normal», «inevitable». Here there is a negative result at the level of *moral* evil in the proper sense, which influences the way of assuming relations placed into existence by the presence of the *malum physicum* provoked by sin, in that the tendency is to justify it, even as far as identifying it with human, natural limitations.

We can say, therefore, that the negative effects of sin as *mala physica*—which always weigh on somebody, as privation, suffering or death—are multiplied by those negative effects that themselves are personal participation in sin (*moral evil*), as free acceptance of it.

On the other hand, and in a complementary way, the growth of the negative effects of objective evil, with its imminent substance and collusion experienced in the structuring of relations, multiplies sin's power of suggestion. It is more difficult to escape; there are risks and costs to pay if one does not «consent». Sometimes it is not even easy to notice that what «everyone approves» is evil, or it is not easy to perceive the link between a seemingly innocuous choice and a greater negative reality, which appears to be practical. In any case, often one tends almost «spontaneously» to «not investigate» what could cost too much.

In such a way the tendency to self-justification imposes itself. The «reasons» that lead to the sinful choice are assumed «in defense», as logical self-affirmation. And this logic will find other reasons, even when the first ones fail. Thus evil grows in its extensiveness and complexity, continuing to further limit the already limited positive human opportunities. And with it grows the inclination to consent.

4
Structures of sin

A social group needs structures and institutions and must organize itself by giving itself rules. That means determining a common good to pursue together and therefore ordering the ways of living to this end. In so doing, it implies sufficient consensus about a framework of values with a certain hierarchy and specific criteria (codified, for the certainty of law), so that the whole range of initiatives entrusted to the creativity of individuals and groups may be in some way ordered to the common good.

Structures and institutions necessarily belong to human life inasmuch as life itself is social. In this sense, not only are they not in themselves sinful, but they also correspond to the «nature» of humanity (therefore to God's will). However, structures and institutions must be the locus and instrument of true humanity, expressions of a correct structuring of relations between people. At issue is the manner of understanding and pursuing the common good, with the subsequent allocation of roles and tasks.

Every structured social group suggests a «common good» defined by the specific goals that determine and sustain the group itself. On the basis of such a specific common good internal relations within the individual areas of social interaction are structured, and on this basis too the exercise of roles attributed to individuals is assessed and mutual expectations are formed. The ethical question permeates the whole process of formation, of gradual structuring and possible modification, that gives shape at the various levels and concrete modes of social interaction. This question concerns the correctness, in terms of *human authenticity*, of the goals pursued and the ways of pursuing them[15].

We also know that in an ideal and perfectly ordered society there would remain space open to the freedom of the individual and therefore his/her possible sinful use even of structures and institutions that are just. But here the question turns on the same «regulating» structures and the «ordered» institutions in a specific social sphere, that is, on the possibility that *they* may be «of sin» and on their subsequent negative effect.

As we speak of «structures of sin», it will help to keep in mind the similarity of terms. In addition to the various levels of «structures», there are also different meanings in the manner of qualifying them as «of sin».

a) Structures of sin *in the strict sense*. The history of humanity seems to have known and still knows ways of structuring social life that in the strict sense can be termed being «of sin», even if this is in a similar way to individual personal

15 Revelation and the tradition of Christian faith provide enlightenment at this level of moral evaluation, with some indication about the ultimate meaning of the social interaction itself of life. Love of neighbor, without restrictions and reservations, is indicated as the interpretive criterion for all the «rules» of relationships between people (cfr. *Matt* 6:43-48; *Luke* 6:27-35; 10:29-37; *Gal* 5:14). From the understanding of the relationship with God in terms of «covenant», to faith in the Risen Lord, the experience of the gifted communion with him highlights the need to assume in one's own free responsibility the historic tension in order to create relationships of fraternal communion. Communion, as fraternal sharing of life, becomes the *télos* of believing human life on earth. This is not saying what the structures of social life must be, at its various levels and in its different spheres, however it is stating what human significance those structures must express and incarnate. This significance is ethically judging the human worth of the institutions and structures; it indicates a «common good» to lean toward, to which specific goals, assumed means, and ways of living in the various forms of social interaction should be ordered. Cfr. the connection between solidarity, charity, and communion in *Sollicitudo rei socialis*, 40.

sin. A law or institution that might be clearly and deliberately discriminatory in its goals, its rationale and the means at its disposal, and therefore, in the outcomes that it seeks to achieve, would be directly and in itself unjust. The fruit of personal sin (of those who instituted it), as an historic result of that sin, would be an instrument of evil (harm, suffering, deprivation, and so on, of the people discriminated against) and the opportunity for personal sin offered (falsely suggested as a good and made «desirable») to all those who —thus solicited— freely and consciously want to use it. Such would also be an economic structure that, based on the law of the strongest, would have mechanisms for always making the strong stronger and the weak weaker.

b) Structures «of sin» *in the broad sense.* There are structures of human society whose aims, means and outcomes one could not say are *necessarily* «sinful»; on the other hand, however, they have been placed in a context of *not accidental ambiguity*, so that the structures lend themselves to spreading and helping not just negative outcomes such as *mala physica*, but also the sinfulness of whoever acquiesces.

Such structures can be deliberately set up, exactly calculating the ambiguity in which they are placed and therefore with knowledge of their desired negativity. Thus this would also be the direct result of personal sins. Financial laws could sometimes arise in this way, as well as economic organizations and commercial structures. There is no need to think of the wickedness of very clear decisions that desire evil for evil. Suffice, instead, to think of the complicity of many «mediocre deceits» for launching a mechanism that produces incalculable damage, but for «calculated benefit» and not without awareness of «not wanting to calculate» the damage.

The structures in question could also be not the result of conscious sinful intentionality, but simply the result of a complex convergence of the historic results of sin, within the sphere of limited human possibilities. They could even be the result of good intentions (which sincerely seek the good that is possible), but in a context in which the historic effects of sin and its present effect do not permit a completely transparent structure. With respect to the ways of co-existence already profoundly structured in sin, they propose to direct these ways toward a humanly authentic meaning/value[16]; however, such direction is only

16 Perhaps in this sense can be considered those institutions called of «secondary natural right» (for example, private property, or at least the ways in which it is protected), in relation to natural law (for example, access for everyone to the goods they need). Cfr. *S.Th.* II-II, q.66, a.2. On the theme of property in relation to the common destination of goods a reminder is contained in *Sollicitudo rei socialis*, 42.

possible within the framework of the conditioned and conditioning historically given objective possibilities.

In this sense, it is useful to recall that even structures that are historically just and necessary for the common good, can have negative effects for specific people (one thinks about the penal code and the problems deriving from it).

c) Structures and the rationale of sin. At this point one cannot avoid the question about the meaning of the phrase «just structures» in contrast to «structures of sin».

The right (just) structures and institutions are not created by «human nature», but rather by a social group made up of real historic people. It is done according to what the group understands and desires as its own good. Choices, the allocation of roles and tasks, laws and institutions, which a social group expresses, will necessarily be an expression of *that* social group[17].

The «justice» that we are in a position to express in our institutions will not be that of «innocent» people, who do not «know» sin. A preceding history of negativity influences our understanding, evaluation, choosing and acting, that is, the exercise of our free responsibility. In creating political and economic structures, in maintaining or modifying them, there is present both an historical negative force that disregards our free assent, and a force of «inclination» or «seduction» that tends to be directed toward the personal assumption of criteria and rationale «of sin».

At the level of *individual conscience* we can easily recognize the sign/criterion of personal sin in «self-privilege», a criterion opposed to that of charity, indeed to that of simple moral goodness. Within the context of *a relationship* this means that the other person is experienced as a potential rival, as a possible enemy, as someone from whom one must above all defend oneself. From this stems a rationale of possession (to guarantee oneself what one needs to live), of defense (against the presence of others in that they can be threatening), and of conflict and domination (sanctioned in the name of «necessary» security), even including the possible «inevitable» elimination of the other person. That fruit and sign of sin that is violence is not only present, therefore, in its more glaring manifes-

17 Of course, people are created capable of recognizing good and the common good, capable also of identifying and choosing the appropriate means to aspire toward it. People are not naturally «sinners». But they are, historically. And we have recalled that the reality of sin is not external to the person, but rather qualifying his/her inner self, that inner self which expresses itself precisely in decision-making, such as in a constituent or legislative assembly, a judging or electoral college, or an administrative council.

tations; it is present at the roots of our co-existence, in simple and complex relations, even within institutions, in the way in which we also «justify» them.

If this *rationale* of self-privilege (and of the group to which one belongs) is in fact present, we will continue to find people's «justice» succumbing to this rationale. In the sincere search for good, therefore, it is not only human/creaturely restrictions that confront us. Similarly, those restrictions that are the historic result of sin on people's lives have the substance and the resistance of what structures thinking internally as well as what socially structures political and economic institutional mechanisms.

Naturally, that does not mean that everything is sin in our world; it simply means that sin and its strength are neither marginal nor simply external to our being and living. They are realities that are deeply present in, and are structuring, personal and social existence, with effects that concern the true capabilities of understanding and evaluation, freedom and decision[18]. The difficulty of overcoming the *structures of* sin is intrinsically linked to the force of negativity present in the more general *structuring in* sin of personal and social life.

5
Conversion of people, conversion of structures

At the level of personal free responsibility, we have considered sin as the internal reality of conscience, always expressed in the «externals» of relations. In the same way, the genuine conversion will be internal reality and external/relation. It is not «substantially» internal reality, which then in some way expresses itself also in relations. Rather, it is a matter of a subject's internal reality that expresses his/her freedom as responsibility, therefore, as a response to objective needs, to the objective possibilities for good. The person who converts is the person who constructs his/her personal morality in the positive exercise of his/her own freedom in just relations.

18 Cfr. FUCHS J., «The "Sin of the World" and Normative Morality», in ID., *Personal Responsibility Christian Morality*, Georgetown University Press, Washington, DC 1983, 153-175; ID., «Strukturen der Sünde», in *Stimmen der Zeit* 206 (1988) 613-622; SCHOONENBERG P., «L'uomo nel peccato», in *Mysterium Salutis* IV, Queriniana, Brescia 1970, 589-719; WINDISCH H., *Handeln in Geschichte. Ein katholischer Beitrag zum Problem des sittlichen Kompromisses*, Peter D. Long GMBH, Frankfurt a.M.-Bern 1980; WEBER H., «Il compromesso etico», in GOFFI T., ED., *Problemi e prospettive di teologia morale*, Queriniana, Brescia 1976, 198-219.

For the Christian, conversion belongs to the reality of his/her relationship with God in Jesus Christ[19]. It is understood and assumed, as necessary and possible, within the gift of communion with him. As a journey of continuous conversion, which is identified with *discipleship* in Christ, it is the responsible assumption of the answer in faith in a lived positive morality. The maturation of a believer's personal morality is realized in the continuity of his/her story[20]. Expressed here is a *believing conscience*, which recognizes the Lord as the foundation of one's action and searching for the good, and which therefore assumes gifted communion as a task of fraternal communion. In order to be a radical response to the Lord, a Christian's morality engages his/her freedom in desiring the good that is truly possible, thus always extending further afield the space for good work.

In interpersonal relationality, the good inner self «lives», that is, it is incarnated and expresses itself, in a positivity that goes beyond the confines of the subject as an individual; it is entrusted to the freedom of the other person; and it facilitates a true freedom (moral, responsible) of the other person. In such a way, personal conversion is integrated into the structuring of relationships, contributing to a story of good that assumes the fullness and historical force of a human society structured for good.

The exercise of personal free responsibility in the making of just choices has some positive results in the sense of the realization of the objective value of someone's life (*bona physica*), which means also a potential expansion of objective possibilities for good, by virtue of the «newness» of the relations that are established. At the same time, there is also the outcome of the truth and goodness of the relationship itself, which proposes in historic «visibility» the human value of the *moral good* as authentic self-realization, as personal human accomplishment. This contributes to the understanding and evaluation of the good as *good*,

19 For a broader and more explicit treatment of moral conversion experienced and understood within Christian faith, BASTIANEL S., «Conversione», in COMPAGNONI F., PIANA G., PRIVITERA S., EDD., *Nuovo Dizionario di Teologia Morale*, Paoline, Cinisello Balsamo 1990, 145-159.

20 This includes responsibility for caring for one's own inner life as a believing person. Even with respect for all that constitutes a commitment directly aimed at the establishment of a better earthly city, the Christian cannot presume to discharge his/her task «alongside» his/her life of explicit faith. The unity of personal life also bears here the inevitable need for a living relationship with the Lord, in an explicit prayer that places daily life and decision-making «in the Lord». Cfr. BASTIANEL S., *Vita morale nella fede in Gesù Cristo*, San Paolo, Cinisello Balsamo 2005, 121-151. On the theme of conversion cfr. MONGILLO D., «Conversione», in *Dizionario Teologico Interdisciplinare*, I, Marietti, Turin 1977, 576-590 (586-589 in relation to political life); RAHNER K., «Conversion», in *Sacramentum Mundi* II, Burns & Oates, London 1968, 4-8.

desirable and *possible*. It is a contribution to the positive formation of sensitivities and thinking by which the structuring of human life is nourished. In genuine sharing of positive morality, the search for adequate structures for the conditions of life will be a search for just structures that are humanly authentic. As with the structures of sin, the good structures, also, can arise and consolidate themselves only by virtue of a genuine consensus.

Furthermore, just structures exercise their strength of mediation with respect to the personal capacities of freedom and responsibility. They present positive relational models acquired in their validity, and with that they suggest prior understanding and evaluation through the support of previous sharing regarding the choices proposed. In the same way that unjust structures facilitate personal evil, just structures facilitate personal good, while in both cases there remains room for individual freedom.

We have seen that this room for personal freedom becomes constrained by the structures of sin, both by the strength of the objective/external restrictions, and by the strength of the internal inclination or seduction. Instead, the positive action of the just structuring of relations in the visibility of the spheres of political and economic life leads to an expansion of the personal capacity for responsibly assumed freedom: by the strength of the objective/external opportunities beneficial to the good and the strength of the internally mediated positive inclinations.

In the historical condition in which the historically effective forces of good and sin are co-present, it must be recognized that no structure is neutral with respect to personal free responsibility, both in the sense that the structure acts positively or negatively on personal morality and in the sense that personal choice in regard to structures contributes to strengthening or weakening them in their positive or negative effectiveness.

As far as conversion is concerned, the alternative «what comes first: personal conversion or the conversion of structures?» is a false option. There are not literally structures on the one hand and people in relationships on the other, but rather humanly structured relationships. It would be misleading to pretend to obtain results from «just» structures without modifying, or before modifying the morality of consciences. But it would be no less misleading to think of a genuine conversion of people, putting to one side for future consideration the problem of the structures of actual co-existence.

There remains the problem of individual inadequacy with respect to the force of the well-established structures of sin. One can certainly not attribute to the individual (and not even to a group) responsibility for a structure much greater than him/her and his/her opportunities. Each is responsible for those limited opportunities for good that are *his/her* actual opportunities. But each person *is* responsible for this concretely possible good. Neglect is not neutrality. Not being up to the capacity of the total good does not provide the right of exemption from one's own responsibility. To assume responsibly the little space of freedom that is one's own, means more than the immediate visible result, because it is at the same time expansion of the space of one's own responsibility as well as of others. This means living in personal moral internal *goodness* in the search for the *just* way of relating, assuming one's proper responsibility in the common search for a just co-existence, that is, in the search for just structures, even in the sense of changing those structures that are unjust. Internal conversion of someone who is unconcerned about the conversion of institutions and structures «of sin» would not be true conversion.

Chapter 11

Punishment, morality, and the common good

The general theme *justice and punishment*, if one wrestles with it from an ethical point of view, raises specific questions. It is a matter of interpreting ethically the reality of punishment and justice, remembering that the same reality of «criminal», on which we also intend to reflect, has to do with the experience of morality, that is, the experience of free and conscious personal responsibility.

Even when we speak of structures of social life, what we focus attention on is the fact that we are people, and we live with an experience of internal unity, which is conscience, unity of awareness, freedom and responsibility. On the other hand, we know that social life is not reduced to simple elements of the internal life, because it is a complex reality. In any case, we ask about the meaning punishment might have by raising a question about the personal inner self of each person, and with our eyes on the reality of co-existence, not just casually but in social structures. What are the implications of our being people, and what does that involve regarding the problems on which we are reflecting?

We wish to clarify ethically the concept of punishment, and in this context ask ourselves, for example, if the retributive element is justified or not. In the reality of our lives, in the reality of complex relations, and with attention on each person's free personal responsibility, we ask ourselves what the meaning is of an inflicted punishment. How can one recognize any value in it? To what end is it directed? It is a matter of verifying, in a specifically ethical perspective, the concepts, arguments and criteria with which we justify or condemn, express assent or dissent, and the different questions implied in the reality that is punishment.

The perception is that the penal reality, as we know it, with some of its problems emerging at times in such a dramatic way as to highlight their seriousness, is one of the tips of an *iceberg* under which there is a much compromised social and cultural reality. If we analyze the usual logic, which can be found in the media, in the arguments we make at table or in the street, or those that emerge from interviewing a sample of the population, perhaps we can recognize an extremely relaxed and uncritical use of important terms such as «justice», «conscience», «honesty», «common good», terms that are humanly and also for believers theologically highly important.

Sometimes one hears talk of justice, or justice invoked, in such a manner and context as to suggest that in reality what is actually meant is revenge. More than once it is taken for granted that, when someone is speaking about honesty or stating that there is a need for honesty, in effect that is what is meant; however, after a deeper analysis, it seems that instead this is not the case. Similarly, it is taken for granted that we understand immediately, at least among those who declare themselves Christian, what we mean by saying that we are Christian, but in this situation also, perhaps it is not true that we understand each other completely.

In an attempt to avoid such misunderstandings and approximations, we posit two reference points for our reflection: that of personal morality and that of the common good. Beginning with such hermeneutical references, it will be possible to ask ourselves about criminal behavior, as well as the reaction of individuals and society to this criminal behavior.

When there is a guilty person, there is also a victim. We will consider, as a personal *figure in relations* the victim, the guilty and, with respect to them, the common citizen along with the magistrate, the competent authority. We wish to understand the meaning of these relations: what is at issue in them about the entrusted obligation of conscious and free responsibility, and what they express about human nature and individual and shared morality, so much shared that we create a culture capable of building prisons in a particular way, capable of building in a certain way an entire penal system.

1
Personal morality. Being honest

We all know something about what it means to be honest. In fact we have a personal experience, on the basis of which we can verify the reality of an internal non-arbitrary need for honesty, present within us, but of which we are not masters. This lays the foundations of our very existence as people who are properly human.

When we speak of ethical experience, experience of the moral aspiration that qualifies the person as good or wicked, we understand the terms of existence as consciously compared with the existence of others. Personal reality, the reality of existence of the human person, is not truly known as such until the human person's unique capacity to make use of reality, or the capacity to understand and reason, to judge and decide, has been affirmed. The existence of the human person is spoken of in personal terms when the capacity, which *every* human subject has, to understand oneself, the world, its opportunities for realization and value, is affirmed, through *sharing with others his/her life.*

In our condition as creatures on this earth, finding oneself a subject face to face with other subjects, recognizing oneself as a person in front of the personal «you» of another, constitutes an original experience, with respect to other comparable ones. It is not like finding oneself in front of a sheet of paper, a table, or a tree. It is finding myself in front of a subject who *like me* exists on earth, who is capable of understanding and desiring, and who, with his/her presence, makes possible for me a life not defined solely by the relationship with things. The presence of the other person means that I am defined (in terms of existence, not simply as a conceptual definition) as fundamentally constituted in interpersonal relationality.

In view of that fact, naturally, human freedom is not just the mental capacity to assess and choose one thing or another. Each person's freedom arises from and develops in the encounter with the freedom of others. By virtue of such an encounter I can live out what makes me a person in historical reality and not as if in a dream. Beginning with the encounter with the other person's freedom, I can understand myself and the world, what is possible, and how it might be possible to orient myself. I begin with the fact that I can decide what I want to be. I can plan my existence, including choosing the concrete course for its realization, verifying the meaning, value, and perspectives that open up to me, and other people as well, who, like me, have from me and others the gift of being able to live as people.

The experience of the presence of others in our lives is, therefore, fundamentally, the gift that is made to us to be able *to be people* on this earth. From start to finish the opportunities of human life on earth are given by the fact that others give us life, make personal life possible for us.

In the face of each of these people, each of us knows (even in more complex situations) that he/she can choose between only two possibilities: to act in such a way that one's own freedom is liberating for the other person's opportunities for life and freedom, or to act in an arbitrary manner, in an attitude of self-privilege that opposes and saddens the life of others. In the first case, my life and decisions will be such as to give the other person the possibility of life, in that I make that person live as far as he/she depends on me. In the second case, by my decisions I repress the other person, even to the point of killing him/her, as far as he/she depends on me. This can also be done through choices and behavior that wound them by ignoring them or going elsewhere.

The alternative is radical. Within my personal inner self, judgment is not according to my will. I know that, as far as it depends on me, if I do not make myself responsible for the life of the other person, I am irresponsible. I know that I am unable to justify rationally neither indifference nor the attempt to avoid the presence of the other person, because these and similar actions would in any case be equivalent to a rejection. Furthermore, such actions cannot be the rule according to which people on earth behave, since by rejecting or fleeing, no one would assume the responsibility for the life of the other person. In fact, it would be committing murder.

To avoid misunderstandings, we stress that responsibility acknowledges its actual limitations with the phrase: *as far as it depends on me*. Naturally in clarifying what depends on me, we are speaking about not being arbitrary. «Depends on me», in fact, means what is objectively possible for me in light of the actual condition in which the other person finds him/herself and my own real condition, in other words, my objective possibilities for intervention, as far as I understand them. I am responsible only insofar as I objectively can be, but precisely to that extent I am ethically bound, and every space of justification for arbitrary decisions is excluded.

On the basis of this discourse, one can hear the echoes of some contemporary philosopher such as E. Lévinas or M. Buber[1]; but we can as well recall, at the foundation of these affirmations, some text or theme belonging to biblical revelation[2]. What is affirmed in these sources is the internal reality, which we can all verify, that is, the experience of conscious and free responsibility. And it is against this reality that we must measure ourselves if we want to have an ethical discourse. If the references are different from these, one could reach a conclusion with even logically correct reasoning, but which have nothing to do with ethics.

1 Cfr. LÉVINAS E., *Totality and Infinity*, Duquesne University Press, Pittsburgh PA 1969; BUBER M., *Il principio dialogico*, Comunità, Milan 1958.

2 One thinks of the theology of the covenant, or the different biblical traditions that speak about it and converge in the faith Traditio. Cfr. AUZOU G., *Dalla servitù al servizio*. Il libro dell'Esodo, Edizioni Dehoniane, Bologna 1976; EICHRODT W., *Theology of the Old Testament*, 1, trans. J.A. Baker, SCM Press Ltd, London 1961.

2 Simple and complex structured relations

Even today it is not unusual to find discourses that place great emphasis on human rights and values, but which are based on a contractual premise. Sometimes also, a rationally coherent ethical discourse is likewise built on this premise. Such a discourse can be seductive[3]. In both cases the rules of conduct would have agreement as a basis.

The condition of pluralism would seem to support these premises. In fact, however, the temptation present in the contractual premise comes first from contemporary pluralism and first also from contractualism. At its basis, even with attention on ethical logical and systematic constructions, is the attempt to fundamentally sanction the option for self-privilege. My life comes first: what belongs to my life, what I have already decided for my life, what I maintain as important and only then, as far as is possible, all the good of others that one can imagine and realize.

We have succeeded in making even the commandment of fraternal charity succumb to the rationale of self-privilege. We think, for example, of the statement according to which to love one's neighbor as oneself, there is first need to love oneself. We can well interpret that statement as the need to think about oneself first[4].

Here there is a fundamental problem, which should appear obvious when viewed rationally. Nonetheless, we often become astute in rationalizing self-justification in the face of the requirement of non-self-privilege. So we call *love* that *of neighbor* and *of self*, omitting that we understand the second in a different way from the first, that is as preference for ourselves. We should not be surprised, then, that there is a prevalent culture of relations fundamentally subjectivist and non-fraternal.

3 To refer to our own times, at some point we have all heard mention of business ethics. It is not unusual for the *business* horizon to lead a reflection called *ethical* and the search for rules, also called *ethical*, but the aim of which remains defined by interests in terms of business. *Ethics of business or business of ethics?*

4 Cfr. GINTERS R., *Valori, norme e fede cristiana. Introduzione all'etica filosofica e teologica*, Marietti, Casale Monferrato 1982, 98-116; SCHÜLLER B., *La fondazione dei giudizi morali. Tipi di argomentazione etica in teologia morale*, San Paolo, Cinisello Balsamo 1997, 79-114; BASTIANEL S., *Autonomia morale del credente. Senso e motivazioni di un'attuale tendenza teologica*, Morcelliana, Brescia 1980.

The question is: if the exercise of freedom in the face of the other person does not have the objective dimension of his/her real need and my real possibility of working for his/her good, on what basis can we sanction such behavior as *moral?* On what basis can moral rules be established? Why not define the observance of rules of conduct based on a relationship to the other person understood as a rival as violence rather than as morality? If the figure of the other person, the image that I have within me while I think of another person (friend or enemy), is that of a possible rival, I have a relationship with him/her in which I first must defend myself and then eventually search for his/her good (as long as it doesn't bother me too much). In that case, what will be the criterion to determine what is *good?*

Conditional acceptance of the other person manifests, insofar as it concerns me, my lack of concern toward him/her, unless he/she is useful to me (and can also be of use in an intelligent way). In fact, if I carry out many charitable gestures, inasmuch as I can without ruining myself too much, I benefit also in terms of public image. Ethics could thus also be of help in business affairs. It is better to give oneself codes of conduct, rules that it benefits no one to transgress. It is better to run a business with «humanity», to care for what makes others happy, so as not to create obstacles to the proper running of the business.

In this way we can also construct a stupendous juridical order, based on the rationale of regulated competition. But will this be better than ruthless competition? To call ethical a way of living in which each thinks first of him/herself, and then if it's not harmful and is useful, thinks of others too, means renouncing a humanity that can effectively be called such. It means sanctioning not just the rationale of arms as tools, but the rationale of *violence* as relational.

This entire discourse could be expressed clearly in reference to the gospel message; however, here we have preferred not to provide an explicitly theological discourse in order to show its radically human value. We are all placed together in a history for which we are responsible. Believers and non-believers alike are called to establish a humanity through a rationale that makes us mutually responsible for each other. Believers and non-believers, we are aware of being able to construct an «inhumanity», a being together always armed regardless, with the gun or the economy, diplomacy or politics, with all the tools we manage to have.

3

The common good and the goal of social life

The reality of interpersonal relationships, interpreted ethically, remains central, also, in understanding complex, structured social relations. Furthermore, the forms of social life have the human quality of de facto shared morality. Every type of «association» structures ways of relating in view of a shared goal. It is clear that a social structure governs itself insofar as a group of people agree on some projects, on some aims and ways of pursuing them. For each level of social interaction one can identify the specific aim, the common good which that specific society intends. Naturally, every type of *societas* has a level of its own aims that are not the ultimate purpose, but are particular goals. The common good will be constructed by these shared purposes that together one attempts to pursue[5].

The question that we raise concerns the ethical character of such shared purposes. Can we indicate a concept of *common good*[6] that *ethically* qualifies social life and that therefore may be a positive critical application for interpreting the various criteria and levels of common good in the different types of associated social life?

It is not uncommon to think of the common good as a massive cake, which is the property of everyone, and it is good for everyone that it be as big as possible, but with regard to which, everyone thinks they should get the biggest slice at the least possible cost. Why is this common good, wich is everyone's property interesting? It is interesting for one's own (at least hoped for) benefit. We are faced with a way of understanding the common good *at the service of the private good*, that of individuals or groups. Within this way of understanding, at the moment in which one glimpses that one can, perhaps with a slight arbitrariness, contribute a little less to the common heritage and have greater advantage for him/herself, he/she will believe it «logical» to look to profit for him/herself out of what is for everyone. If then, this is a matter not just of some individual who thinks in this way, but rather groups and societies, it will not be difficult to look for and establish rules for mutual satisfaction. And if the rules are not at the service of the private search for the good of important parties, then many peo-

5 Cfr. BOBBIO N., *Il futuro della democrazia*, Einaudi, Turin 1984.

6 For a broader treatment of the problem see BASTIANEL S., «Moralità e politica», in CANANZI A., ED., *Politica come servizio*, Piemme, Casale Monferrato 1994, 43-60.

ple can agree to slightly change the rules and thus, because these people are stronger and able to ensure that the rules are observed, they consolidate their own advantage.

But the *human* significance of social life is an entirely different matter. Ethically understood, the common good indicates the meaning of our living side by side, the ultimate goal of every form of social life, the goal toward which we are moving, in the *sharing of existence*. If positive personal morality is expressed in the relationship of the gratuitous acceptance of the other person and in making of one's own freedom some responsibility for the life and life opportunities of the other person, the morality of social life will be expressed in the sharing of existence. Thus it indicates an *ultimate goal* of society, its *utopia*, in such a way that the intermediate aims will be critically evaluated in their being conformed toward such an aim of communion[7].

We speak of *communion* within the Christian tradition, interpreting the utopia of life together on this earth in the perspective of Christian charity according to God's intentionality and his salvific interventions, remembering Jesus[8]. We know that we are at a certain point in history, that we are not prior to original sin, and that we have known salvation in Jesus Christ. We recognize ourselves in an historic condition that lives under the sign of his saving presence, even if we are still on the journey in the acceptance of this salvation.

We speak of *communion* within ethical language, because the term communion authentically expresses what *common good* means in an ethical perspective. We speak of *utopia*, meaning with this term the ultimate goal to which we are aiming as co-existent people: our human life on earth in socially structured relations that are continually structuring themselves in the concreteness of history, in the continuous interweaving of freedoms. We ask ourselves if our human life has a utopian social perspective, at the level of personal intentionality and at the level of shared human culture.

With respect to the various tools of social life, with respect to the various institutions and ways in which we live in the institutions, with respect also for the juridical instruments, including the penal system, the question about such utopia becomes a question about the way of structuring relations between us.

7 Cfr. BASTIANEL S., «Carità e politica: problema etico», in *La Civiltà Cattolica*, 3341, 140/3 (1989) 345-358.

8 God's intentionality is expressed in his salvific interventions, from Exodus to Jesus' resurrection. They create communion and call for communion, as a reality of true solidarity which nourishes faith and translates faith in gratuitous care for the other person. Cfr. RIZZI A., *Pensare la carità*, ECP, San Domenico di Fiesole (fi) 1995.

4

Behavior judged by the penal code

When there is criminal behavior there is someone who bears the wounds in his/her flesh. There are consequences of objective evil[9]; there is a person, a victim, damaged by this criminal behavior.

In the usual way of arguing, the emphasis is on the fact that there is an innocent victim, but we must clarify the use of the adjective «innocent» in this case. This adjective is not an indicator of the moral innocence of the one attacked, but of the fact that it is a person unjustly attacked: guiltless with regard to the aggression, not having sought, caused or provoked it.

Let us imagine the case of a person cheated out of money in his/her bank account or someone who suffers a robbery, the stealing of a good or the deprivation of the opportunity to procure it. Let us imagine someone who, through violence, suffers a physical wound or some other trauma that sees that person deprived of father, sister, son, friend, because of his/her being attacked, kidnapped, killed. There can be many examples; the levels and objective seriousness of the damage provoked are highly differentiated. In each case, the force of evil exercised and the consequences of the objective evil procured are not limited to the physical level. The damage inflicted concerns people and the relationships involved, in their meaning, their inner selves, in their most profound human qualities. From the point of view of the meaning of his/her personal life, the one who has suffered the attack can have been ruined by the evildoer for the future, as well.

Naturally, we must understand the meaning of «ruined» in that context. If the meaning of human life were understood and assumed in ensuring that one's own freedom becomes life opportunity for others, if the ethical quality of our life were truly understood as the capacity for gratuitous relations (which means a humanity that creates humanity), we must state that no evildoer, not even with the most sophisticated weapons or the cleverest tricks, will ever be in a position to ruin the meaning of this existence. Whoever understands this must not forget it—and perhaps never be silent about it.

9 For an overview of Catholic thought see RAHNER K., «Guilt—Responsibility—Punishment Within the View of Catholic Theology», in ID., *Theological Investigations*, VI, Darton, Longman & Todd, London, 1974, 197-217.

In this sense, even basically clear juridical categories (such as that of the innocent victim) are used on the moral level in a critical way and not emotionally, without consenting to the fact that they become legitimization for easy individual and social self-justification. Thus, it is a question of determining if we believe in human values or not, if we interpret their specific relevance through the unconditional application of moral value, and if the moral value of honesty is understood as inalienable or if we merely place it among so many values, as one among others and with the possibility of enduring their rivalry.

We must all ask ourselves these moral questions and verify them. Even the victim should understand them, and if he/she doesn't, we must help him/her to understand. If we ignore these issues when we are harmed, it means that our culture and our social life have suffered a serious setback from the ethical point of view and that basically we do not know how to distinguish *ethically* good from evil.

5
The victim

From the moral point of view let us now consider the person harmed and the guilty person, and social responsibility toward both of them.

From the point of view of the person harmed, is there something the person can do? Or is she/he denied any possibility of intervention, not only by virtue of the aggression, but also by virtue of the shared culture of human relationships? Let us suppose that the person has not died, but is still alive on this earth, still capable of making decisions. What good can this person do, as far as it depends on his/her free responsibility? Given the circumstances in which the criminal behavior happened, given the objective conditions, what will be the way to create, as far as it depends on him/her, a more authentic humanity on earth?

There is the evil that has been suffered, as well as its continuing relation to society. There is the relation of the aggression suffered and its relation to another person who is guilty of it. There is the meaning, the achievement of the victim's life (in theological terms of salvation), which is built within the human quality of his/her inclinations, choices, and concrete ways of relating.

If I am harmed by an evildoer, what is still asked of me is to build, as far as it depends on me, an authentic moral relationship in wanting and searching for the evildoer's good, human growth, and life. Insofar as I can, within the limitations of my understanding, through the freedom of which I am actually capable, I am requested to look for and do the good that is genuinely possible for the other person who is with me and for the relations in which I find myself, so that our relations *become* more capable of humanity, by nature more liberating.

In this situation, authentic morality encounters forgiveness. Even if one can be effectively heroic in some situations, we cannot silence the sign of forgiveness, as not paradoxical, but as a normal and logical path of our human relations[10]. To care for the life of another, because it is the life of another person and not because it suits me, should be the «normal» way to be morally honest in relationships. To be ready to forgive, understanding its meaning correctly, not as a cancellation of the abuse carried out, but as a contribution to someone else's human and ethical reintegration, should become the normal «way» to basically overcome, individually and socially, the culture of self-privilege and self-defense.

6
The guilty

It would not only be historically objective, but it would also be morally mystifying, to speak about aggression and victims and to avoid speaking about guilt and the guilty. The juridical requirement, in this sense, is not only at the service of the affirmation of objective correctness, but also at the service of moral truth and the personal responsibilities always implied in relations.

In the situation of the guilty person there is the evil inflicted and its relation to the victim; there is the evil inflicted and its relation to society; there is the non-meaning of decisions that have failed the authentic meaning of existence; and there is punishment reserved for being guilty.

Furthermore, in this condition the guilty one is called to be a person, insofar as it depends on him/her. It does not mean that because he/she has caused damage and become a criminal, that he/she must remain a criminal. In order not to remain a criminal, he/she also needs to look for and do *good* in the search for and realization of that *good* that is concretely possible for him/her. Additionally, it belongs precisely to the interests of his/her humanity to know and understand

10 Cfr. GENNARO A. DE, ED., *Amore e giustizia*, Giannini, L'Aquila 1980.

that there *is* a good possible for him/her, which, therefore, is then asked in conscience of him/her.

The good of the guilty person requires above all that he/she not be dishonest; that he/she becomes a person capable of exercising his/her freedom responsibly. It is of this that he/she has greatest need[11].

In order to be genuine, the assistance that comes from others should be *gratuitous*, even in the sense of not being conditioned by the pretense of any prior guarantees of conversion. And yet, it is true that something new happens in someone's conscience and human existence when the manner of other people's presence mediates the raising of the personal question: insofar as I am able, here where I am, with all that I have done and the ways of experiencing relations, what can I do to create a more authentic humanity in these relations?

Naturally, it will not be true that the guilty person is genuinely trying to be honest and to change if, being able to repay, he/she does not repay; being able to help does not help; being able to do something to repair the damage created he/she does not; being able to encourage the growth of the other person he/she instead continues to privilege him/herself. In any case, what he/she must do at this point in order not to continue to miss the meaning of his/her own existence is precisely to assume, in responsible freedom, care for the other person and others in a way that basically is not self-interested and self-concerned, but gratuitous.

7
Society, punishment, and the common good

The society in which criminal behavior takes place has suffered a setback, in that when there are offenders, it means that we, as society, do not succeed in living a genuine sharing of existence. The analogy with the reality of poverty and the various forms of poverty is clear. As long as there are poor people on this earth, it means that we are not up to the measure of humanity, and our life systems need converting[12].

11 Cfr. BASTIANEL S., «Conversione», in COMPAGNONI F., PIANA G., PRIVITERA S., EDD., *Nuovo Dizionario di Teologia Morale*, Edizioni Paoline, Cinisello Balsamo (MI) 1990, 145-159; GINTERS R., *Valori, norme e fede cristiana. Introduzione all'etica filosofica e teologica*, Marietti, Casale Monferrato 1982, 192-210.

12 Cfr. SCHOTTROFF L., STEGEMANN W., *Jesus and the Hope of the Poor*, Orbis Books, New York 1986.

The analogy with the situations of poverty allows us to clarify something that seems to be ethically important: the privilege of the weak is the first step toward justice. If there is a needy person, leaving aside the fact the person may be good or bad, preference goes toward that person by the fact of his/her objective condition of weakness. If this preference is not expressed concretely in the care for that person's life, it means that we are not truly searching for justice.

When there is criminal behavior, there is a *needy person who is harmed* or exposed to harm. There is also, however, a *guilty needy person*. For both of them, their personal good and their common good need to be integrated. For both it is a matter of wanting the good, beginning with actual conditions, in discerning what is actually possible. But, precisely from this point of view, looking at the person-to-person moral relationship, it is important to remember that the guilty person is, for that reason itself, also objectively needy, humanly and morally needy, weakened by the very punishment within the failure of lived relations.

When we consider what would be the correct personal and social relationship to have toward the guilty person, a punishment «inflicted» per se does not, therefore, have any ethical justification. Indeed, if we do not release this person from his/her condition of weakness by offering, insofar as it depends on us, the opportunity to contribute to social life through his/her free responsibility, it means that in our search for justice there is an element of insincerity, a rationale of defense/attack that is radically unjust.

If this is the case in the person-to-person relationship, it is likewise the case in social relations. It is not only a matter of remembering that a punishment inflicted as vendetta has no moral sense, but it is also a matter of clarifying that the social task of justice is not at all realized by simply inflicting punishment and marginalizing[13].

If the criminal can, from a certain point of view, be considered the poor, the weak person, he/she will become even more so if we de facto marginalize him/her. So he/she will become victim not because he/she may be innocent, not because it is as if the person did nothing wrong, but because of the fact that we now become aggressors through indifference, explicit denial, and condemnation. The rationale of inflicted punishment does not resolve the damage caused, does not cancel guilt, does not overcome the conditions of the guilty, does not recognize social co-responsibility, and is not directed toward the goal of building the common good (sharing of existence).

13 Cfr. VALSECCHI A., *Giudicare da sé. Problemi e proposte morali*, Gribaudi, Turin 1973.

At the level of shared social culture, restricting oneself to punishing expresses and sanctions a rationale of violent relations, with the aggravation of the cloak of legality. Furthermore, such actions risk producing, in turn, relations that tend to legitimize themselves on the basis of arrogance and the victory of the strongest. In this hypothesis the society we build will be the child of such a shared culture, with the rationales present in it[14].

Obviously, from this point of view, the issue that moral requirement presents to the current juridical penal system cannot avoid the question about various forms of punishment, their validity, their significance, and the open opportunities for changing them. What are we attempting to do? What is the aim, and what are the fundamental criteria of the current penal system?

It is said that a concrete gesture expresses and realizes a person's goodness when it effectively translates his/her taking on assumption of, in conscious freedom, the responsibility for the *good* of the other person. Similarly, a specific social structure or an institutional instrument expresses and realizes morality when it effectively translates co-responsibility for co-existence aimed at the *sharing of existence*. In the horizon of the common good, understood as common reaching out to the sharing of existence, and beginning with where we are, it is right and proper to ask ourselves about the social and institutional structures in which we live today, and whether they are to be effectively adapted or not in order to move toward an increased capacity for the sharing of existence. This becomes a question of whether the reasons by which we justify a civil and penal institution, or a specific structuring of life, or specific choices, are effectively directed in transparency toward the common good and the promotion of the person who is objectively needy, or whether they are pseudo-reasons that have nothing to do with that aim of humanity.

This is not a discourse that should cause alarm. There are some significantly positive aspects in our institutional systems that we need to recognize if we are to contribute to an authentic legal and moral development of our social life. However, our questions are raised with honesty, and in particular the question of if by chance there is not a problem of a warped mentality (with respect to all religious creeds and various cultural forms) of shared self-justification, as when faced with criminal behavior of individuals and groups, one is led to say that

14 Cfr. BASTIANEL S., «Strutture di peccato. Una sfida teologica e pastorale», in *La Civiltà Cattolica*, 3328 140/1 (1989) 325-338.

there are crazy people and criminals, but nevertheless, society is sane. And yet, we know, a plant only grows in suitable ground.

The guilty party can also be identified without turning him/her into a scapegoat. In the same way, identification of the personal moral responsibility of each of us will also be without mutual condemnation. Such identification of moral responsibility means first of all the free assumption of consciousness and the free commitment to place ourselves under the spotlight. If we do not do so, a situation can occur in which first of all we self-justify. We declare ourselves to be just (possibly because of the fact that we suffer provocation or aggression), instead of considering that if by chance the «justice» we share is not such as to kill or to produce indignity and degradation of the opportunities for human existence on this earth[15].

8
Conclusions

In attempting to reflect on the ethical dimension of this theme, the intent was not to claim to reach some propositional direction in the area of penal law but rather to come to the point of suggesting a positive stimulus about the need for formation of conscience.

Moral formation of conscience and the commitment to contribute to forming consciences on an ethical level is, both personally and socially, an extremely important and urgent task and must be recognized as such at this moment in history. There is an immediate need to patiently work on a task that perhaps will not bear great fruit while we are still alive, but is necessary for the humanity and social interaction of those who come after us.

What is needed is the patient work of *paideia*, being careful not to create confusion, to recognize human values for what they are. It is necessary to assume, in a conscious, free and responsible vision of utopia, the effort of overcoming our diversity of opinions, helping us to discern the objectivity of the values at issue and to propose solutions that are fundamentally within the bounds of authentic humanity.

15 Cfr. the dossier «Entre le pardon et la punition: la réhabilitation des détenus», in *Le Supplément*, 197 (1996) 5-80.

Chapter 12

The reaction to evil

BASTIANEL S., «Come reagire al male? La risposta cristiana», in AAVV., *Perdono e giustizia nelle religioni*, Humanitas 2, Morcelliana, Brescia 2004, 298-319.

The theme proposed, with its dramatic topicality, seems to highlight in an obvious way a question about justice that concerns the correct way of interpreting its meaning and the opportunities within our current societies, in complex cultural, religious, political, and economic conditions. The question, as it is formulated in our theme, however, does not concern per se the veracity of one or another theory about the *just*, nor even justice in general. Rather, it is about the meaning of justice in certain specific conditions, that is, with respect to a context of relations in which one takes for granted that evil is already present through someone's work. The question is about *how* one should react and respond to evil.

When faced with the obvious setback that the provoked evil causes for our humanity, the question about the way of reacting bears with it an understandable need or desire for effectiveness. If we consider seriously the life of others and our own life, it involves this need and desire; it is not a matter of confusing the search for justice with the renunciation of freedom and rationality or with the resignation to arrogance. Yet, this too raises questions for us: *What effectiveness* are we seeking? With what criteria of effectiveness do we evaluate just action and the possible good?

This reflection intends to highlight the theme on a properly and directly *ethical* level, that is, with respect to the personal involvement of consciences. We will examine the implications of the question posed from the point of view of a person's inner life, in his/her conscious being, in his/her exercising personal liberty, therefore in his/her being involved in personal responsibility. The question, then, will be stipulated in this sense: faced with a provoked evil, what response constitutes genuinely free assumption of responsibility for the good that is possible?

The need to qualify the authentically ethical character of this question is associated in our reflection with the necessity of understanding the *specific contribution of the Christian traditions* and how this specific contribution can be explained, communicated, and argued in such a way that it not be understood as a possessive and hidden treasure, as the exclusive possession of one party. In fact, we are aware that the condition of our globalized societies, characterized by a necessary pluralism of perspectives and ways of existence, allows the fact of mutual dependence and conditioning between the different ethical cultures and religious traditions to be seen more clearly today than in other historical eras, as far as horizons of understood meaning, criteria of value, and models of experienced conduct are concerned. Often, in declaring instrumentally or sincerely pursuing the desire for a dialogue capable of mutual understanding, ample reference is made to the influence exercised by the various religious traditions and different anthropologies on the formation of a shared ethos, on the criteria for decision-making, life-styles, and the very way of thinking about the coherence and correctness of concrete choices in the different ethical fields[1]. In the light of this knowledge, to speak of our theme and the specific contribution that the Christian traditions can offer to the sincerity of interreligious dialogue, also becomes a matter of asking ourselves how it might be possible to think realistically of a synergy between the different religious traditions that might be fruitful for an ethical culture capable of sustaining all those who attempt to sincerely seek justice, that is, to seek the good because it is good.

1
A type of relating

Can responding to evil with evil be just? The reality with respect to which similar questions are posed is a manifold reality, with many variants, each with its own relevant specific import. However, it is always a matter of *someone who has done wrong to someone else.* That is, we are not in a situation of damage caused by natural calamities or in the presence at any rate of an evil that is not due to someone's free decision, nor is it possible to blame adverse nature, the stars or evil divinities, for the damage realized. The evil we are speaking about is that which is

1 One thinks about the debate on inter-culturality, currently in progress in our multi-ethnic societies, with the challenges and opportunities that such a reality places on the overcoming of individual distinctiveness in the search for a basically universal understanding about the values that fundamentally concern human life. Careful secular reflection, too, recognizes the role that the various religious traditions can offer in this regard. However, there remains the question about understanding such a contribution in an ethically correct manner, not in a functional and utilitarian sense. There remains above all the ethical problem of understanding and living the meaning of ethical dialogue, explanatory and not enforced, as on-going formation of identity, personal and collective, through the *encounter with that which is different.* Even within the Catholic Church the debate, which arose in the 70s, under the great conciliar movement, as a question about the «specific character» of Christian morality, and developed in the 80s through discussion about the «autonomy of morality», focused in the 90s on this theme, obviously connected with the fundamental issues of moral theology, such as the relationship between ethics and politics, ethics and the economy, ethics and law and also that between ethics and theology. On this question, cfr. BASTIANEL S., «"Autonomia e teonomia" and "Specificità" (della morale cristiana)», in COMPAGNONI F., PIANA G., PRIVITERA S., EDD., *Nuovo Dizionario di Teologia Morale*, Edizioni Paoline, Cinisello Balsamo 1990, 70-82. 1271-1278; HABERMAS J., «Fede e sapere», in *Micromega* 5 (2001) 7-16 and the articles by TRENTIN G., BONDOLFI A., BRENA G.L., in *Studia Patavina* XLVIII (2001).

more or less glaring, which is caused by people. It is that totality of damage, burdensome in present daily life and with effects that last in time, which someone has intended, and which is of concern precisely *insofar as* it has been intended and desired by some people[2]. This places in the forefront that evil which is people themselves in their arbitrary action, and thus, it is a matter not just of a disaster, but an obvious setback for our humanity and for our claim to humanity.

Someone has done wrong to someone else. Expressed in this way, the formula is deliberately simple, but the terms of the question that it poses are not at all simple. Who is that *someone who is the originator* of evil? The cause of evil could be an individual, a more or less numerous group, a social class, a people, different peoples, a generation, a totality of well identified or even unidentifiable subjects. The *evil* caused can be a slap, a wound, a death, people killed, a massacre, but it can also be humiliation, marginalization, or deceit. It can be a matter of violence visibly carried out, but it can also be suffering, poverty, ignorance, or hunger caused for generations of people, in a certain area or in a part of the earth's hemisphere. Those suffering the evil, also (the *someone attacked* who, we remember, is objectively victim, aside from his/her moral qualities!) can be an individual, a group, a social category, a people, different peoples, some generations[3].

Someone has harmed *someone.* From here stems the question, precisely because it is about responding to the existence of human beings. One is not responding to the evil that is created, because the evil created does not speak. Instead, evildoers speak; those who live with them speak; those harmed speak; and I speak, I who respond not to evil, but to the one who has seen it, if necessary to

2 We recall the classical distinction, from the ethical point of view, between *malum physicum* and *malum morale*, in reference to the free responsibility of consciences involved in the face of an objective limitation or negation of value. The distinction, developed in the contemporary ethical and ethical-theological field also as a difference between the ontic limitation and the moral limitation and between the human value (or pre-moral or ontic) and the moral value, is necessary precisely in the sense of a consideration of human actions concerned with the objective worth of concrete gestures, but not limited to the parameter of simply material measurement of them. The distinction places as central the question of the *relationship* that the subject builds with the values and concrete opportunities and, even in the face of an inevitable evil, the objective difference between desiring it and tolerating it. Cfr. JANSSENS L., «Ontic Evil and Moral Evil», in *Louvain Studies* 4 (1972) 115-156; FUCHS J., «Diritto naturale o fallacia naturalistica», in ID., *Ricercando la verità morale, Teologia morale*, San Paolo, Cinisello Balsamo 1996, 32-69.

3 Cfr. BASTIANEL S., «Pena, moralità, bene comune: una prospettiva filosofico-teologica», in ACERBI A., EUSEBI L., ‹edited by›, *Colpa e pena? La teologia di fronte alla questione criminale*, Vita e Pensiero, Milan 1998, 161-177. For the distinction and connection between the figures of the unjust aggressor and the objective victim as such, in given circumstances, see the «principle of legitimate defense», as understood and expressed in the Christian ethical tradition. Cfr. CHIAVACCI E., *Morale della vita fisica*, Edizioni Dehoniane, Bologna 1979.

the one who has done it, and to the one who is witness to that evil and my reaction. That is, the relations that are the source of the evil caused and the relations set in progress by that evil, they are the ones that speak—relations that are never neutral and that call for a response.

When faced with the other person, the others, who are human beings like us, we are responsible. If we are believers, in the exchange of interpersonal responsibility we are responsible before God. Human evil, the evil that is at the same time a damage caused and the wickedness of a heart that has decided to cause the damage, this evil that is a setback for our humanity, that makes us recognize that we are not being able to live humanly on this earth, this evil caused «to someone» asks us: What do you decide? How do you exercise your freedom? To obtain what? How do you respond to people like you who live with you? How do you respond in the face of those harmed, damaged individuals and people, faced with this need for good that you have seen contradicted by the one who has done an evil deed against you and others?

Out of these questions arises the ethical question. It witnesses to the reality of conscious freedom called to become responsible. From here stems the ethical demand for justice, with a question about its effectiveness. The question about justice, in fact, as it is formulated by our theme, is of course an indicator of the virtue of justice[4]; not, however, in the sense of a perfectionist tendency close to the hearts of only a few, nor in the sense of a legalistic reference to the observance of rules that necessarily guarantee co-existence, but in the sense of an answer that everyone, and we personally, are called to give when faced with the other person, in the experience of social interaction. Who is just? How does one respond when faced with a situation in which there is evil caused by someone?

Naturally, in our reflecting we must consider that, in the complexity of situations and operative concrete choices, the properly ethical point of view is not identified directly with the juridical one, and that the respective fields have their autonomy that is recognized and respected. But the presupposition of non-coincidence between ethics and law is, at the same time, also a pertinent presupposition between ethics and law, in the sense that law must take into account

4 For a general overview about the issue, cfr. COZZOLI M., «Giustizia», in COMPAGNONI F., PIANA G., PRIVITERA S., EDD., *Nuovo Dizionario di Teologia Morale*, Edizioni Paoline, Cinisello Balsamo 1990, 498-517. Cfr. also THOMAS AQUINAS, *Summa Theologiae* II-II, qq.57-80; KEENAN J.F., *Goodness and Rightness in Thomas Aquinas's Summa Theologiae*, Georgetown University Press, Washington, DC, 1992; MOSSO S., *Il problema della giustizia e il messaggio cristiano. Elementi di teologia morale sociale*, Piemme, Casale Monferrato 1982.

aspirations that cannot be reduced to some fundamental principles. Law will need to be the translation, in regulated co-existence between people, of what precisely the aspiration of humanity suggests, in the way in which it guides the historic journey of the search for a life fundamentally accomplished on this earth[5]. Faced with an injustice caused deliberately, the ethical question will involve, therefore, the inner nature of people, which expresses and guides the outward appearance of the gestures. It will concern the objectivity of our answer and the placing in history of what we think and desire, the criteria, goals and expectations of honesty and justice that we effectively seek.

2
What justice?

The reference to the terms honesty and justice, to which the question we are examining leads, often appears today in the religious and political, social and economic language of individuals and peoples, so often as to give the impression of abuse through the frequent and indiscriminate use of the concepts. It is not uncommon to hear discourses or find oneself faced with public statements and programmed declarations, evaluations and personal judgments, which place great emphasis on the defense of justice and legality, on human rights and values, but which begin with premises that openly conflict with (or cunningly avoid taking into consideration) the experience that is basic to our existence as people as far as we are properly human, that is, what we can verify, faced with a moral requirement of non-arbitrariness and free responsibility that is present in us and of which we are not the masters. Even the question we are posing, about the «just» way of responding to the harm caused by someone, finds its explicit reference (and clearly verifiable) not in one or another strategic action, nor in one or another theory, but in such personal original experience that qualifies the person as good or wicked on the basis of the manner of his/her conscious relationship with the existence of other people, because the «just» refers to the jus-

5 Cfr. BONDOLFI A., «Diritto e giustizia», in WILS J.-P., MIETH D., EDD., *Concetti fondamentali dell'etica cristiana*, Queriniana, Brescia 1994, 58-82; CAPRIOLI A., VACCARO L., EDD., *Diritto, morale e consenso sociale*, Morcelliana, Brescia 1989; CATTANEO M.A., «Il diritto come valore e il problema della pena», in *Società, norme e valori. Studi in onore di R. Treves*, Giuffrè, Milan 1984, 167-224; DEMMER K., «Tolerancia y cooperación. Una pregunta a la ética del derecho», in *Moralia* XV (1993) 97-108; HABERMAS J., *Morale, diritto, politica*, Edizioni di Comunità, Turin 1992.

tice of a subject or of many *human* subjects, *co-living people*, different and similar, on this earth. But how? In what sense?

The reality of the human person is not truly stated until one can exclusively or largely affirm a person's functional capacity to make use of reality so that such capacity forms the faculty to understand and decide and establishes the validity and efficacy of one or another normative system. A person's existence is expressed in personal terms, just as, likewise, the existence of a group or society can be called *human*, when the capacity, which every subject has, to understand him/herself, the world, the opportunities of realization and value, is affirmed, *sharing with others one's own existence*[6].

Beyond the specific anthropological routes of the foundation or reflected expression of a meaning, which can be at times so differentiated as to seem so distant from each other, we all on this earth find ourselves as subjects in the face of other subjects and all of us on this earth have the opportunity to recognize that this finding ourselves before another person is not like finding oneself in front of a table, a piece of paper, or some other thing. The possibility of recognizing people begins when faced with the personal existence of others. But, if we don't wish to be generic, this means that *personal human* existence begins for each person, for me, faced with the personal «you» of another subject who like me exists on the earth. He/she is capable of understanding, and caring and asking to be recognized in this capacity. Faced with me, with only his/her objective presence, he/she makes possible for me a life that is not defined just by the relationship with things. Faced with him/her, I understand that I am called to choose and the choice is objectively between only two possibilities: free responsibility *or* arbitrariness[7]. In this sense we must not call the simple capacity we have to choose, take action, and plan *human liberty*, if this choosing, taking action and planning does not arise from the conscious assumption of a co-existence with others that has brought us to the possibility of living as a people, and if it is not

6 Cfr. BASTIANEL S., *Teologia morale fondamentale.* Moralità personale, ethos, etica cristiana, (for students' use) PUG, Rome 2005, 23-40. The category of *interdependence*, morally interpreted in the sense of rightful *solidarity*, is often found in the post-Conciliar Magisterium of the Catholic Church. See, especially, the Encyclical *Sollicitudo rei socialis*, in *Enchiridion Vaticanum 10.* Documenti ufficiali della Santa Sede 1986-1987, Edizioni Dehoniane, Bologna 1989.

7 For the original character of the moral requirement, the uniqueness of the moral alternative and the novelty and irreducibility of the *experience* of conscience with respect to the different anthropologies and reflected ethical formulations, cfr. BASTIANEL S., *Autonomia morale del credente.* Senso e motivazioni di un'attuale tendenza teologica, Morcelliana, Brescia 1980; FUCHS J., «L'assoluto nella morale», in ID., *Ricercando la verità morale, Teologia morale*, San Paolo, Cinisello Balsamo 1996, 15-31.

liberating the opportunities of life and freedom for others, not only for ourselves, and not for ourselves through others.

If we speak of the objectivity of the moral requirement, and not simply the sense of justice, it is right to remember that we cannot hide behind «feeling» and not even behind the cover of «just» rules of co-existence, which avoid any reference to one's personal inner nature and the personal way of understanding and living one's own freedom. The objective acceptance and the objective rejection of the moral requirement of free responsibility are verified in the concrete response given to the other person in his/her objective need, that is, by the way of understanding and living one's own freedom, either as a gratuitous choice of the good or as the choice of self-preference. Either one chooses in such a way that one's own life and decisions are responsible, that is, such as to offer the other person the possibility of life by making him/her live insofar as it depends on us, or by choosing the repression of the other person, even as far as letting them die insofar as it depends on us[8]. The alternative is radical, but within personal conscience the judgment is not at the free will of the individual, just as it is not at the free will of one or another group, or of one or another cultural or religious tradition.

Of course, in specifying the measure of objectivity of the moral aspiration of free responsibility, the conditions that need verifying are those of the actual need of the other person, that *someone* who is before us. But this is not enough. Precisely in order that the response may be true and correct, the objective possibilities of the person who responds to that *someone* must be verified as well, that is, my actual possibilities of intervention in favor of the other person, as far as I understand them. In this sense it should be noted that there is no good objectively asked of us that exists apart from the historical real conditions of the other person and ourselves. Therefore the formula that reminds us to do good «insofar as it depends on us» is intelligent and realistic; and therefore each person, even in clarifying what truly depends on him/her, must not be arbitrary but gratuitous[9].

8 The manipulation of the other person and self-preference or preference of the group to which one belongs do not happen only in open conflict with someone else's freedom, but also in each expression of prejudicial and conditional acceptance of the other, through a rationale guaranteeing one's own advantage that sometimes also direct humanitarian correct and effective plans. On the question, cfr. BASTIANEL S., «La fame, una sfida allo sviluppo solidale», in *La Civiltà Cattolica* 148/1 (1997) 330-343; RAWLS J., *A Theory of Justice*, Harvard University Press, Cambridge MA 1972.

9 The specificity of moral objectivity, in the proper sense, therefore implies priority attention not just to the different elements, but also to their unification in the claim of conscience. Cfr. FUCHS J., «Moral Truth between Objectivism and Subjectivism», in ID., *Christian Ethics in a Secular*

Therefore, it is specifically a matter of understanding the full personal achievement of freely making oneself responsible in the conscious commitment to the true fulfillment of someone else. The proposal that moral aspiration makes to our conscience is the desirability and possibility of good, not simply the search for one's own benefit. It also proposes the reality of a fundamentally unconditional acceptance that is not concerned in assessing what is concretely possible or the laying down of prior guarantees about the other person, but instead, with accepting him/her simply on that guarantee of being accepted and respected by him/her.

Understood within this experience of conscious and free responsibility, of which we are made capable, and which we can all verify and against which we can all measure ourselves, even the answer we give to the question about intentionally caused harm declares to those with whom we live our reading of the human reality and, at heart, who we are, what humanity we represent and cooperate to create, insofar as it depends on us. Furthermore this question and this experience have found its root of meaning and foundation in many religious traditions and, in them, have found clear words of expression and normative guidelines. In our reflection we intend to consider the texts from revealed Christian tradition.

The fact that the Christian traditions clearly indicate that evil can only be overcome with good seems to belong to a normally unquestioned given of shared knowledge. What does this mean? By what rationale of human relationships is this declared possible? The way in which overcoming evil with good is proposed, along with the fact that in history there is no lack, and never has been, of temptations to avoid its import, not just on the part of «outsiders», but precisely on the part of those «belonging» to the tradition of Christian faith, calls for critical attention to be paid to what is commonly meant by «justice» and also to the way of profoundly understanding the moral demand of honesty. Remembering Jesus of Nazareth, remembering what happened in the relations that he created, we will attempt to understand what his disciples experienced and understood in the relationship with him.

Arena, Georgetown University Press, Washington DC 1984, 29-41; ROTTER H., «Soggettività e oggettività dell'esigenza morale», in DEMMER K., SCHÜLLER B., EDD., *Fede cristiana e agire morale*, Cittadella, Assisi 1980, 231-246.

3
The Christian interpretation of the human: the memory of Jesus

Christian faith is not a totality of theories about the Christian life; nor is it simply a collection of religious news and experiences. At the basis of Christian belief lies not only a human effort, but God's gratuitous initiative, not simply the revelation of one or another truth, but God who communicates himself in the man of Nazareth, in his gestures, words, his human way of living out relationships on this earth, in his living and dying, in his remaining present through the gift of the Spirit.

What does it mean to state that in the humanity of Jesus is revealed the closeness of God who loves and saves? What does it mean to say that Jesus is the revelation of the Father? Conceptual terms such as incarnation, the passion and resurrection of the Lord, help to understand these realities, beginning with the understood experience of those who directly encountered Jesus of Nazareth during his visible existence, according to what we can gather from the New Testament texts. These were written precisely so that the testimony of those who «have seen», «have heard», «have touched», have recognized God in the face of Jesus of Nazareth, makes the encounter with Christ possible for others. The history of this mediation becomes living *traditio*, becomes the church. To be part of this *living traditio* does not mean simply that someone knows that others have had a certain experience, but that, through the lived and explained mediation of those who encountered Jesus Christ, it is possible to meet and recognize him personally, so as to be able to live this reality of encounter, so that in living it one is able to mediate and transmit it to others.

In this sense, what is specific about the ethical tradition of Christians is the fact of being Christians, not the theories about Christian life nor a specific cultural affiliation, even if the recognition of this human reality in the interpretive memory of Jesus is nourished and expressed in manifestations of faith and historical cultural understandings before the beginning of the life of the first Christian community, and moreover, as had already happened for the people of Israel. What is specific about a Christian's moral life is the vitality of his/her relationship with the Lord, just as for the disciples the freedom of outlook and the gratuitousness of life develop through continuous conversion, founded and continually nourished by communion with Jesus. Therefore, if we wish to consider the response to evil in a Christian interpretation, we do not find ourselves faced with just the Christian specificity of the content of values and normative indications, perhaps to be lived as the exclusive property of one party, but we find ourselves first of all faced with the reality of a relationship, a presence, a living word that we, too, can welcome, remembering what happened in the relationships Jesus created, just as his disciples internalized and attempted to realize them on earth.

In reading the experience of the disciples in the various New Testament texts[10], we can say that what they saw, in the relationships that Jesus had with them and with others, was encouragement, patience, mercy; it was finding themselves always before him and placed in conditions to be able to extend the space of possible communion. For them Jesus was above all and to the end the one who cared for sinners and poor people. He took the initiative in creating familiarity; he did not expect their perfection, but from the start he trusted their journey, not just when they understood, but also when they did not understand, helping them to understand. For them he was the one who accompanied their uncertain development, gave them time, attention, support, pardon. From the testimony of the disciples we can grasp the awareness of being accepted by God's gratuitous goodness working in Jesus and not because of our own merits. Therefore we say that the experience of Christian faith fundamentally belongs to the experience of being forgiven, not being forgiven in a pious sense, but in Jesus' making himself a neighbor, in the gratuitous closeness of his gestures, his word, and his ways of relating.

Paraphrasing the words at the Last Supper over the bread, we can say that the disciples understood that Jesus gave them his «body», that is, his concrete existence, in the visibility of relationships, as their nourishment; in the sense of the salvation of God, which in that giving over of self he revealed himself; and in the sense of the fullness of humanity that in him became possible on this earth[11]. Jesus has given this «body», this his existence, without prior guarantees, without prior conditions from the beginning to the end, in order to make real people live, to give them life. And precisely in this, his way of establishing relationships with them and others, in the criteria that guided his decisions, gradually

10 Cfr. ABIGNENTE D., *Conversione morale nella fede. Una riflessione etico-teologica a partire da figure di conversione del vangelo di Luca*, Gregorian University Press-Morcelliana, Rome-Brescia 2000; BASTIANEL S., *Figure di preghiera nella Bibbia*, Edizioni ADP, Rome 2005.

11 Cfr. BASTIANEL S., *Vita morale nella fede in Gesù Cristo*, San Paolo, Cinisello Balsamo 2005, 153-171.

recognized in familiarity with him, the disciples were able to recognize a *human* way of living: true, just, complete, beautiful, desirable. Gradually, understanding their own concrete existence in relationship to this Jesus, the disciples have «seen» that to live like he lived on this earth is possible and is a life entrusted to them.

In the light of this rational experience, communicable in its gratuitousness and its human possibility of realization, we can understand those words, so clear in the New Testament, about the meaning of a true and not merely pious forgiveness, about the fact that evil can be overcome by good and not by evil: «Never repay evil with evil but let everyone see that you are interested only in the highest ideals. Do all you can to live at peace with everyone» (*Rom* 12:17-18). Whoever has encountered Jesus and assumed the criteria and interiority of that encounter, has seen that for Jesus the world is not divided between friends and enemies, because to him no one has been an enemy. We are reminded of the outcome of the encounters with Jesus that the gospels narrate for us. We are reminded of the evildoer who recognizes Jesus beside him at the moment of death, of Zacchaeus who encounters him on the last stage of his journey toward Jerusalem, and we are reminded of those who lay snares for Jesus, deny him, and betray him. «Love your enemies», is the gospel phrase (*Matt* 5:44; *Luke* 6:27-28) and whoever encountered Jesus remembers well how someone has in effect been an enemy of Jesus, totally rejecting him, but for Jesus no one was an enemy in the sense of being rejected by him.

Confessing to being a believer in Jesus Christ means expressing an awareness that comes from this experience, which is not simply one among the many experiences of life. The possibility of recognizing and assuming the intentionality of God's work in Jesus comes from the encounter with him, comes from perceiving in his presence the gift of being accepted by him and being called to a basically gratuitous, faithful, unconditional communion. But journeying toward this communion for the disciples meant following Jesus in conversion, gradually understanding being made capable of converting one's own thinking, assuming and sharing the Lord's outlook in relating to others, in a concrete story.

The point of view of the conversion, as constitutive experience of the disciples' following the Lord, allows us now to shed new light on the theme of our encounter. We are attempting to question different religious perspectives, and in particular, the specific contribution that can come from the Christian tradition (understood as lived experience and also a totality of normative formulations) for the understanding of justice in the possible ways of responding to someone who has wished and carried out an evil deed. It seems that one essentially can respond to the question in only two ways: either one accepts that the realization of evil justifies (or even demands) a retaliation according to the evil carried out, or one seeks an alternative to the evil in responding to it with good. We can be satisfied in asking which of the two responses is an authentically *Christian* response. In the preceding reflection we first understood which response of justice would be not only authentic from a Christian point of view, but would also be *humanly honest*, in terms of human moral experience of free responsibility, in which all can be united and which we recognize as the work of God and accomplished in the existence of Jesus Christ.

The answer, therefore, would seem to be unmistakable. And yet, when faced with this statement of unmistakability, our reflection cannot cease, because we must recognize that the alternative of retaliation, the answer of evil for evil, has many times, even in the history of the interpretations and past experiences of Christians, claimed to be founded on faithfulness to the tradition of faith. We can recall various historical moments and expressions of gestures and words of Christians in their relationship with other Christians and in their encounters with those who were not Christian. Primarily, we are thinking here of the many ethical and theological interpretations of the Christian tradition that have, in the course of time, contributed to strengthening a secular concept of justice and cohesiveness, so far removed from the ethical aspiration of gratuitousness and so far removed from Jesus' way of living: a concept of justice that is neither human nor Christian[12].

12 Cfr. RIZZI A., *L'Europa e l'altro. Abbozzo di una teologia europea della liberazione*, Edizioni Paoline, Cinisello Balsamo (MI) 1991; TANZARELLA S., *La purificazione della memoria. Il compito della storia tra oblio e revisionismi*, Edizioni Dehoniane, Bologna 2001.

Of course a religious tradition is not born without or apart from history, isolated in regard to an ethical context, and independent from shared economic, political and social models. We must carefully remind ourselves also to be aware of the double character of *opportunities* and *restrictions* that the same religious traditions can represent: positive opportunities, because of the good and historical efficacy of the good mediated by the opportunities, and restrictions, because of sin and its effect, which also conditions interpretations of it[13]. We can recognize it also with regard to our concern: If posing a question about how to make a just response to an evil caused, what do we actually mean by «justice» and what justice do we think is possible on this earth? With what criteria have we read or do we read the word that the biblical tradition discloses and entrusts to us?

It is easy to trace in the New Testament texts and in the subsequent Christian traditions, clear indications about the fact that evil can be overcome by good and not by evil. In speaking of the praxis and words of Jesus, scholars agree, for example, in recognizing the centrality of the commandment to love, proposed by Jesus and handed on in radical gratuitousness, as manifestation and realization of the Father's intentionality, as sign and acceptance of the kingdom of God on this earth. «Which is the first of all the commandments?» the scribe asks Jesus, according to Mark's gospel, and he replies with the key words from biblical memory and knowledge: «Listen, Israel, the Lord our God is the one Lord, and you must love the Lord your God with all your heart... You must love your neighbor as yourself. There is no commandment greater than these». And the scribe, instructed in the traditions of the fathers, recognizes this: «Well spoken, Master; to love the Lord with all your heart and to love your neighbor as yourself «is far more important than any burnt offering or sacrifice» (*Mark* 12:28-33)[14]. The

13 Cfr. FUCHS J., «The "Sin of the World" and Normative Morality», in ID., *Personal Responsibility Christian Morality*, Georgetown University Press, Washington DC 1983, 153-175.

14 In this and in numerous similar New Testament phrases, the single commandment of love of God and of neighbor, «with all» oneself and «as oneself», translates into a unity the words of *Deut* 6:4-5 and *Lev* 19:18, interpreting the sharing in God's intentionality precisely in continuity and as the foundation of the gratuitous gift of fraternal closeness, according to the same rationale of the «beatitudes». It is the unifying center of the whole of biblical revelation and the experience of the fatherhood of God in gratuitous closeness. It is also about the non-legalistic authentic accomplishment of the *Torah*. Nevertheless, even the ways of interpreting this tradition have shown, in the history of Christianity, the historical strength of sin and how it has expressed itself. For the interpretation of *Lev* 19 and the history of the reading of the text, cfr. DI PINTO L., «Prossimo, straniero, nemico: il comandamento dell'amore in Lv 19», in CATTANEO E., TERRACCIANO A., EDD., *Credo Ecclesiam. Studi in onore di A. Barruffo sj*, M. D'Auria, Napoles 2000, 13-35; MARTHYS H.P., *Liebe deinen Nächsten wie dich selbst.* Untersuchung zum alttestamentlichen Gebot der Nächstenliebe (Lev 19,18), Universitätsverlag-Vandenhoech & Ruprecht, Freiburg

doctor of the law presented by Matthew and Luke repeats the same thing. «On these two commandments hang the whole Law, and the Prophets also», says Jesus in the first reference (*Matt* 22:34-40)[15], and «do this and life is yours», he says in the second (*Luke* 10:25-28)[16]. It is one of the only times that Jesus expressly cites the ancient Scriptures and offers an interpretation of them. Perhaps for us it is particularly significant to remember this moment and this word, because the conversation is with «experts» of the tradition, guarantors of its correct interpretation. In addition to this moment, however, Jesus has interpreted and proclaimed the primacy of gratuitous love of neighbor always, in every one of his words and with the whole of his life. Thus the various phrases that in different New Testament contexts place the emphasis on love of neighbor as the fundamental criterion of relations between people should be interpreted in the light of what Jesus understood, lived, and gave. By virtue of salvation given in him, with the specific emphasis that comes from the incarnation, it is the very humanity of Jesus that interprets the normativity of its meaning. His human way of living on earth, the manner of his relations, become the paradigm for the life of every disciple[17].

Through his words and actions, Jesus has shown that the foundation that motivates and makes possible this unique *love* (as John calls it: *John* 13:34-35, etc.), is God himself, his work, his plan. It is about accepting the gift of communion

Schweiz-Göttingen 1986. For the meaning of the commandment interpreted by the life and proclamation of Jesus, cfr. BASTIANEL S., «Un'etica delle beatitudini per la cultura contemporanea», in COMPAGNONI F., PRIVITERA S., EDD., *Vita morale e beatitudini. Sacra Scrittura, storia, teoretica, esperienza*, San Paolo, Cinisello Balsamo 2000, 182-207; SCHNACKENBURG R., *The Moral Teaching of the New Testament, 1*, Jesus' Moral Demands, Burns & Oates, London 1965, 81-156.

15 «The whole of the Law is summarized in a single command: Love your neighbour as yourself», Paul will say (*Gal* 5:14; cfr. also *Rom* 13:8-10), radicalizing the ethical importance of making oneself a neighbor to the other person as integrity in the adherence of faith. The same sharing of God's outlook in care for the other person is found constantly in the New Testament, from the Synoptic gospels (one thinks in particular of the Lucan care and the figure of the Samaritan in *Luke* 10:25-37) to the letters (one thinks, for example, of the *Letter of James*). It is John above all who manifests the foundation of such liberating love in the «how» of Jesus' love for us. Cfr., in particular, *John* 13:34-35; 15:12-17; *1 John* 7:7-21.

16 Emphasized in the Lucan account is the specifically ethical element of the answer not just for the necessity of «doing», but above all for the reference to the motivation of the Samaritan's behavior, which is immediately recalled afterwards. Cfr. ABIGNENTE D., *Conversione morale nella fede.* Una riflessione etico-teologica a partire da figure di conversione del vangelo di Luca, Gregorian University Press-Morcelliana, Rome-Brescia 2000, 182-186; HORN W.H., *Glaube und Handeln in der Theologie des Lukas*, Vandenhoeck & Ruprecht, Göttingen 1983, 107-115.

17 Cfr. BASTIANEL S., «La normatività del testo biblico», in FERRARO S., ED., *Morale e coscienza storica.* In dialogo con Josef Fuchs, AVE, Rome 1988, 197-203; SEGALLA G., «Quattro modelli di "uomo nuovo" nella letteratura neotestamentaria», in *Teologia* 18 (1993) 113-165.

with him. And how does God work, where does he speak, how can one accept him? Jesus' answer about this was clear: standing with him and being like him on this earth is every person who is an example of *human* conscience. We recall the Lucan parable of the Samaritan, a man who is neither priest, nor Levite, nor scribe, nor doctor of the law, a man, plainly a man who sees, stops, responds to the other person, giving to that person his time, his goods, his life, precisely like Jesus, with the capacity to mediate the memory (*Luke* 10:25-37). Love of neighbor means making oneself a neighbor, which is the same as being merciful[18]. The person who in conscience assumes and lives out of gratuitous neighborliness, assumes in his/her own free responsibility God's operative intentionality. That person's criteria are those recognizable in the life and work of Jesus.

5
Faith tradition and conscience

Unconditional love of neighbor, the love of neighbor that is worth «more than any burnt offering or sacrifice» (*Mark* 12:33) is, therefore, a clear New Testament prescriptive expression. So how does one explain that the question posed by the doctor of the law «and who is my neighbor?» continues to be raised in a *traditio* founded on knowledge of Jesus? And how does one explain, through the centuries and up to the present day, those various forms of temptation which, with degrees of sweetening or justifications of human impotence, have convinced or still convince to thwart, or at least strongly reduce, the practical import of these same expressions?

In effect, the gospel context in which this story is presented to us for the first time, and is thereafter incorporated into the concrete history of the Christian traditions, reminds us that even those clear words can be not understood or

18 The link between love expressed in closeness and forgiving mercy is highlighted especially by the evangelist Luke. See, for example, the affinity between the discourse on the Plain, where, in *Luke* 6:36, it is said: «Be compassionate as your Father is compassionate» and the reaction of the doctor of the law, at the end of the parable of the Samaritan. This man recognizes the truth of making oneself a neighbor «who took pity» and showed mercy (*Luke* 10:37). The terms used by the evangelist are not the same in the two cases, but their similar significance stands out. In *Luke* 6:36 the adjective *oiktirmon*, which usually translates the Hebrew *rahamin* (the maternal uterus), indicates the external expression of mercy. In *Luke* 10:37 the term *eleos* (translation of the Hebrew *hesed*) indicates the internal feeling of emotion. Cfr. FAUSTI S., *Una comunità legge il vangelo di Luca*, Edizioni Dehoniane, Bologna 1994, 184.

misunderstood. We have found a thousand different ways to avoid the clarity of the stipulation of love of neighbor by stating that it is paradoxical or by referring to the exceptions and even saying that the rationalizations of reservations expressed about it are prudent. Thus there has been and still is a need to emphasize that, in the life of the just person and according to God's intentionality, love of neighbor means to genuinely love the other person, and it has seemed necessary to add something so as to avoid any misunderstanding: even one's enemy, the one who does you harm.

Making the other person neighbor by making oneself neighbor to him/her is valid for every other person, be they ill-treated in their objective need for help, or be they evildoer in their objective need to become a neighbor. The word is clear: be a neighbor! Who is the enemy? Is it someone who is objectively an evildoer, someone who has done wrong or has done you wrong? Well, even this person needs your love, expression of God's love for him/her, not so that the person who has done wrong may do some good, but precisely because the fact that he/she is an evildoer speaks of the person's need to be helped to become an honest person. We recalled the figure of the Good Samaritan. What did he do? He saw, stopped, and what he could do he did. Nothing more or nothing different was asked of him than this good concretely and sincerely possible, but this was asked of him in conscience and this he did. As for him, so for each of us, the criterion of good and just conduct is that love which *makes the other person be a neighbor*, according to that good which is now concretely possible. What you can do for the good of the other person, do it; do what you can within the bounds of what is actually possible for you, but with the criterion of his/her good, wishing to make him/her be a neighbor.

What is asked of us is to genuinely desire the good of the other person, to genuinely want the good of the other person as if he/she were are a family member or a friend, and to desire, not just in words, but rather in seeking out the good of the other person, even when he/she is an adversary. In Jesus' time this was difficult to understand, and is even so today. The gospel word stipulating love of enemy arises precisely because there is a difficulty, ancient and ever new, which has its clearly visible cultural and social value, spanning across the specific faith traditions[19].

19 Cfr. BARBIERO G., *L'asino del nemico. Rinuncia alla vendetta e amore del nemico nella legislazione dell'Antico Testamento* (*Es* 23,4-5; *Dt* 22,1-4; *Lv* 19,17-18), PUG, Rome 1991; RIZZI A., *Pensare la carità*, ECP, San Domenico di Fiesole (fi) 1995.

Why these difficulties? Why the ambiguity of interpretation of the very clear faith traditions? In different ways, with different traditions, but also with elements common to the different traditions, we are accustomed to understanding the person (with the values and personal rights linked to the person), in a fundamentally individualistic manner, or focused on the individual person. Thus, we understand social interaction, relations, in a subjectivist parameter, as something that comes after the value and good of the individual person. In this way the stipulation of gratuitous love is scandalous if it pretends to be prescriptive, because my individual good can be understood in contrast with the individual good of another person. When we say «love your neighbor as yourself», we can be tempted to look for justifications, for example explaining by a not totally sincere problematization that, *naturally*, one must first love oneself in order to be able to love one's neighbor *as* oneself[20]. And there remains a potential division between the two loves, as if making oneself neighbor, gratuitously caring for the other person, were not the true realization of one's own life. So we define an individual right as *natural* and say that the other person does not have the right to damage it, whereby it comes *naturally* to defend such a right by privileging oneself, one's goods and generally what is of use: one's own life, not the common life and the common good.

Without examining them in great detail, I think that we can already see in the different Mediterranean cultures impulses that have built up in time in a fairly radical manner about the justification of defense and self-privilege, despite adherence to faith traditions such as the Jewish-Christian faiths, which openly proclaim their foundation on God's gratuitously making himself neighbor to humanity. It is not difficult to recognize strongly «partial» impulses in the widely accepted way of understanding justice, in our proclamations of rights and our expectations, in the criteria of evaluation and appraisal judgments, in national and international juridical and economic regulations. With the usual criteria of privilege and strength we regulate conduct and commitments that we call, often a little ambiguously, *communitarian* and *extra-communitarian*. It is not by acci-

20 I. Kant focuses attention on the ethical deceptiveness of such argumentation, in a perspective of the autonomous foundation of the moral claim. In this regard see above all, the arguments presented in *Fundamental Principles of the Metaphysics of Morals*. Even more so should this challenge the disciple of Jesus. Cfr. GINTERS R., «Il punto di vista della morale: altruismo o egoismo», in ID., *Valori, norme e fede cristiana. Introduzione all'etica filosofica e teologica*, Marietti, Casale Monferrato 1982, 98-116; SCHÜLLER B., *La fondazione dei giudizi morali. Tipi di argomentazione etica in teologia morale*, San Paolo, Cinisello Balsamo 1997.

dent that when speaking of justice often the first thing that instinctively emerges and comes to mind is the proportion of benefit. And, we can add, in the case of lack of respect, it is retaliation.

We have been speaking of the Christian tradition in reference to Jesus Christ. The problem with the above ways of responding is that the theories we have sometimes formulated and still formulate reveal their weakness specifically with respect to having recognized in Jesus Christ the salvation given by God. The Christian is not just a person who knows he/she is created by God. He/she knows that God creates with a purpose, and the purpose is that of a life lived in communion, as a human family, not as individuals. Salvation in Jesus Christ is given so that even if I have been a sinner (I, not only others), even if we are sinners and have not lived according to God's plan, he maintains his fidelity. He continues to make us capable of understanding and desiring, recognizing and pursuing the good. God, the Father, makes us capable of this through the coming of Christ. He makes us children and friends reviving in us the capacity for communion on this earth through the human existence of Jesus.

6
Responding to evil with good: how effective is it?

Where there is *someone* who causes harm *to someone*, it means that there is not a genuine sharing; it means that we, as a society, do not succeed in living a truly human existence; it means that there have been and there are now possibilities of life and conscience denied, not seen or not accepted, gestures of abuse and enmity that generate evil and that produce fruits that are generators of evil. Perhaps it is important to remember this in order to recall the need for an answer that the assumption of free responsibility always demands be given, within the bounds of an unavoidable consciousness, when faced with an evil caused by people. We must consider the objective weakness of the victim, to which one cannot remain indifferent, and the objective weakness of the one who has carried out the evil deed, through the collapse of the authentic meaning of existence, expressed in concrete decisions. There is a personal relation between individuals and the life of a society, with ways of relating and shared thinking that are at the origin of that evil and in which that evil has taken shape. To our humanity, this proposes in an obvious way a radical question about the *jus-*

tice of our structures of co-existence and the actual responsible *effectiveness* of the reaction to evil[21].

At the beginning of our reflection this legitimate claim or desire for effectiveness was noted. Nevertheless, faced with this, we know that the self-justifying of reservations, on a personal and collective level, can arise through the very means of understanding the historical effectiveness of good, the interpretation of the correct answer to give, the verification of the results of an action, and the way of reacting to what appears as failure. Perhaps from this point of view, too, the assumption of a human response faithful to the human way of Jesus' life on earth becomes important. «If anyone hits you on the right cheek, offer him the other as well» recalls the Matthean antithesis (*Matt* 5:39), and of course, it will need to be clarified that this does not mean wishing that the aggressor continues to be so when faced with a victim. But, when I myself am the victim, would presenting myself again without any defense to a guilty person be resigned endurance? Would it not be rather to continue to trust that person and call him/her, specifically in this way, to be a person and to make that person truly a neighbor in a new possible assumption of responsibility?

What the disciples of Jesus did not manage to understand right up to the end, up to when they themselves died to their expectations with the Lord's death on the cross, was the fact that this Jesus decided not to do what the logic of worldly victory held to be right and proper, useful, and urgent, and that is to condone the death of the enemy and the imposition of strength in reaction to the wicked person. Basically, we say something similar when we consider Jesus' behavior to be heroic and his attitude a stupendous demonstration of God's love, but we then continue to interpret the defeat and death that can derive from it as failure (although deserving of a future reward). This is the scandal that runs the risk of rendering short-sighted our criteria of effectiveness, the paradigms of justice, and our expectations of perfect life.

In speaking of the incarnation and expressing the reality of humanity in terms of the incarnation, we Christians must remember that in the human face of Jesus, complete humanity is present and recognizable on earth. And reaching out for complete humanity is possible in him, in communion with him. For the Christian, to live like Jesus has lived, including the day of his death on the cross,

21 Cfr. BASTIANEL S., «Strutture di peccato. Riflessione teologico-morale», in ID., ED., *Strutture di peccato.* Una sfida teologica e pastorale, Piemme, Casale Monferrato 1989, 15-38.

should be reasonable. It should be reasonable to live, not defending oneself, creating fraternity, being trustful, without in any way using one's own strength to violate the freedom of the other person or even merely to constrain it. For a Christian, this life and this death represent the fullness of humanity, not failure, and this humanity is the effective reaction to evil because it is the overcoming of arbitrariness with the possible creative alternative of solidarity. For, if we have made the world in such a way that there are those who are first and those who are last, those who can and those who cannot; if the world is so made that there is evil caused by people, then those in this world who desire to be with Jesus, the Word of God made flesh, should never, for any reason, be on the side of those who create this evil. For me as a Christian this should signify that, if evil must weigh on the shoulders of someone, it will be mine, because this is true solidarity, because this is the way to create a humanity that makes the other person live and not die.

Furthermore, the situation in which the societies of our world currently live, with the usual oppression of the weakest, the crisis in democratic systems, the relentless risk of violent solutions in the most familiar relations and in economic and political relations, should open our eyes. Considering with objectivity the results of historic choices and strategies, perhaps we must be more able to say today what we have understood to be the true effectiveness or failure of humanity, in terms humanly understandable by people and people of different faiths, secular and religious. Whenever did the violent response create peace? So many juridical and economical, political and philosophical theories have attempted to justify the use of force as necessary, but in the history that we know, what has happened through the use of force? What are we in a position to say in giving a violent answer to the violence of others? At least sometimes, don't we say that in order to obtain one's own ends it is beautiful to be stronger; it is good and just to be able to show and use one's own power? Historically, hasn't this meant affirming that good is one's own, it is that of one's own side, it is the good understood by one party, the good that can impose itself because at that moment it is the strongest? Is this legitimate? Is this justice? What will the children of those killed because of this justice say? What have generations of orphaned children said? What has our history, that of the century just finished, continued to recount in all the regions of the world about the pretense of finding another way that is not that of love, a love capable of forgiveness, to change this humanity?

We risk meaning and suggesting self-privilege as honesty, often defended with cultural efforts, rather than defending the ethical aspiration of free responsibility. And in this way we risk nourishing false expectations of efficacy, misleading paths of privilege for ourselves, our structural guarantees, our security, our future, our children, all understood as our property and legitimate possession. Thus, the question about the effectiveness of justice and the just response to evil caused becomes an invitation to ask ourselves, in the honesty of conscience: What do we genuinely want? Honesty or something else? Do we want a «human» humanity that builds fraternity on the earth, or do we pretend that other people are fraternal in such a way as to leave our privilege unjudged? What use do we make of proclaimed rights, of juridical and social structures, of international bodies, of economic and political plans? What expectations of such a humanity do we actually propose?

7
Toward truth and good

To understand and succeed in seeing the effectiveness of good in terms of true humanity, therefore often calls for conversion of the criteria of effectiveness and achievement. Christian faith and the various faiths in dialogue can be of great help in encouraging this conversion, not just for the renunciation of false expectations, but also for the formation of consciences in the development of the capacity for trust. To accept and decide on the good, for the purpose of giving a sign opposed to evil, means always de facto to trust. The moral requirement is not to be reconciled with egotistic calculation. The choice of gratuitousness in this world entails costs, even if one isn't dying at every moment. It is also costly having to establish that the readiness given often does not produce fruits of acceptance and that the results of gifted gratuitousness might not lead to the development of humanity, because arbitrariness and manipulation of the other person, self-privilege and self-benefit endure, despite the possibilities opened up by witness.

In considering the reality of an historic journey toward the truth and the good, the fact cannot escape us that morality in the true sense cannot be produced or programmed, nor is it the precise result of a cause highlighted by teaching, example, and communication. Of course, memorable and provocative arguments and examples from life are put forward, but what must happen so that personal responsibility develops in freedom toward the good is an event of conscience. And it is always thus, each time someone makes her/himself responsible. However, the Christian statement that one lives on earth in the fullness of humanity by living like Jesus, does not simply say this. Remembering the internal effectiveness of grace that is recognizable as God's work in us, grace recalls as well, a fullness that happens according to the plan of God who saves, according to the word of which he makes himself guarantor, not according to our forces, our times, and our ways. We are asked to accept God's action, searching and building communion on the word of the Lord. We are not asked to save the universe; we are not even asked to look for a security that does not rely on this dependence on God. Certainly, there are signs that confirm and signs that disorient, but the sign, especially performed in a perspective of trust and believing dependence, does not represent all we can do, though it has an impact beyond that small bit of good that in concrete terms we can do and is asked of us.

We see that there is little we can do, but would it be necessary and possible to be able to walk «two miles» with the other person instead of «one» (*Matt* 5:41), with the aim of carrying out gestures of justice and formation for a life in conscience, patience and intelligence? We do what we can; it is the way of living today in the fullness possible, and it is the way in which tomorrow a step of greater fullness of justice and humanity might be possible. We know, in fact, that every step contributes to forming a direction, on the personal level and on the social, juridical, economic and political levels. There is the step (or agreement) that creates better opportunities for dialogue and sharing, but there is also the step that nourishes self-defense and the rationale of greater benefit at minimal cost; there is the compromise that creates fraternity and also that which creates conflict and which therefore only vainly can claim to be an advocate of peace. Christians, like all believers, are called in their specific religious traditions to live out the authenticity of their faith in searching for the possible step of authentic justice, manifesting and sharing the meaning of human life on earth in its full worth, assuming, in sincere dialogue, what the means of human understanding and the human capacities for conscience indicate as the overcoming of unrest and privilege.

With the consciousness that comes from belief, Christians can perceive the commonality of their task and their task of communion in helping this manifold search for humanity and ethical principles, which perhaps even the very con-traditions in which we live suggest again that this search is urgent. Humanity's search is entrusted to the coherence of everyone's response, in the unity between private and public conduct, between religious practice and the care for the good of the other person. This is valid for the individual and for the multiplicity of cultural and religious traditions. To speak of justice today, specifically the duty to overcome a mentality of retaliation and conflict, means hoping to be able to find with yet a stronger reason this common ground of the authentically human, recognizing what, from the point of view of the various faith traditions, we know to be the will of God, the goal of his creating our humanity, the *télos* given and entrusted to us: the possibility of a humanity not divided or shattered or humiliated, but rather, a just humanity because it is fraternal and shared.

Part Five

Morality and the structuring of relations

Chapter 13

Conscience: autonomy and community

BASTIANEL S., «Coscienza: autonomia e comunità», in *Didaskalia* 31 (2001) 3-20.

We will now address two dimensions of personal moral conscience: the dimension of its necessary *autonomy* and the dimension of its *social interaction* or *community aspect*. We will discuss how these two dimensions co-exist and interact, that is, if and how the two dimensions may in some way be related to each other. However, before responding to these questions, it is worthwhile clarifying in what sense we are speaking about personal moral conscience, how a person matures in moral conscience, and how the formation of personal moral conscience occurs. We must then pause for a moment to recall the fact that we live in a history in which evil, too, is present and effective, and evil's efficacy influences the human capacity to live with a moral conscience. Finally, we will attempt to consider what might be the role and task of the Christian community in regard to the formation of Christian moral consciences and to the search for morality, which the entire human world is in fact undertaking, that is, the search for morality that is experienced in the history of humanity.

1
Personal moral conscience

When we speak of personal moral conscience we intend to indicate not a person's capacity, but the actual person in his/her existential unity of consciousness, freedom and responsibility. The term «moral» connotes a specific field of experience, not reducible to anything else: the experience of good and evil and one's own involvement in them; the experience of free and intelligent responsible living. Such experience of conscience connotes the personal life as such, as well as a person's life of faith: the encounter with God in Jesus Christ and the response to him[1]. We will see of what such personal unity consists and what it means to speak of consciousness and free personal moral responsibility.

1 Speaking of conscience as a unitary experience of the person, we intend to place the emphasis on personal morality, underlining the fact that only beginning with that, will it also be possible to think of each ordered and systematic complex of principles, values and hierarchy of values, criteria of evaluation and norms, which is what we mean when we speak of ethics or morality. Likewise, when speaking of conscience of faith, emphasis is placed on the reality of the moral experience interpreted in faith, lived in faith, qualified by faith, as soul and foundation of the Church's living *traditio*. It should be possible to understand terms such as «autonomy» without any misunderstanding by considering them in relation to the manner of such an experience of conscience. That there should then be a close relationship between the necessary autonomy of conscience and the autonomy of morality seems obvious. For its part ethics (and ethical-theological reflection), as a discipline distinct from and in relation with others, will have the task of

Self-knowledge, which every person capable of understanding and desiring in fact has, speaks of the existence of the human person as not a blank and not at random. Our personal lives as human beings do not exist without knowing why, since they manifest a recognition of ourselves within a world of relations and a capacity to take action within a world of relations that is a given, that is not created by us, and that in fact molds us, and without which we would be lost or blind or incapable. It is about knowledge and a knowledge of ourselves, even if this knowledge will not necessarily be explicit, reflected, and thematized each time. Sometimes we do not speak explicitly about a specific type of behavior, and yet we are aware of doing it. The level of knowledge present will not be reflected in the act; however, it will involve becoming aware of self and the reality in which one lives, the world and oneself in relation to the world; it will be intelligence of otherness and self in relation to otherness[2].

This capacity to live consciously, knowing who we are, what we want, and why we want it, this capacity to understand and desire, assumes its truth, its truest and most profound meaning, when it is marked and qualified by the consciousness of one's own living with others, that is, when the experience of human otherness, personal otherness, is placed at the root of self-knowledge. More precisely we can say that when we wrestle with the opportunities for action that concern not just things or the infrahuman world, but concern the presence, life, and life opportunities of others, in such cases our liberty is called to become responsibility. Thus, if in general the meaning of a decision, or the significance of a type

interpreting ethically what the other disciplines illustrate with their specific investigations. More broadly speaking, on the primacy of the autonomous experience of conscience and the relationship between the various disciplines, see BASTIANEL S., *Il carattere specifico della morale cristiana. Una riflessione dal dibattito italiano, Cittadella,* Assisi 1975; ID., «La dottrina sociale della chiesa come teologia morale», in AA.VV., *Teologia e dottrina sociale.* Il dialogo ecclesiale in un mondo che cambia, Piemme, Casale Monferrato 1991, 51-73.

2 Attention to clarifying the various levels of knowledge and consciousness seems necessary in order to understand the relationship between individual behavior and the inner profundity of the person, in reference to the recognition of sin, goodness, and the properly moral character of personal action. In the ethical-theological field, one sees how such attention occupies a central place in contemporary reflection about the «fundamental option», which has developed in the European area, and also, with different emphases, about «virtue ethics», which have developed above all in Anglo-American culture. However, this attention is not new in the Christian moral tradition, but belongs to its original nucleus. Furthermore, it had already been explictly formulated by Thomas Aquinas. See, for example, the distinction between *actus hominis* and *actus humanus,* which became a classical distinction in the later ethical, philosophical and theological tradition. Cfr. *Summa Theologiae* I-II, 1, 1.3. On this matter see also BERNASCONI O., *Morale autonoma ed etica della fede,* Edizioni Dehoniane, Bologna 1981; BOELAARS H., «Riflessioni sull'atto umano effettivo», in *Studia Moralia* 13 (1975) 109-142; FRANKENA W.K., *Ethics,* Englewood Cliffs, New Jersey 1973.

of behavior can be measured and assessed on the basis of our attitude toward realizing the goal we set for ourselves, and therefore, if our relationship to reality can be pragmatically assessed as a means or tool for the realization of the intended aim, then in the relationship with human otherness, in the relationship with the personal «you» we encounter, the very exercise of freedom is placed at issue as to its meaning. The truly human exercise of freedom cannot be measured simply by the effectiveness of pursuing a goal, because faced with the other person the goal itself is at issue, even who we are is put at issue: the value of our lives, specifically on the basis of the relationship that we realize as being an interpersonal relationship.

We take an action, but if what we do concerns someone's life, presence, freedom, opportunities for existence and living conditions, then the question that we find ourselves internally faced with is not simply: with such behavior do you or do you not achieve your goal? Rather, the question is: what is your goal, in your decision-making, and in your behavior, toward who the other person is for you? In this sense, in the understanding of what we decide about practical behavior, in which some way directly or indirectly interests the lives of other people, we cannot avoid the question about what we make of the presence, existence, and possibilities for existence of these other people, in other words, the question about who the other person is for us. With respect to this question we cannot pretend that it is we who declare that a given behavior is all right because we say it is all right or it is bad because we say it is bad. Faced with human otherness we cannot pretend to arbitrarily qualify the meaning and value of our decisions and our corresponding actions. This is necessarily so, not because we are searching for it, but because we are constituted in our authentic humanity as co-habiting, co-existent[3].

Of course, when faced with the other person, we can choose to ignore her/him, to act as if that person did not exist, or we can even use him/her for our own purposes. In both cases that means that the other as person does not interest us; that, insofar as it depends on us, the other person is not there or, if he/she is there, can die, because he/she interests us only if the person benefits us; in other words, if the other person causes harm or is of no use, then he/she in essence is not there. In this way, even if the person continues to be there, he/she is not there as a person, and what interests us is only to be able to use this presence like any other

3 On the original character of the moral phenomenon and its origin, as history and meaning, in an inter-subjective event, see for a broader treatment, BASTIANEL S., *Autonomia morale del credente. Senso e motivazioni di un'attuale tendenza teologica*, Morcelliana, Brescia 1980.

presence, just as with the whole of worldly reality. The alternative placed before our conscious freedom, faced with the other, is only this: either to accept his/her presence, assuming as goal of one's own life and decision-making a perspective of co-humanity, therefore seeking the accomplishment of his/her life as belonging to the goal of one's own life, or to want someone else's presence as a tool, assuming oneself and only oneself as the goal of one's own life, to which all others are subjected. Personal moral conscience is specifically self-conscience marked by an awareness that freedom, when faced with the other person, is either being responsible for that person, his/her life and opportunities, or it is being arbitrary, which means assuming and understanding the fact that in the quality of relationships with the other person, clearly at issue is the quality of our own being, our own lives as persons.

Freed from the condition of withholding oneself, however, personal responsibility is necessarily measured by a person's true freedom and consciousness. As we are traditionally accustomed to saying, what a person is not capable of is not attributable to him/her: *ad impossibile nemo tenetur*. This also means that the true conditions of a person's freedom, that is, not perfect liberty but that liberty which de facto belongs to the person, limited by his/her story and made possible by that story, that capacity for personal liberty which has been formed in the course of history, is precisely the measure of personal responsibility. In fact, we speak of responsible liberty, of free responsibility, but this likewise implies the fact that we are not free to choose what we do not know, and only the measure of our actual knowledge about what is offered for our choice, about the possibilities of good and evil that we have before us, is the measure of our responsibility[4]. In any case we are responsible for the good that is genuinely possible here and now, and this also means, not secondarily, for the good that is known as being possible, as both good and possible. Of course, in stating that it is important to recognize the actual and imperfect opportunities in order to not attribute a responsibility that is not within a person's bounds, it must also be said that the good that is actually possible here and now, understood as such, is entrusted to personal responsibility. For the good here and now that is genuinely possible, we are responsible, and it is a responsibility that cannot be delegated

4 See, in this sense, the respect traditionally given in moral theology to mistaken conscience. Also in this case, in fact, personal conscience remains the ultimate claim and authority for our action. Cfr. FUCHS J., «Cosa significa "coscienza erronea"?», in ID., *Ricercando la verità morale. Teologia morale*, San Paolo, Cinisello Balsamo 1996, 226-237; ID., «Coscienza, legge, autorità», in AAVV., *Coscienza, legge, autorità*, Atti del XXIV Convegno del Centro di Studi Filosofici tra Professori Universitari (Gallarate 1969), Morcelliana, Brescia 1970, 54-66.

to anyone. What belongs to our free and conscious responsibility binds us in an unconditional manner, that is, not if it pleases us, or when it is convenient, or when it corresponds to our plans. The good possible for us binds us, placing before us our possible previous choices or previous directions.

To state that responsibility for the known good, for the other person, and for the actual opportunities present, constitutes the center of the moral experience of conscience, also means affirming that the internal reality that is indicated by the terms of moral conscience is necessarily the locus of personal autonomy. Precisely the unconditional character of the link to the concretely possible objective good and to avoiding the concretely avoidable evil, truly the unconditional character of the ethical bond, affirms, involves, and demands that only through the mediation of moral conscience can there be for us a moral duty. In this sense one speaks of the autonomy of moral conscience, autonomy in the sense that the moral need is not the result of and is not identifiable with an external law that is imposed on humanity from the outside. Even when it is a matter of laws recognized as such or enacted by recognized and legitimate authorities, even when it is a matter of God's laws, on the moral level it is understood that only through the mediation of moral conscience, that is, conscious inner freedom, is a person responsible. Ethical normativeness, with all that refers to such normativeness and can be recognized and formulated in history in terms of moral laws, moral norms, moral authority, in reality is what is manifested in and corresponds to practical judgment or, as it used to be said, to the «ultimately practical» judgment of personal moral conscience. This means that, when with sincerity, in the search of right conscience, with sincerity in assessment, in reaching conclusions, one in fact says that this is the good that I recognize as possible for me, it is impossible not to say that in this case I must act in this way. In this moral judgment that the subject makes lies the concrete norm of his/her action, and no one will be able to relieve the ethical subject from the bond of seeking to understand and the bond of acting according to what he/she has understood as concretely possible[5].

5 Hence respect for conscientous objection, or however convictions of conscience are presented, is imposed as necessary and morally binding, in a given historic cultural climate, as being different from those shared by the majority. Cfr. SCHÜLLER B., *La fondazione dei giudizi morali. Tipi di argomentazione etica in teologia morale*, San Paolo, Cinisello Balsamo 1997, 54-101; BÖCKLE F., «Normen und Gewissen», in *Stimmen der Zeit* 111 (1986) 291-302.

In this sense the autonomy of moral conscience is above all not a principle but a fact, and not a new affirmation. *Autonomy* is simply the quality of that consciousness which we indicate by the adjective *moral*. By the term autonomy, one wishes to underline that free personal responsibility, with respect to the good or evil of which one is aware, is the reality that connotes ones inner being. The norm of conscience is the inner norm, and precisely because of this, it cannot be delegated and cannot be rejected; it is not like the judgment about me that someone from outside me can make if necessary. I could have reasons for rejecting an external judgment, but that internal judgment about the quality of my life, my deciding, my action, which my very own conscience shapes and offers, is a judgment that I know cannot be rejected for any reason.

Furthermore, the responsible exercise of one's own conscious freedom cannot be delegated to anyone, nor can it be substituted by any other claim, even when it may be understood in terms of God's will. For the believer, the will of God will be precisely what he/she, in communion with God and in sincere adherence of conscience and freedom to him, recognizes as possible good and understands as having to do it. In this sense the will of God will be the responsibility that informs the person, who understands him/herself to be called to communion with God, toward the world, for a correct knowledge and correct realization of values, «in the light of the Gospel and of human experience» (*Gaudium et spes*, 46).

2
The formation of personal moral conscience

Reflection on the reality of personal moral conscience as the inner unity of consciousness, freedom, and responsibility, immediately poses some questions: Isn't this something vulnerable? Aren't we perhaps aware of limitations in our true knowledge of the good and true, of the wicked and false, aren't we perhaps aware of mistakes? Isn't our knowledge of what belongs to the universe of human values important for moral responsibility perhaps something that knows doubts and not definitive clarity? And again, our capacity for liberty, our capacity to seek to understand what is true and good in order to realize what is true and good, is it not a liberty, a fragile liberty that we do not inherit in a beautiful, whole, transparent condition with no undercurrents and nothing blurred? When is a person truly internally free? We all have experience of a story of personal freedom in which many limiting factors are present, but often it is difficult to identify the boundary between the free and the not free; often it is difficult to clarify the boundaries of a person's genuine capacity for freedom, and therefore, the true substance of his/her responsibility. Isn't this image of moral conscience as inner unity, unity of liberty, consciousness and responsibility somewhat ideal?

When we speak of the human capacity to understand and desire, we are already indicating in some way a threshold that is not easy to determine when it has been reached. Perhaps it is clear to us that a person is not capable of understanding and caring eight months after birth; perhaps it is not too difficult to recognize that at forty years of age, except in the case of serious mental illness, a person is capable of understanding and caring, but at the same time we recognize that the measure of this capacity can be subject to so many restrictions that are also difficult to envision. Furthermore, on the level of external influence, another note should perhaps also be added, namely, that personal life is from all points of view, an historic reality; the capacity to understand the meaning and the truth of the interpersonal relationship is something that matures in time, through the exercise of interpersonal relations. If a person becomes capable of personal morality, it is because in reality others have helped him/her to know how to understand and decide; others have helped him/her to comprehend and to understand him/herself, to understand him/herself in relations and to explain a meaning for his/her own existence; others have helped him/her to understand what is of value and what is not, what is of more value and what is of less. All that dwells in the consciousness of an adult moral conscience is a reality matured in time, through the mediation of relations. They constitute the locus of our possible comprehension and understanding of ourselves, the cultural environment in which we grow and become what we are, the context that offers us, already pre-understood and pre-interpreted, nearly all the elements that belong to our lives, the reality of relationships that forms the vocabulary on the basis of which we give words to what we understand, how we explain ourselves and what we see, what we feel, and with respect to which we take action. A story of mediated experience makes accessible to us an interpreted universe and allows us to interpret, in our turn, the reality in which we live, the reality that we are.

Therefore, from the point of view of knowledge, we are not originally autonomous in the sense of independent. The world, even the interpreted world, does not begin with us. We grow and are born within a world already read, already interpreted, already suggested to us according to a certain interpretation.

And this is true not just for knowledge. Likewise, from the point of view of liberty, we become capable of liberty because others mediate to us the possibility of liberty. The ways of relating that constitute us are the basic experiences that shape and structure our internal direction, our preferences, our making of decisive gestures. Even our freedom, in its historical development, is not something with which we are born, something shaped by us, dependent solely on us. Being able to say that I decide this, I decide that, because I see it is good and I take on responsibility for this decision, is the result of a history and of manifold influences. In our deciding, in our assuming of one or another way of deciding, therefore in our concrete exercise of freedom, we are in some way shaped by others. The space for freedom, which in practical terms is given to us, is a space constituted by a network of manifold relations, in which the same way of understanding our freedom, its opportunities and how best to direct it, is something that comes to us mediated and interpreted by others.

We call to mind the influence of the models we encounter in our existence and of the influence of negative or positive experiences. From the point of view of a liberty that makes us responsible in our consciousness of good and evil, we call to mind how personal interiority is shaped through the actual experiences of relations, through what was over time interiorized as possibility, positivity, and negativity. We learn to be able to understand and assume the very meaning of responsibility, that is, the fact that it is good. It is realization of one's own existence to be able to understand and assume the gratuitousness of the choice of good, that is, to choose the good because it is good and not for any other reasons (not if and when it interests me or if and when it benefits me, but because I recognize its meaning and value) and to be able to freely assume responsibility for others. These are understandings that mature in the context of relationships. It is necessary to have experience understood by the fact that life has been given to me and that freedom has been given to me by others. In the reality of my existence I must recognize that I am the result of gratuitous relations, that others have permitted me to live, have made my freedom possible. The experience of a love gratuitously received is usually necessary so that a person can recognize the value and meaning of a love gratuitously given. And this is at the heart of personal morality.

Therefore all that belongs to the development of a personal moral conscience is a reality that does not become a story that begins with the individual independent of others. The reality of personal moral conscience is made possible by the context of relations in which the person is constituted. The actual story in which we live makes it possible for us to become persons with our own interiority, with our own capacity for consciousness and liberty and our own call to responsibility. What we are, what more intimately qualifies us as persons, our being moral subjects, our being persons in the strict sense, is the result of a varied, complex network of relations, of interpersonality.

This possibility of a personal life formed within the context of relations, history, and social interaction that is ours, also means that only by beginning out of this rootedness can we develop our autonomy. The development of adult moral conscience, the development of autonomous moral conscience, the development of this personal inner self comprised of consciousness, freedom and responsibility, all of this is the result of a history. The true history, that of the relations that have been and are built for us, is the totality of proper opportunities and limitations of the autonomy of personal moral conscience. In this sense, fundamentally, the autonomy of moral conscience is never, and never can be, independent[6]. Our autonomy is in some way contextualized; that is, it cannot proceed in just any way whatever. All that is originally ours, personal, individual, and all that can develop, will always be marked by the space of knowledge and freedom which is the space of a specific historical and cultural context. Thus, autonomy does not mean arbitrariness; autonomy does not even mean independence. Autonomy means to have developed in private, a conscious conviction, a meaning, a perspective of value, and a capacity for assuming responsibly the space of one's own liberty.

The living of a personal moral conscience in the historic context in which one finds oneself means therefore, that no conscience is «unrelated» and that every autonomy of conscience is constitutionally important and relational; but this also means that, precisely by virtue of the social interpersonal make-up of each person's life, the autonomy of the individual personal moral conscience has its influence on the history of the same context of relations that shapes it, in its life and self-expression. We are children of a concrete tradition, of a story of

6 This would be relative autonomy, which also necessarily means in relation. In this way the concept of moral autonomy comes to be understood in contemporary moral theology. On the constitutive relationality of such moral autonomy, in the triple dimension of the natural historical, and transcendent, cfr. AUER A., «L'autonomia della morale secondo Tommaso d'Aquino», in DEMMER K., SCHÜLLER B., EDD., *Fede cristiana e agire morale*, Cittadella, Assisi 1980, 32-61; PINTO DE OLIVEIRA C.J., ED., *Autonomie. Dimensions éthiques de la liberté*, Ed. Univ. Fribourg Suisse-Du Cerf, Fribourg-Paris 1978.

social interaction, of a culture, and in the degree to which we become capable of freedom, in the degree to which our life is an expression of free responsibility, our life influences the presence, sensibility, and life of other people, who have equally autonomous moral consciences like ours. This means that in some way, in the history into which we are placed, what most intimately, most personally constitutes us, is the place of the most profound influence on the history, life, freedom, and capacity for the free responsibility of others. As children of a cultural environment, we are, in this same environment, in a future perspective, responsible for its development and therefore co-responsible for the opportunities and limitations with which the personal story of other freedoms and other autonomous moral consciences is constructed. This concerns the immediacy of relations and the mediated relations, the relations that one structures, and those relations that one commits oneself to within institutions.

In the immediacy of a simple relationship (the «I-you» relationship), the lasting of this relationship in time tends to structure itself, in the sense that mutual expectations, shared attitudes and criteria, specific roles and tasks are created[7]. Then, when it is a matter not just of individual relations, but of complex ones, this forming of mutual expectations, de facto attributed roles, creates a whole network in which each component is dependent on other components, and the space of true freedom and autonomy, the space of each person's actual assumption of responsibility, influences the capacity, opportunities and restrictions of each of the others. Thus, when over the course of time interpersonal relations are structured socially, this composing of relations in the ways of co-existence becomes a place that makes possible as well as limits the growth, development and expression of moral consciences and capacities for freedom. Therefore, from the point of view of personal morality as well, from the point of view of what is most profoundly singular or individual in a person's reality, that is, from the point of view of his/her inner reality of liberty, responsibility and consciousness, it is easy at least to discern the fact that the dimension of social interaction is not at all secondary, but is constitutive of the personal reality itself. The relations in which we live are the relations of which we are comprised. Without them we

7 A careful ethical reading of the reality of relations, in their dynamic of progressive structuring, is central for a correct understanding of the meaning of the terms «structure» and «structure of sin», as used in the Church's social Magisterium, and especially in the Encyclical Letter *Sollicitudo rei socialis*. On this theme, see BASTIANEL S., ED., *Strutture di peccato. Una sfida teologica e pastorale*, Piemme, Casale Monferrato 1989.

would not be, we would not become persons; without them we would not be able to develop our own original inner self. In the context of immediate relationships, in the context of structured relations, in the context of an actual history, we become persons, we become moral consciences. This context offers us the possibility of being and limits our personal interiority.

This leads us to serious consideration of the reality of history, the reality of the human community, and the reality of the Christian community in which we are placed, as the reality that shapes personal moral consciences. Of course, such a reality does not determine consciences *ad unum*, but it contributes to the formation of the concrete ways in which life in conscience becomes possible. A context of relations experienced in gratuitousness facilitates the understanding and assuming of gratuitousness as a value. On the other hand, context of relations in which individual benefit is normally recognized as a legitimate criterion, if not even as the ultimate criterion of decision-making, facilitates the assumption of a distorted conscience, specifically with a prior option, prior direction, and with prior judgments that necessarily will condition a person's possible decisions, beginning with what the person him/herself understands and, therefore, how the person understands him/herself.

Therefore we must recognize the seriousness of the historical conditions in the exercise of our always-situated freedom. We must recognize the seriousness of the responsibility that is possible for us and that has been entrusted to us. We have experienced the fact that our consciousness, while being thus demarcated, is nevertheless *our* consciousness; we have experienced the fact that in our concern for knowing the true and good, *we* are involved —not just others, not just culture, not just what on average everyone thinks. In fact, when our thinking is connoted by our own distinct particularity, we tend to say that the thought is ours and not simply shaped by others, and so for our decisions, also, when a decision matures in inner conviction we know, and if need be claim, that that decision is ours. We do this not without being aware of the conditioning, but precisely with consciousness of the liberty exercised. Therefore our responsibility does not mean unlimited liberty, but is a responsibility for that concrete space of conscious freedom that is ours. There our responsibility is exercised positively and negatively; there our possible contribution to the maturing of that understanding, of freedom, of the good of others, is realized.

3

Faced with the historic force of moral evil

To recall history, the complex of relations in which each person's moral conscience is developed and formed, is also to recall that precisely in this context we see, not marginally but present and effective, moral evil, that is, the malicious exercise of conscious freedom. The fact that the developing of relations, structured relations, constitutes and produces a way of living, thinking and assessing, should help us to reflect on the shared experiences and thinking that in reality also mediate the result of many justificatory rationalizations and lie at the basis of the structures of life and social institutions. Herein lies the theme of the world's sin, social sin, the structures of sin. It belongs to the ambivalence of human history, to the ambivalence of every actual context of our living and growing as persons, as ethical subjects.

We have spoken of the reality of the structuring of relations. From the moral point of view, this reality possesses a positive as well as a negative aspect, the first being an aid in the positive exercise of conscience, and the second being an obstacle to conscious and free responsibility. In fact in the experience of relations, the good and evil of many people have their historical effectiveness at numerous levels. A person is facilitated or inhibited in the external conditions of life, whether just or unjust, and is also facilitated or inhibited in living personal morality in the history in which one finds oneself. Even concupiscence, in fact, comes communicated through the concrete story in which a person finds him/herself. Furthermore, if moral evil means the refusal to acknowledge oneself in the face of the task of taking on in conscious responsibility one's own possible freedom with respect to values, and if the consciousness of one's own autonomy of conscience challenges the pretense that sin is inevitable, we therefore experience also the fact that self-privilege and its rationale is communicated to us by the same history of relations in which we find ourselves.

What is easier to identify as the influence of history on personal morality is what in many ways belongs to a current mentality, to the de facto shared ethos, made up of conduct and styles of behavior, interpretations of values and hierarchy of values, principles and formulation of rules and norms. To say that a story of evil is effective in our world, or more precisely, that in history evil, also, and not secondarily, is effective, means recognizing that in the formation of the inner self of each person certain pre-evaluations or pre-judgments, which are proposed as normative and typically shared evaluations and judgments, have their importance. When it is a matter of mediation of evil, this means that something has been proposed to us in the context of our life with the illusion of being good, something has been suggested to us as good when it is not good, as a human criterion when it is not human, as necessary when it is not necessary. We can recall, in this sense, the clear reflection that runs through the Scriptures, from the account of the origins to the temptations placed before Jesus. The reality of the temptations presents itself as a deceitful suggestion in the style of what is good and desirable, something that in reality is neither good nor desirable. It is the image of the garden and original sin, the invitation about the desirability of the forbidden fruit[8].

At this point it is perhaps not harmful to recall some important basic temptations that we find again in the cultural understandings of our times and that concern specifically the relationship between autonomy and social interaction or community, from the point of view of personal moral conscience. Sometimes we assume that in a context of a plurality of values, of proposed moral truths, to find ways of imposing one's own world vision, framework of values, one's own hierarchy and truths, is important and effective. Above all, while we live in contexts in which there is a crisis of values, the desire to see one's own framework of values prevail can definitely be a strong temptation. Instead, we must recall that

8 In the account of *Gen* 2:4b-3:24 sin is presented as an historic condition of the relationships that are no longer of communion. Adam and Eve, living first in a condition of communion desired by God and recognized by their human capacity of conscience, according to God's creative intentionality (*Gen* 2), succumb to a reality that reveals itself as inviting, desirable, effective, triumphant: the illusion of wanting to build their own lives, deciding «in their own image», that is, independently from God and from good in its objective substance (*Gen* 3:1-6). The result is a falsified relationship with God, but also between themselves and with the earth. People no longer live in the «garden», relationships between them are of possession and defense, with the fruits of death, which immediately afterwards, begin to appear (*Gen* 4-11). The same worldly rationale of self-privilege manifests itself in the suggestions the tempter makes to Jesus before the beginning of his public ministry (*Matt* 4:1-11; *Luke* 4:1-13). They portray paradigmatically what corresponds to the current mentality, not just at the time of Jesus, permeated with expectations and worldly criteria, but also shared within a believing community, in the same way of thinking about the image of the Messiah. What is insinuated is that on the earth, in order to be able to realize something good, it is necesary to pass through the contradiction of solidarity, gratuitous good, in order to obey this world's rationale of power, illusive actually in its apparent effectiveness. By refusing to kneel before Satan the worldly ruler, Jesus denies the pretense that salvation passes through the rationale of power; it is not by strength and self-privilege that one can reach truth, the gospel, and salvation. When one begins to rationalize one's own self-reservation, the objective possibility of moral goodness is already denied, the meaning of gratuitousness and the very meaning of Jesus' making himself neighbor is already contradicted.

all that is of value, all that is important to assume as the understanding of life and what gives life, all that is important from the point of view of the free assumption of conscious responsibility, actually needs to be seen through the lens of free conscious assumption of responsibility: that which belongs to the universe of human values, and which is available for people's decisions, must be recognized by people's consciences. Therefore the manner of suggesting what is of value must be such that the communicative relationship itself effectively expresses the desire for good, the acceptance of the other person, and the giving over of self to the other.

No morally important human value can be imposed. The result of the imposition of values or moral truths is a delusory outcome. Depending on the measure for which it is imperative, this manner of communicating is inevitably unsuccessful from the point of view of ethical communication. The correct way, therefore, is the way of dialogue[9]. But, keep in mind that dialogue is only genuine if it is dialogue between consciences. Dialogue cannot be instrumental, cannot be prejudiced on the basis of an outcome that one wants at all costs, that is, that the other person consents. If dialogue is true, what one wants to achieve is that the other person sees and freely accepts what is recognized as good and just. Dialogue means listening to the word of the other person and speaking one's own word to the other person: to listen to understand and to speak to make oneself understood; to listen to recognize the reasons and to speak to allow one's own reasons to be recognized. The aim of dialogue is to achieve a better understanding of what concerns one's own life of responsibility and to offer oneself to the better understanding of others in what concerns their free responsibility. Dialogue is the search for the true and good, with the attitude of one who wants to learn if there is something to be learned, to comprehend better and to better recognize, assume and offer one's own reasons, in the desire to hand over one's own understood experience, so that it might help the other person to build his/her own understood experience, understanding, freedom, opportunities and responsibility.

This does not suppose just any way whatever of understanding human coexistence, or the good of people, but in particular, it supposes a life perspective

9 On dialogue as a virtue, cfr. RAHNER K., «Reflections on Dialogue Within a Pluralistic Society», in ID., *Theological Investigations*, vol. 6, Darton, Longman & Todd, London 1974, 31-42; BASTIANEL S., «Presenza cristiana nella società: per una coscienza di dialogo», in *Quaderni di Azione Sociale* 30 (1981/14-15) 81-94; TOGNOLO A., «Persona e dialogo», in *Studia Patavina* 2 (1986) 321-338.

in which the common good is understood as the goal, not as the sum of goods beneficial to many, but as the common striving for concretely possible communion, with actual potential methods for realizing it, as well as with its present restrictions. Thus, dialogue becomes an expression of this search for communion beginning with the current conditions, including the differences, difficulties in understanding, and the conflicts that continue to arise. The way of dialogue is to realize the communion possible today, and to move toward fuller communion.

Faced with the historic effects of sin on personal moral conscience, it becomes highly important to recall the positive construction of morality that is realized through dialogue, in striving toward the common good. To understand the common good in the sense of the search for communion and a path toward communion, will mean not cunningly twisting the idea of the common good itself to the service of the private good and its possible justificatory rationalizations. For example to search for peace in order to avoid damage to oneself is not yet searching for the common good. To search for peaceful co-existence through institutions and laws, only because in this way we receive better protection, is still not searching for the common good. The reality of concrete history, like the continual structuring of relations, including institutions, is a reality that demands a change of mentality, of a considered and shared rationale. To understand communion as an end, and therefore to assume the pathway possible for communion, and to extend its possibilities, is something that will be of interest not only to the common life in the sense of limiting damage or reducing the majority's costs (or those of the strongest), nor will it be of interest only to the external aspect of life with others. Instead, reaching out for communion will be something of interest to the very way of self-understanding and one's own personal good.

Perhaps we are still tempted to understand autonomy as a private space in regard to social interaction. To the extent that this understanding is true, it means that autonomy is interpreted in the sense of arbitrariness and social interaction, and community is understood as something incidental, secondary. For us believers this way of thinking is at the same time illogical and contradictory because of our honesty and our faith in conscience. At issue is the possibility of taking seriously the fact that charity is the foundation, synthesis, and criterion of all that is good.

4
The role and task of the Christian community

The discourse about the autonomy of conscience, constitutionally social and communal, finally poses a question to us as believers. We wish to understand the role, the task of the Christian community in regard to personal moral conscience. The question can have two levels: as Christians' personal moral conscience and in regard to the moral conscience of all people.

A Christian community is a reality of sharing in faith what concerns life, values, the meaning of existence and its accomplishment. Its task is specifically that of transmitting a morality that might effectively be such and be effectively shared in faith. Those who have learned to recognize themselves on the basis of knowledge of the Lord and to share this, those who have learned to take responsibility for good, understanding it in the Lord, and therefore taking on the criteria and aims that are those of the Lord, will also be generators of life «in the Lord». The Christian community, to the degree in which it is born and develops in the lively reciprocity of personal experiences of conscience, in the sharing, even explicit, of personal searches for the good and true, within the accepted communion with God in Jesus Christ, will allow the maturing and living of moral consciences stemming from profound inner stature, will consent to the formation and expression of autonomous consciences in a profound way, capable, that is, of assuming the responsibility for one's own understanding in faith and, on the basis of this understanding, assuming responsibility for deciding in faith. In this sense the Christian community can be a place of possible responsible assumption and maturing of a heritage of faith and shared morality. Naturally, the ethical quality of this Christian community will be the ethical quality of the Christians who constitute it, just as the quality of faith will be the quality of faith of the Christians who make up that community. Its aim, however, is that of handing on a history of shared morality in faith, with the opportunities that this offers.

Since the Christian community lives in the world, the maturing of relationality and of structures of relations within the church is something that in any case always happens in a history constituted by a humanity, by a social interaction broader than the confines of the church itself. From this point of view, the assumption of shared morality in faith will be able to become a contribution to the history of the understanding of the moral life of the whole of humanity. This will mean, not incidentally, that we recognize not only one's own ecclesial environment but also the human story itself, redeemed in Christ and living out of this redemption, in the objective search for good and in cooperation with the historical force of good, which goes beyond the boundaries of the visible church and is realized by many, believers and non-believers[10]. This will also mean that we make memory of the Lord the interpretive criterion of human values, assuming and recognizing the necessary cultural understandings of the gospel message and the fact that it can never be identified with the cultural product of a particular tradition. In the face of what others propose as human value, faith will have to animate reason in discerning what is true and authentic, in order to assume it, critically interpret it within a horizon of understanding, and re-propose it to cultural communication. The Christian community will be able to provide its contribution to the «human» authenticity of the world of humanity, beyond the confines of explicit faith, in understanding and testimony, in conscience and for the benefit of consciences. Furthermore, in this it knows in whom to place its own trust and hope.

10 From this point of view one recalls the claim dear to the Gospels and restated persistently in the emphases proper to Vatican II theology: the image of the yeast, with the spiritual attitude it indicates, to express the meaning of the testimony of believers as care for the potential «human» fullness of life in the world. In this regard, see FUCHS J., «Vocazione e speranza. Indicazioni conciliari per una morale cristiana», in *Seminarium* 23 (1971) 491-512; RAHNER K., «Storia del mondo e storia della salvezza», in ID., *Saggi di antropologia soprannaturale*, Edizioni Paoline, Rome 1965, 497-532.

Chapter 14

Freedom and responsibility in family life

We now address the theme of the family from a specific, defined point of view. We consider the family as a place of social interaction, in that it constitutes a particular level and form of living together. Beginning with that, we will reflect on the relationship between this level of living together and the other levels of social life in order to indentify the positive opportunities therein that challenge people's free responsibility.

1
Family structure and socio-cultural diversity

In the structuring of Italian social life of just a few decades ago, the family was something different compared with what we see now. The difference between the *patriarchal* family in a rural environment up to the middle of the last century and the family comprised of three or four people in an urban situation today is such that at this level the term *family* is an *analogous* term. We are not interested here in an analysis of the factors behind the change, the distinguishing elements, and so on. What interests us is simply highlighting the fact and noting that where there is *a socio-cultural diversity in the structuring of the family there must be a corresponding diversity in the internal allocation of tasks and roles among the members of the family itself.* There is a difference between one era and another, between one geographical location and another, between one cultural environment and another. There is diversity in the relationships and bonds that constitute the family, as for example when one family consists of husband, wife and child, while another is comprised of the parents, a series of married siblings, each with respective children.

There will be a need, which *is not just a fact but becomes an ethical task*, to redefine competency and roles on the basis of concrete reality; and this has an impact, obviously, upon detailed aspects. For instance, if the wife works and must also look after the children, the «things to do» attributable to her and those attributable to the husband will not be the same as in a situation in which her task would be simply that of looking after the children and the house. This fact can be well-received or not, but it is a genuine fact, and as such it appeals to free responsibility; that is, at issue is the sincerity of consciences in searching for behavior or models of behavior that correspond to the objective reality. Such a task involves realizing the fundamental *task of objectivity that is primary in the respon-*

sibility of conscience as moral conscience. Thus, in defining competency and tasks, what «has always» been the case, what was before maintained to be good, will of course be important but not decisive; it is a matter of evaluating the actual co-presence of a plurality of needs, values, and opportunities. In any case, in the diversity of the individual cultures there will be a relation between the way in which the family is structured internally, in its composition, and the way in which the society within which the family lives is structured.

A very simple example for us in Europe is the connection between the family and a social structure that has progressed through focusing itself on the basis of criteria of production, urbanization at the service of production, and large settlements in small spaces. A society that is organized in this way creates, desires, and postulates as utilitarian to itself a small, flexible family, in which the space of *privacy* is reduced to a relationship between a few people, and which becomes functional to support the burden of the customary denial of *privacy* for personal conscience, of the lack of personal time, and of the denial of gratuitousness. Such privacy is constantly denied —and not accidentally— in a society structured on the basis of aims and rhythms of production. The amount of available free time is extremely limited, and therefore a greater intimacy of the small nuclear family —which has its small, well-confined place— is functional. If there are risks in a society thus structured, risks in the capacity for people's free responsibility, it is necessary not to confuse the satisfaction that the level of this type of intimacy can give, with its range of involvement with humanity, in which this structure becomes a functional constraint to unacknowledged all-engaging aims. This is an illustration to indicate the possible reflections on those things that seem to be self-evident and that perhaps need to be reconsidered.

Paradoxically, the needs of social interaction, which are structured *in a certain way*, can lead to wanting the small society of the family to be such that it renders its members incapable of social interaction, but still *spontaneously* capable and determined to obey the rules of such way of social interaction thus constructed, and capable also to internalize those rules in order to become *functional people.*

To a certain extent, therefore, the socio-economic structure is determining the very structure of that reality we call family, its styles of life, mediated values, and life preferences. We must not forget that, just as between individual conscience and society there is a relationship of receiving and giving, so also, between large societies (civil community or international state) and society-family, there is a relationship that is both of *receiving* and *giving*, of being conditioned and conditioning; therefore there is *space for free responsibility, and a space to «occupy»*.

In this context, the central issue I wish to emphasize is that of the *specific role* that the family is in a position to undertake and is called to undertake, with respect to human society (and likewise, with respect to the ecclesial community), that is, a role *of mediation*.

2 *The role of mediator in regard to human society*

We often use the term and concept *family* to indicate the social dimension of life, connoting and manifesting its *human* character. When one speaks of the *human family*, one is specifying something regarding the term *humanity*. It indicates a correct manner of relations; it refers to *true humanity*. When we speak of the *family of believers*, here, too, we wish to indicate a type of relationship. In some way family life has assumed the capacity to indicate—as significant image or model— what it really means to stand side by side. In the preceding discourse, we have frequently used the term «family» precisely in the sense that God's intentionality in creation is that of creating a people, a human family; it is a creation of solidarity, fraternity, and communion.

Thus, we must discern how the level of social interaction possible in the family —even though differently expressed in, for example, the patriarchal family and the small nuclear family— may be in a position to mediate the images, figures and capacities of humanity that the wider society needs, without itself producing them. The family has its own unique possibilities, not completely to be replicated at other levels of social life. Even given the fact of cultural diversity, it is in any case a matter of the life together of some people, a few compared with the whole of society. A family is a small group of people whose relationships are bound to a type of foundational relationships —which constitute the family as such— that in themselves are privileged with respect to the other usual relationships of life, because it is in the family that one is born, grows and is formed. The bonds are those of consanguinity, of relationships that develop over time, in closeness and progressiveness, in a long and continual *association*. Being gratuitously side by side develops *familiarity*, comprised of customary daily frequency, experienced reciprocity, and stability and strength of relationships.

In such conditions, the family becomes the *environment in which, more or better than elsewhere, there is the possibility of genuine formation in the capacity for correct and diversified relationships.* Within the family one experiences —in a verifiable range of social interaction— the possibility, capacity and need to correctly build relationships with different people having different characteristics, qualities and «roles». Let us take the example of a growing child. He/she discovers, assumes, understands, through the diversity of figures, the possibility/capacity of having a *good* and nevertheless significantly different relationship with mother, brother, father, grandparent, sister.

We turn now to a discussion of *correct and different relationships.* To verify the fact that there is value in diversity and to learn to live it means establishing that it is possible to have a correct relationship, to be able to see and experience it in its effects so that the *range of relationships is verifiable and testable* (for instance, these relationships are obviously not like my relationship with the head of state). Through these relationships I see what happens when individuals act in one way or another; I see what happens to me if the other person has a particular way rather than another of relating to me, so that I am able to learn to evaluate diversity through personal experience and the fact that this diversity is not purely accidental but also depends on me to the extent that I can create a change in relationships and I can verify what this change entails. All of this makes me capable of discerning what may be more or less human, what is good and what is evil, experiencing it within a daily familiarity of diversified relationships, understanding my responsibility seeing the assistance or hindrance the other person offers me, and thus seeing opportunities for openness and formation in the capacity for human co-existence. With respect to universal society, the individual finds him/herself faced with something that is disproportionate with his/her possibilities of feeling active, present, responsible in practice; he/she is not in a position to verify, as an echo, the result of one or other way of relating. In the dimension of the family, on the other hand, this is possible, and it is possible in conditions of continuity.

The *particular element* in this situation is to be able to live, experience, and understand, to have an understood experience of free responsibility lived in a verifiable reach (both in terms of the significance, the meaning of building relationships in a particular way rather than in another, and in terms of effectiveness). It means *having an understood experience,* not just intelligence and not just living through something. It is to learn to live with the other person, not in just any way whatsoever, but rather in *understanding and evaluation of the true objective situation of the other person, with his/her capacities and needs, comparing one's own real opportunities and capacities.* It is learning to live as *co-subjects*, learning to see how the result of co-existence is the result of personal gestures and choices, responsible or irresponsible decisions. Here the dimension of morality as the capacity to give oneself over can be aided by the previous liberating experience of others who have surrendered themselves to me, that is, by an at least partial experience of my life as given to me by someone whom I can recognize in his/her giving gesture. That person is the one who offers me the daily opportunity for life, the one whose face is a face of goodness. To have experienced it close at hand and familiarly, progressively and with continuity, makes me capable of being able to understand that the giving over of myself—that is, I myself becoming the face of benevolent presence— is not a losing of self, that the giving over of myself is not necessarily a loss of one's own life. So, here there is mediation—through known figures and models— of the possibility of internalizing the meaning of morality by experiencing and understanding it. And this *place* of living morality has those conditions of privilege (such as opportunity, capacity) compared with the presence of a large society as noted above.

Usually interactions such as these do not happen in a straightforward, harmonious way without problems and conflicts. But, once again, the type of specific social interaction possible in the family is privileged in being able to mediate and verify the possibility of *living conflicts by overcoming them.* The experience of conflict is something difficult, but it is not the death or end of the world, and it is not even the end of a relationship. Rather, it can even help the relationship itself develop, so that it becomes more solid, more capable of liberating the opportunities for one's good and that of others.

The experience of the presence of conflicts and their possible surmounting becomes the capacity to understand conflicts themselves, to assume them in an active and responsible manner; that is, having the capacity not to flee from everything that is presented as conflict, but being able to sense that conflict itself is called to become a *place of humanity.*

In the sphere of an extensive civil society, the individual as individual can live with conflict as the presence of a «hostile society that crushes him/her» (and in fact when there is not sufficient mediation of family life this is usually the way in which one senses and lives with social conflict). It is difficult to recapture elsewhere the possibility of family social interaction if this is not sufficiently present. To the experience of conflict and its possible overcoming —in some way it is worth recalling the role that conflicts have in personal growth— is linked the experience of actual received *solidarity*, of received benevolence, that is, the experience of integral social interaction and a capacity for gift as a possible reality, as a reality that is to be built ever new, entrusted to people's free responsibility.

In this context a mediation becomes possible that in some way renders transparent the *assumption and transmission of socially recognized human values*, that is, an *ethos* already present in the cultural sphere in which the family finds itself living its experience of family. Thus, the cultural and ethical data are not experienced as if coming from outside, from the unknown, from the anonymous, because they come communicated in the figures of belonging to the family itself, in their personal assumption and interpretation, in their personal tendency to live these values. Therefore, even in that experience the mediator role in regard to human society ensures that the individual does not find him/herself as if constrained to enter into a society that is foreign to him/her and imposes rules. Rather, he/she reaches that society through a personal mediation of civil and social life, through the level of humanity that is called to be incarnate in the social interaction of each situation. The importance of a similar *place of experience of social interaction as possible humanity* seen and verified in continuity, in the diversity of situations and relationships, is obvious.

There are also implications concerning the diversity of roles within the family on the part of the adults with regard to the little ones, but the reality we are speaking about indicates wider opportunities than the simple education of children, by virtue of the *dynamic of reciprocity* that concerns all the individual members. Children become such not simply by birth, just as one becomes father and mother not just through procreation, and a son becomes more than just being son, and so on within the family relationships. In the diversity of roles, complementarity and reciprocity that unite one with the other, constitute, within the family structure, a *de facto solidarity*, in which there is an intrinsic dynamic of *mutual and reciprocal enrichment* (in a positive system of assumptions).

We are accustomed to considering the help that an adolescent or young person receives in order to become an adult. Let us present the case in which this happens correctly, on the basis of the relationship that the adult has with the young person. When this happens, the young person —with what he/she has to contribute as young person— helps the adult to be an adult; adults, too, *become such*, even after they already are. A case in point is the relationship between a young person and his/her father or mother, a number of years older, at the moment of inevitable change of sensitivity (which is socially visible and of course can also bring a strongly-marked confrontation of life styles, due to a powerful socio-cultural change in a short time). The young person is born and grows with the changes of society, and therefore is a child of this movement and is at ease in it; but he/she might not notice that there is something else, that there are historic roots from which he/she has to learn. In short, it is the family presence of the parent (or grandparent), which is capable of placing alongside the young person's growing youthful experience a wisdom, which is the experience of a life begun earlier and now rich in memories, and which is useful to him/her. On the other hand, the adult (the mature adult or an old person) can have difficulty in understanding the meaning of novelty, can feel him/herself cut off from the youth. Here it is not just a question of the possible level of frustration in feeling oneself cut off, but rather the fact that he/she can be rightly present with his/her contribution as an adult (or older)person, precisely at the point where the young person—in formation and growing toward maturity—knows how to mediate to him/her a positive understanding of the novelty that is arising and growing, knows how to make him/her see that in this way the world is not being turned upside down, that is, the young person knows how to *keep the adult alive*, at ease. The way of formation, therefore, is not a one-way experience; it goes *from parent to child and from child to parent.*

Obviously, this does not happen automatically; if it did there would be no need for discussion. We have personal experience of the difficulty of living that social interaction that is family life, and yet, from the ethical point of view, it is important to point out these opportunities of the family's mediator role, because to the extent that they are actual opportunities, they engage our free responsibility and they become a *task*. We are called to live these possibilities, with the knowledge that *these possibilities normally are not replicated elsewhere*; that is, it is a specific mediator role proper to family life itself. To carry out a role of mediation belongs to the meaning, to the *ratio* within life.

3

The role of mediator in regard to the church community

This point is not properly distinct from the preceding point. Here I address again some of the aspects that emerged above, making them clear from the point of view of the relationship to the church. For convenience, I also introduce some elements not highlighted before, but which likewise are valid to civil society.

Basically, all the elements that emerged in speaking about mediation on the part of the family in regard to human society, everything that was said positively—or implicitly said negatively— is also valid from the point of view of the capacity for mediation related to the church. The ecclesial community, as well, (despite the term *community*, itself an analogous term) is something sufficiently large, vast, made up of many qualities, many people, many subjects. It is a reality sufficiently broad so that the individual feels as if faced with an anonymous *quid*. Here too, at any rate, there is need for a mediation that can also be obtained elsewhere, not only in the family. It will always be a mediation of figures, made possible in our case in the relationship with believers. Nevertheless in the ecclesial community, also, there is a mediation that is in some manner typical of the family, which cannot be completely and easily recovered in other spheres of mediation. The motive of the specificity and distinctive quality of the family as mediator is due to the type of community and co-existence, the unique possibilities of social interaction that the family as such makes possible by virtue of its constitution, through the type of bonds, and the continuity and *familiarity* of relationships it establishes. This does not happen elsewhere. Even the closest relationships (of friendship, of life in groups, associations or others) for all their grandness and nobility, for all their importance and strength, do not have those characteristics that the family has. Therefore the role of making possible a true internalization of those values, those meanings, that sense of experience, is proper to the life of the ecclesial community, as is likewise the capacity to assume all this as one's own, in free personal responsibility.

In manifesting the faith dimension, the role of the family is viewed as *communion of life*, *communion of values*, and *communion of faith*. What has become a common expression refers to the family as a *domestic church*. Of course, the term is analogous, and thus reminds us precisely of the fact that a portion of the church—and a portion of church is always where a group of believers are gathered together— has the possibility of taking on overtones of life that are domestic, those of the *domus.*

In this way one wants to show that the life of believers in the family environment is fully the life of the church, that is, of the believing community (not in the sense of being self-sufficient as church, but in the sense that it shares the life *of church*). Thus, belonging to the church does not concern just individual believers as individuals, the sum of whom then constitutes the family; but much more than that, this group is as such a believing community. The life of each person has the possibility and task of expressing the reality of church through mutual relationships. We can review the elements that emerged in the preceding section and read them in the light of a meaning that is given by revelation and salvation: that reciprocity of relationships, that mutual help, those opportunities to live humanly, which in the family can be made visible and experienced in a verifiable range, all of these have the opportunity of being expressed in explicit terms of faith, and it is to such an expression-manifestation that the believing family is called. Within this family is the possibility of verifying, on the basis of the experience of the other person and in the experience of life with the other person, what it means to truly interpret, in life, a specific human value as a Christian value, as capable of expressing one's own adherence of faith, capable of liberating a transparent morality because it is rooted in Christ. One also calls to mind the virtue that we call *hope* and that we qualify as a *theological virtue.* It must not be built in a vacuum, but rooted in a human experience of trust. Beginning with the understanding of trust in the other person, from this capacity to trust —which has arisen and has been experienced and in which it is seen that one's own life can develop through the other person— a greater trust can be understood and also manifested, a trust that comes from on high and is theological hope.

Here once again at issue is the relationship between human and Christian, natural and supernatural. The *supernatural* is defined as such by us not just by the fact of being higher and greater than which is natural, but also by the fact that it is inserted and rooted in what is natural. *Gratia non destruit, sed supponit et perficit naturam.* This statement is also valid from the point of view of ethical experience and ethical experience lived in faith, of being humanly capable of morality and having a morality redeemed by God's intervention, by grace, by the strength of the Spirit.

Obviously, this discourse on the mediator role of the family in regard to the believing community is a somewhat demanding topic, which today seems to hark back strongly to the fact of a specific responsibility. It draws attention to the importance of a genuinely experienced unity between the social and ecclesial dimensions, a genuinely experienced unity between what one usually does and the internal understanding or the spiritual life, between the moment of secular action and the moment of prayer, between the secularity of daily life —the many tasks, obligations, and so on— and the liturgical gesture.

I am able to speak to an adult person about the Christian role of commitment in social issues, but this discourse could be understood as a juxtaposition between a duty in the secular field and a duty that belongs to the responsibility of witness as a believer. How different, though, is the situation in which there is a pre-understanding of the lived experience of human values and a plain and immediate sense of commitment to social issues, which he/she has seen grow alongside the search for sincerity in faith. From the figures alongside him/her in the family and in the course of his/her development, a person may have learned to see how a public matter (positive or negative), a problem about the neighbor (or the area, or the city, or war on another continent) can become an object of concern, attention, commitment and prayer, and how this last element is not added by accident, but can be the entrance to the pathway of understanding. A similar integration between human value and value of faith, between living the human experience and the various levels of social commitment, manifests in a faith context that which gives ultimate meaning to this commitment itself, namely that it requires a lengthy mediation to become a reality that touches our intelligence and hearts. It must appear in figures of conscience, in human faces, in real people, in styles of life, in daily attitudes; this is what becomes mentality, which becomes the capacity to *structure* one's own conscience. The contribution that the family at this level can give is, according to the reasoning of the previous point, entirely its own, characteristic and specific, only partially accessible through other places of experience and conscience. Of course, in saying this the limitations and negative aspects present when there is not an authentic experience of family are implicitly underlined.

There is yet another aspect, still linked to the mediator role. The family is called to be a *place of internalization* and at the same time to have an *openness to human problems* broader than just *to understand in faith*.

To be at once both the place of internalization and of openness means that the moment of lived understanding —made possible in a privileged manner within the sphere of social interaction which is the family— also concerns at the same time becoming aware of the fact that one's own innermost being, just like the close relationships with the people with whom one is living and the satisfaction linked to that, are not everything in life. It is a question of sensing how taking an interest in the other person who is not close as a family member, or to have responsibility and commitment external to the family, are not in competition with loyalty, sincerity and communion of life within the family; external responsibilities can even assist in ensuring that closeness does not become a direct demand for satisfaction, that is, the search for self, because when this happens, closeness itself can *explode* (in fact it only takes two people to become intolerant, two people searching for themselves). Instead, the capacity to be at the same time present and responsible elsewhere allows for a more balanced understanding of the problems within family life itself that one lives through. It helps to understand the problems that affect me closely, my capacity or incapacity to relate, my reactions and non-reactions, the expectations I have toward the other person. To understand one's own affairs in a broader perspective means a greater capacity for objectivity, greater freedom.

There is therefore an internal link of meaning between what we have called internalization and openness. To be able to experience this connection, to be able to live it, is a fact that is liberating for growth in maturity, for a capacity for responsibility, and to allow me to live without fleeing. Now, the faith dimension, if it is capable of integrating these elements, ensures that in a basically harmonious way one can live one's own presence within the family nucleus, in the wider society, and in the church. Thus one can live the various levels as mutually interdependent, as mutually whole. It is a matter of establishing the bases of experience and understanding for that *personal unity* by virtue of which the subject understands that stopping to pray is important for the effectiveness of one's social action and that social action is important for the sincerity of one's prayer, and that both are important for the possibility of true unity within the family.

To live all of this, however, does not happen spontaneously when one is externally exposed to the attraction of a thousand different tendencies. Here one reconsiders the various elements from our previous point, including that of the relationship between adults and the reciprocity of the relationship between adult and non-adult and between adults of different generations.

The importance of being mindful of *contemporary attention on inner solidarity and external participation* thus seems obvious in that the other places of social interaction and the other places of church must be present with their specific characteristics and possibilities; they must be correctly integrated between themselves, so that they become integral to the personality of the subjects, whether as human growth and development or as a journey of development in faith. This also becomes a problem of having (of finding, because usually it does not come by itself) sufficient space and time to defend against an all too common intrusiveness of anonymous and, even worse, hidden planners. Here too the emphasis is on the capacity to assume in free responsibility, individually and together—this *together*, in regard to the family and from this point of view, is of extreme importance— the various elements of one's own choices and decisions, the various guiding elements in the concrete use of time, interests, what concerns me and what does not concern me. Life, commitments, and choices, cannot be honestly entrusted to chance. The term *chance*, then, from a social point of view, does not mean what was once termed *fate*. In truth it refers to choices and activities not openly visible but real, which are programmed by *whoever can* program the life of others. It is not worth lamenting the fact that others program me if I allow myself to be programmed; therefore the problem of defending sufficient space and time is correlative to that of the preceding discourse. If it is true that external presence is necessary for internal endurance and strength, it is also true that this will not be so without the necessary space and time to care for the internal relationship between family members; it will therefore be necessary to assess and make choices, establishing criteria for suitable and sufficient bounds, rhythms and ways (ways, too, because it is one thing to be together going to see a film or a match on TV, and it is another to be together with attention focused on what more directly builds up relationships between individuals). In effect, to decide on these elements is to assume care for family life as one's own; to not decide is to leave to others the decision about what provides the quality of internal relationships in the family, and it is fairly clear that, given the current structuring of co-existence and given the relationships between society and the family, it would be easier if all that one does in the family would basically be programmed from outside, even up to the hours devoted to it and how the time is spent. Basically one is persuaded to live the space given to so-called free time in a certain way, always functional to a society organized so that everything, even closeness, can possibly be programmed, targeted to *other* aims in regard to family life (and to other, that is different aims in regard to the meaning of human life). It is certainly not concern for people's humanity and morality that leads to the choosing of the objectives of these hidden planners.

These hidden planners, however, are not demons; they are identifiable personal realities, even if it is difficult to identify the specific realities, because often they consist of many things and above all, the confluence of manifold interests.

This capacity for planning (the topic links to previous themes) is linked to submission, to the practical acceptance of a rationale, to the assent of many, because the effectiveness of that planning is the effectiveness of concrete results that are obtained precisely through the «yes» given by individuals. Thus, however much it might be difficult to overcome these problems, it must be noted that if the space for personal freedom is not great, it becomes even smaller if we allow it to escape; and the place we call family is a place of social interaction in which, despite the difficulties, it is easier to overcome these forces, because one is not individually exposed to them. Internal solidarity is both an element that helps *to protect oneself from* and an element that one protects, because the family's resolve for other goals tends to assert itself precisely against this type of internal solidarity. This reality also applies to the family-church relationship, because the church, too, can be understood and experienced as a social reality to be made *efficient* in its structure, in what it does. In this case there is an obviously positive aspect in that it is necessary to seek ways of effective presence, to create structures. But there is also an inherent danger, because what could easily surface again (the models are intercommunicable) is the style of relationship between civil organizations and the family, so that all things considered, the organization church lives and the organization family lives, each as basically utilitarian to themselves. Now, precisely through the meaning that the church's life has, it is necessary to overcome this temptation, because the *role* of individuals and the family itself in the church is not a functional role, similar to internal roles in a business organization. It is strange that sometimes the confusion between the ends and the means becomes so persuasive, so capable of permeating sensitivities that one doesn't even realize when the aim has been manipulated to various and sundry ends.

In this entire situation there is clearly present a question of major formative value (which is valid for young and old) in regard to the growth of free personal responsibility. In fact, it is important that one can sense and see how the growth, the maturing of free personal responsibility be entrusted to us and be for us a task that is possible to accomplish. Not only am I free and responsible, but I am called to be so; and I will *no longer* be free and responsible if I am not examining, understanding, internalizing, not closing in on myself and therefore caring for my inner self. In regard to this responsibility for one's own formation, for one's own growth and, once again, for the mediator role of the family—even toward the Church—becomes a reality that is difficult to replace.

4
Advantages and difficulties in generational encounters

We begin with two simple reflections. The first reflects on the fact that generational encounters are *to be protected* and the second on the fact that they are encounters of *mutual formation.*

In reference to an encounter to be protected, in a certain sense it might seem inevitable that this is the case, even though there may be some difficulty about the way it is so. In reality, however, even family structuring and the manner of living family life today, pressurized by a series of influences, tends to assume a significant limitation from this point of view. All things considered, and always having in mind the so-called nuclear family—the small or very small family—there is a tendency to ensure that the encounter between the generations will be as restricted as possible, basically concerning just parents and their children. At the same time there is a tendency to ensure that little ones avoid experiences of grief, sickness and death, as if almost wanting to make the family a *nest*, a place in which one is protected from any disturbing element or *extraneous* factor. Sickness is a reality to be kept out of the family, something to come into contact with only indirectly, and as soon as it is something serious, it belongs elsewhere, all the more so if it is a sickness that might last, which would therefore present a handicap, a burdensome presence. Death is better if it does not happen in the home. The fewer signs there are about this reality the better. The child must not know these things; it would be a trauma. This becomes so much more obvious, so much more felt in fact—even if not theorized—when it is a matter of this inconvenience possibly occurring in the house and involving for example, grandfather or grandmother, perhaps old, perhaps not self-sufficient.

There are incidental factors—of an economic, psychological, logistical nature, and so on—that make difficulties of this kind easier; but the idea also seems to creep in that a presence like that of a very old person, someone not self-sufficient, someone seriously ill, someone dying is at the least useless, from the point of view of the formation of the child. (We are using this perspective, which is not the only one, but perhaps the most obvious). At times the presence of a very old person is felt not just to be useless, but even counterproductive, negative, as a reality from which the child should be protected. It is a foreign body in the *nest*, a cold body, something disturbing. In this case, the reflection to be made is that *we do not learn to live if we do not know death.*

We must consider —not as a marginal issue in a fundamental moral theological reflection— the necessity and possibility of overcoming fear of death, and with that, the fear of suffering, of difficulties, of all that basically destroys, constrains, restricts. *Knowing* (in the Semitic sense of the word) suffering, sickness, difficulties, and obstacles belongs to life, to the wisdom of life, to the human capacity to be responsibly present. Seeing that life is not to be identified with the absence of obstacles, we understand that hope and trust, although perhaps difficult, are necessary presuppositions.

This understanding constitutes the first level of *difficulties and advantages in the encounter between the generations*, because obviously if an elderly person is present, there is another generation in comparison. It is clear that the elderly person cannot always be present concretely, due to particular conditions of family life; however, in this case, there is always another way of making the person *present*, of not being a stranger to that person, of not making that person totally absent as if he/she did not exist. The sensitivity indicated a short while ago, that of wanting to protect the growth of children regarding this reality of life, carries within itself a somewhat strange attitude. It is a bit like wanting to teach someone to swim but avoiding all risks, even to the point of hiding the reality, and so the baby is held —out of the water.

Such an attitude means deceiving oneself with the idea that life is an endless game in which others think of all that is onerous, and I must defend myself from difficulties. Thus, I will learn only how to escape, to expect from others, to accuse others. In this way the family does not mediate a capacity for social life, because to social life belongs, not in a marginal or subsequent way, not subordinate but essential, the ability of succeeding in living through difficulties, of succeeding in taking into account these daily realities even when we seek to exorcize them, and of trying to build a protective environment for life in regard to all that has a ring of suffering and death.

Even if at a different level, internally close to this in meaning, the problem is raised about the value, difficulty, and limitation coming from the possible hardship of the encounter between the generations. In such an encounter one truly must contend with a mutual understanding that does not come about spontaneously, that instead must be sought, created and built. One is actually contending with a diversity that is objectively comprised of biological and psychological life rhythms, with the multiplicity that we constantly meet in human life. One is constantly confronted with the difficulty that comes from the fact of being born and living in a specific, concrete context marked with a precise date and a precise environment and relationships; the difficulty I will have in regard to the other person in order to succeed in understanding, in developing dialogue, to succeed in being able to listen so as to be able to speak meaningfully with someone who has been born at a very different time, and with all that this entails in terms of relations, experience, understanding of values and opportunities in life.

We have experienced, especially in recent years, this difficulty of the relationship between the generations, which also seemed to be *the* problem of co-existence. The *underlying temptations*, or rather the temptations always present when faced with this type of difficulty, are the usual ones: that of *denying the fact*, or that of *declaring it impossible to be responsible for the situation and thus to escape it.*

At the end of the day the outcome is the same. To act as if the person or the difficult situation did not exist, to live *as if the person did not exist*, to do everything so that problems are not created, is obviously a form of *denying the other person* as such. It is withdrawal in on oneself, even when it is done by a group instead of individually.

A family that tends to avoid these realities fails in its precise role, because at the point at which the encounter between the generations is problematic (in the sense of difficult), the family structure is implicated for its failure to recognize that its significance and specific possibilities, as recalled previously, constitute the privileged place for making these tensions visible, for experiencing the possibility of overcoming them, learning not to flee from them, learning not to give importance only to what is immediately useful and fruitful, learning not to hang on to what and whose presence can be previously evaluated as positive in its outcomes. The family should be a place for making possible an *acceptance/assumption of the limitations themselves*, experiencing and understanding what is possible, and that even the limitations are not just limiting, but rather also a way of surmounting and transcending. Growth by internalizing these opportunities, these perspectives that become significant for a subject's life, is undoubtedly one of the most important elements in the family's mediator role. Without it, it will then be difficult when in the social sphere the conditions of elderly people are taken very seriously, when they cannot earn and are no longer useful in terms of functionality or the economy. When this occurs their presence will be easily viewed as a burden, and it will be difficult to see their positive role as people in society. The perception of older people as a social burden is already present, and perhaps we must recognize the fact that it will become even more so, given the tendency in the western world to differentiate between the elderly adult and the adult population, in which it is primarily the latter that performs work and production and decision-making.

In light of these realities, a role that the family can promote at a radical level of formation of conscience is truly the positive possibility, from the ethical point of view, that this place of experience that we call family teaches not to privilege ourselves (and one's own group) and not to assume one's own benefit as the decisive criterion in making choices. If that doesn't happen, it seems obvious there is a possibility that at least close conflicts will not only be «generational», but might also extend and become greater depending on the incapacity to focus on shared and commonly pursued goals and aims, with all the connected political implications, in the sense of even more fragmentation and division, aggravating the tensions, and so on; because obviously the rationale of all that is supportive of me, while at the same time of nothing —basically— of what hinders me or places restrictions on me, will make quite problematic (and makes it so already) a correct social life in a situation in which the one who decides and the one who needs are not the same person and do not belong to the same group or the same age group.

Let us now consider the fruits of pulling apart the interests in the relationship between genuine need and the possibility of suitable decisions. One thinks of pressure groups, the manipulation of information, and economic-productive and political-administrative power groups, and at the level of small societies, individual states, and also at the level of international relations. In this context, the perspective of a worsening of difficulties in the relationship between the generations raises the possibility of an additional level in the pulling apart of interests and possibilities for decisions, with the consequences that one can perhaps already imagine.

In any case, this is a discourse about possible consequences; and it is opportune now to return to the discourse about the fundamental meaning. There is a formative value in the role the family is called to undertake, which is intimately linked with the capacity to become responsible, and therefore with the capacity of freedom as morality. This formative value consists in *learning to accept actual, concrete limitations*, seeing that they are not just burdens and obstacles, but *the locus* of our life, of our possible humanity.

This means learning to accept the limitations that come from the difficulties of understanding, from the diversity of mentalities, eras, cultural worlds; a formative value, therefore, in learning to overcome every temptation to escape and every temptation to deny the reality of objective difficulty. From this one understands the fact that in the encounter between the generations there is a relationship that basically can be—it is not automatic and it must be nurtured—of *mutual formation. One becomes* father, mother, brother, sister, cousin; *one becomes* son, daughter, nephew, adult, old person; *people become* such with diversified relationships that can always be appropriate, relationships with the other person in the diversification of roles and tasks, bonds, ages and mentalities, personal capacities. The young person can mediate the experience of the present, the adult and old person can mediate the experience of the past-present, which is never a pure past because it is present in them. They can mediate appreciation of the positive that is now present; the young can mediate to them the experience of the positive present and that which is expected, the goals toward which one is heading; and it is only through the integration of these two directions of mediation, that one can find a way, a way of sharing, a means of planning goals, a structuring ordered to the goals of the ways of co-existence even including the institutions themselves; a way of living the existing institutions from within —and the dynamics of relationship, strength, trends that there are— so that one can speak of a human way of co-living. Here too it is worth recalling that the fact of the «leaving-out-of», or someone's «not-interested in» is always a situation of not being free, of not being capable of humanity; it is, at one and the same time, an offense against the other person and an *offense* (in the sense of internal wound) of one's own personhood as human, as moral; it is a failure in one's own task of humanity, of ethical conscience.

When the encounter between the generations is realized in a positive way, it becomes the place for *mutual help in living in a reconciled manner and therefore also for being reconcilers.* To live in a reconciled way means living with an internal deepening unity that does not come from the prospective exclusion of what one encounters as contradictory to one's own personal free growth, but rather from the capacity to *order* one's own life and one's own co-existence with others. We suggest that the capacity to be reconciled with people of another generation (with all that this entails) is reconciliation with oneself; it is the capacity to not lose one's way, to not be concerned, to not live in fear —once again— of all that *destroys* and of the destroying realities, in the sense of those things that restrict in our daily lives and are not just beyond ourselves, but rather within us as well. There is a relationship between succeeding and being at peace with the other person and succeeding and accepting oneself, because what we are —even to ourselves— is not a sort of ideal *that we can fashion and desire for us; it is rather a being*, a *given being*, which comes to us also and not incidentally from the cultural environment that is constructed and modeled by the manifold relationships with other people.

When I project an ideal image of myself, it is not identical to what I see, so to speak, looking in the mirror, nor what I recognize in looking at myself in conscience and truly understanding who I am, with my limitations. The personal limitation is not external; it belongs to me. And the capacity to accept one's own limitations is linked to the capacity to accept someone else's limitations; it is fundamentally linked to the capacity to accept the *limitation* that comes to me from the fact of another person's being.

In what sense here can one speak of *reconciliation*? Since it concerns seeing that the limitation whose name is *you*—that is, the other person— is not just a limitation, is not even primarily a limitation, but is a value for me, makes me a person, liberates me, makes me capable of liberating. Therefore we can speak of reconciliation. And so the capacity to accept the otherness becomes capacity to accept the otherness that I discover already within myself, because I am not the fruit of my hands. From the point of view of the capacity to assume them, as from the point of view of their genesis for the person, external and internal limitations are very close and linked between them. Paradoxically, then, the encounter with the other person (and the capacity for dialogue between the generations) shapes me, makes me possible, facilitates self-understanding and self-acceptance. Thus, reconciliation with the other person is reconciling for me, with my inner self.

Regarding the fact that someone internally reconciled may be a reconciling presence, it is sufficient to recall what has already been said about the influence that through the concrete ways of living and through the concrete ways of speech, we exercise in shaping the relationship between consciences, portraying a figure of conscience that presents itself in speaking, doing, and being in relationship. Once again at issue is the *relationship between interiority and externals*: the spirit that makes up the body, the inner personality that makes the *social body*, and the personal individual experience that becomes a contribution to the constitution of social corporeality, in the sense of conditions, structuring, and the foundations of history. It is fairly obvious the extent to which an internally reconciled conscience may be a condition of the true capacity for responsibility and true capacity for freedom.

Passing reference has just been made to the fact that obviously this discourse is similarly valid both for the mediator role of the family in regard to civil society and for its role in regard to ecclesial life. In regard to this role and ecclesial life, ecclesial life is also a level of social interaction, social interaction *in faith*, but which becomes visible and historic in a community. Here as well, there is a connection with a past (at least we are all somewhat aware of it). We can be tempted to exorcize the present burden of this past, but it would be like wanting to erase from the lived and daily experience of one's own responsibility the figure of the *grandfather*'s presence, so to speak, and the works of his generation. It is like wanting to avoid considering the fact that we are children (and grandchildren and great-grandchildren) of this past of the church, in good and bad.

To want to forget this —at an ecclesial level as well, just as at a social level— would be to want to cut off one's own roots. In a certain sense such a temptation is quite strange, because it seems that we would be living our present existence in a negative way, without appreciating the value of the past that gives us meaning and authenticity as believers today, without seeing that the past is, in its inner reality and not as simply historical-chronological succession, a gift interwoven with what the preceding generations handed down to us (not just to the first generations). If today we understand something from the Gospel, it is made possible for us by that visibility and historicity, that *social corporeality* that constitutes the past experience and reflection of faith and historical behavior lived by those who went before us. Even when, in the name of the Gospel or in the name of transparency of conscience, we challenge something that belongs to the heritage handed down to us, in its historic forms and expressions; even such a possibility of criticism is because of the links that we have with the past, which are the thousand ways of mediating an experience of a *traditio*, both of faiths and ethics. In the name of faith —that is, with the possibility of faith experience historically handed down to us by this church— we challenge the actual validity of certain expressions from the past. It could be said that the temptation of rejecting the past is basically suicidal, a tendency toward futility. An inadequate expression from the past may be like a tool that is basically contradictory to its purpose, but it nevertheless can assume capacities for communication, opportunities for the transmission of values, of human authenticity, Christian truth, and both human and Christian truth about life. One cannot see how one can live in the present with little interpretation of the past beginning from the present, without an interpretation of the present, which is understood beginning with and by virtue of that past, which is still present because it is becoming present, and which is the wisdom of those who, having experienced before us an authentic search for faith and morality, are in a position to hand it on to us *faced with the new that is developing.*

We can also verify how incapacity in the encounter between the generations is usually transformed into a similar incapacity within the same generation. A simple illustration: Someone who has lived for ten years of his/her life—for example, between the age of 20 and 30— incapable of living out a correct, calm, reconciled relationship with those who are twenty or thirty years older, most likely at thirty will not be capable of having a correct and reconciled relationship with someone who is five years younger. It seems that with age this dynamic worsens. If one imagines a person who begins to walk, in the world or in the church, trying to create the capacity for relationships *ex novo*, where objectively relationships are difficult, what will it be like for that person? If instead we are accustomed to forming relationships in an environment that permits a style of relationships whose range and daily character is verifiable, and therefore, one has the capacity in the family for effective familiarity in relationships, here one finds a mediation that is not theoretically necessary, but certainly difficult to access in other contexts or environments.

At this point we can recall the objection: yes, this is wonderful, but the families we know are not like this; the families we know are on average incapable of undertaking such a role, at least in the full sense of the mediation expected; families tossed here and there, hardly consistent, incapable of finding their own space, incapable of establishing themselves according to a reasonable, thought-out and furthermore always correct and suitable plan; families that collapse, married couples that separate again and again, with the consequences that stem from that for children, and so on. Therefore, in reality, what mediation is there?

Usually when we present an ethical reflection we begin with the negative experience, the experience of injustice, for example, which prompts us to speak about justice. Thus, it is a matter of identifying an evil of which we are aware, to see where it is rooted, recognizing thereby that it is not unavoidable. This will not be done without identifying positive possibilities that at least in embryo we have historically seen and experienced. From these possibilities the morally important value perspectives can be identified.

The aspect from which I have attempted to view the problematic area of *family* in its contemporary situation (and undoubtedly today there are significant problems concerning the family), prompts me to reflect in the way outlined above: that of underlining specific human values, important for morality, that normally happen in one's own story when one has a strong experience of the absence of those values.

The problem in this case is not that of deciding *which locks* to put on an institution or life style; it is not a question of finding remedies as an answer to symptoms; the problem is not that of a symptomatic cure. Awareness of a negative reality leads us to as calm a reflection as possible, which is not caught up in the difficulties perceived, but which may actually be a reflection about meaning. It is a question of identifying the indications that are able to free the capacity to find suitable ways and means, not for a symptomatic cure, but for introducing positive elements about healthy life in regard to the sick reality. This is the meaning of the reflection we have carried out.

There is a *weakness* itself about ethical reflection. From the viewpoint of a general reflection on a value or an issue, the reflection does not provide a concrete solution; this is a weakness, but at the same time, a great *opportunity.* The so-called, oft-invoked *concrete solution*, more often than not is not a concrete solution, due to the fact that it is only concrete and not a solution. That always happens where important human values are concerned and one gives in to the temptation of the pretend solution of a *symptomatic cure*, which is never a solution.

Chapter 15

Authority and obedience

1

The analogous use of terms

The concepts of authority and obedience occur in ethical and theological discourse with similar meanings. The *similitudo dissimilis* in meaning calls for attention to the diversity of these terms and the subjects and relationships being discussed in reference to God, conscience, and human co-existence (in the church and in society). In reference to God's authority the believer interprets the meaning and value of every other authority; all authority comes from God (*Rom* 13:1). This entails the need for believers to understand and assume the task of conscious and free responsibility both in the exercise of authority and in the exercise of obedience. Human authority does not replace that of God; it is not placed alongside it nor in competition with it.

It can be said that, as giving significance to the meaning of *auctoritas*, the *analogatum princeps* is the authority of God. This also means recognizing that, when we continue to use the same term with reference to human authority, precisely because it is analogous, we must not forget the *dissimilitudo*. When we speak of *God's authority*, we mean a term of absolute reference; when we speak of *human authority* we mean a term of reference that, important though it is, is never absolute. When we speak of the *authority of conscience*, we speak of a term of reference that is not absolute in the same way in which we speak of *absolute* God. On the other hand, it is not even relative in the same way in which the term «authority» is relative when we use it with regard to a civic authority. The authority of conscience speaks of a *human absoluteness*, in the sense that faced with it, we are absolutely bound, while in the face of human authority we are indirectly bound (and the correspondence works precisely through conscience). In this sense, the authority of conscience is actually what can be called *delegated* from God's authority, inasmuch as the ethical normativity, the normative worth of a value, in the mediation of conscience is recognized as God's will. Obviously, that also concerns the correlative term *obedience*.

With regard to the term obedience, it is worth recalling that we are speaking about it inasmuch as it designates a *human* behavior, or rather a free and responsible one, in regard to a particular type of relationship due to specific roles (as we will see later). Only as free responsibility does obedience belong to the *moral* experience. If the term were leaning toward a suggestion of meaning in which one of the aspects —freedom and responsibility— were excluded, it would no longer be a *virtue;* it would no longer be a morally significant term.

2 *Authority as a social reality*

The fact that there are people in authority roles reminds us that we are in the presence of a social phenomenon. Authority and obedience are realities belonging to the social structuring of interpersonal relations. In a different way, in regard to its concrete expressions and the way of sanctioning it, the being of an authority is a phenomenon present at all levels of life as a *social body.*

In the family, in civil society, in the church, in every institution that has come into being creating a structured form of co-existence, the phenomenon of *authority* always appears, even though in different forms. It is a fact which within a social group, because this social group functions, gives itself something we can call *exercise of authority.* Its development and the multiplicity of its forms of being are a fact. The diversity of forms is connected with different historic moments. An historic moment does not refer simply to a date, but rather to a complex totality of social and cultural factors that structure the ways of life, its opportunities and restrictions, from the way of thinking and feeling to the ways of behavior. One thinks of the «historic moment» of the family in Ancient Rome, of the so-called patriarchal family of 50 years ago in the rural areas of the Veneto, of the situation today of the very small family living in a city apartment. We rightly give the same name «family» to an institution which, however, has assumed different forms. The corresponding authority figure is itself diverse, even if we rightly denote it with the same term «authority», as rightly we call «father» the different figure to whom authority is attributed. One thinks of a family today, living in a city apartment and with a housekeeper; toward this person the father of the family has a role that is different from that which the little son has toward the housekeeper: but that is not the same as the role (the relationship between the two people) that the *paterfamilias* of Ancient Rome had in regard to the *famulus* member of the family.

In time, every institution tends to modify its way of expressing and justifying itself. Internally, even the role of authority varies, corresponding to the variations of the institution itself. The diversity of forms is linked to the changeable self-understanding of the social groups, for example, the authority of the absolute monarch is not the same as the authority—sometimes even hardly identifiable— of a government in a democracy. The different ways of understanding society, and therefore the different ways of structuring social institutions, bring a diversity in the *way of exercising* that same function. It can be said that variation in the exercise of authority is linked to the meaning of authority, which is functional to the society in which it is exercised.

3 *Authority as meaning*

The constancy in the discussing of the phenomenon of authority in relation to society indicates that we are dealing with a function that reveals itself as necessary to human co-existence (that is, as *societas*). Even in its development in history, it shows itself to be necessary. In this sense we can say that authority (the being of an authority, respect for it, laying down conditions for its correct exercise) is something that belongs to *lex naturae.*

It may be said without misunderstandings that human co-existence, social interaction of our lives, belongs to the *lex naturae* as such; authority belongs there as a function for the possibility of manifesting and bringing about reasonable social co-existence. *Lex naturae*, therefore, as a function ordered to a goal of human «nature», which is the pursuit of the common good of the *societas*, is at heart, the very being of this social interaction of life *as social interaction.* In other words, the being, the exercise, the respect of authority as such, is an opportune task in terms of natural law, inasmuch as it is (tends to be, is protected as) a function of the *social being* of a social body. Thus, it will de facto be conditioned by social consent within the individual society (in which is always expressed a specific way of authority). Social consent on the basis of authority itself and the way of exercising it and its being targeted to the common good appears de facto necessary.

This does not mean that such consent must necessarily be manifested in a formal manner, and even less that it must be so in the usual way in contemporary democracies. It means simply that, for example, at the moment in which within a specific society there is no longer the consensus previously present about an authority shaped as a monarchy, because that form is no longer believed to be suitable for the society itself, at that moment such authority is no longer justified, and another form of authority must be found, precisely for the same reason for which the one before (the monarchy) was believed and judged to be valid and therefore was sanctioned.

The judgment about the fact that a form of authority is or isn't suitable is based on its working for the common good. Authority is not modified simply on the basis of a common and sufficiently socialized judgment about its working or not; the exercise of authority must be judged on the basis of its pursuit of the common good and its functionality to the common good, because herein lies its meaning and its human *goodness*, reasonably suggested.

We have already mentioned that the meaning of authority says something about basic needs so that its exercise may be morally positive. Authority, as a specific task of caring for the common good, engages personal free responsibility in this task. It must be a specific expression of solidarity, as care for the common reaching out for the common good.

4
Obedience to human authority

In the case of *obedience* as a human reality (of course «human» should not be confused with «non-Christian»), the context for any discourse is that of a form of *structured social life:* a specific society (in one way or another) and, within it and at the service of it, a way of relating that we call obedience. *Obedience* means free responsibility for the common good on the part of every person, in relation to those people who have as a specific function and task the «care of the community». Obedience is fundamentally an expression of solidarity. To be a morally positive reality in each case, it will have to express personal assumption, in conscious and free responsibility, of the needs of human coexistence, with its actual implications in the context in which one lives. The need for «coordination» of the common striving for the common good is one of the *actual implications.* Therefore, the meaning of obedience as a virtue will be that of *privileging the common good compared with the individual good,* understood as private and privately pursued (that is, understood in an individualistic way). More specifically, the understanding of the individual good itself will be as internally linked to the common good, which is defined by the *interpersonal nature of human life.* Thus, obedience as virtue will be the expression-realization of interhuman solidarity.

An element within the fundamental significance of obedience is that any form of «realization» that is not an avenue of concrete, free and responsible assumption of one's own co-responsibility toward the common good would not be obedience.

Clearly this means that from the outset it is already obvious (given that we know a bit about life together) that to obedience belongs something that is expressed in the vocabulary of *renunciation* (with regard to will, desire, ones own intentions).

However, it must be noted that it is «renunciation» in the sense that calls into question free «responsibility». In this sense, someone who in no way wishes to renounce him/herself, will not be capable of obeying, due to the simple fact of being unable or not wanting to seek the moral good. The same dynamic applies in assuming what here and now is good and just for me (and one will not succeed in understanding this for-me aside from the for-us) that gives meaning to obedience as a *virtuous attitude and gesture*. Thus, just as care for correct obedience (where «correct» means *true*, not disguised, not barely done, but sincere and adult) is part of the correct exercise of authority, so also care for the correct exercise of authority is part of the responsibility for correct obedience. Just as with the law and moral norms, so also we say that the person is not simply responsible *in the face of* authority, but rather is also responsible *for* authority, that is, so that it may be correctly exercised, insofar as it depends on his/her free responsible contribution. Thus, just as with the ethical norm, here too is valid not just obedience in that it is commanded, but obedience as far as it is *justly commanded*, and this implies that responsibility is suited to the possibilities of each person, with care so that what is commanded be *correctly commanded* (that is, because what is commanded is just).

These clarifications are important for understanding authority and obedience and their relationship, just as it is important that the same clarifications be understood and experienced in such a way as not to thwart authority and obedience. We can say that probably, if both roles are experienced in a correct manner, historically *conflicts* will arise, due to the objective difficulties and different interpretations of them. In this context of experience as well, it is essential that conflicts be neither avoided nor disguised, but that one attempts to discover their *meaning* and their *correct resolution*. It will be said that this does not make things easy, but we are not looking for the facilitation of things or their simplification, nor for the negation of the human depth of our lives and the ethical importance of our responsibilities. The terms of reference that come up again are always the same: what it is to which one aspires (the end, the *bonum commune*), what is useful to this end, and with what tools that end is pursued. The description and identification of the end, as common good, in the concrete assessment will have some *variations*. Variations in the goal, in the concrete assessment, will lead, with lesser or greater importance, to variations in the identification of the means and the way those means are used, and therefore also in the determination of the truly correct manner of the exercise of authority and obedience. With the respective possibilities, capacities and roles, no one can avoid the responsibilities (and the co-responsibilities) of the function of roles, the exercise of roles, the use of means, and therefore of the real pursuit of the end (otherwise it would be *flatus vocis* to say that pursuit of the common good is a common task).

5 *The foundation of authority and obedience*

For a believer it is fairly clear that for authority and obedience, as well as for everything that has meaning and value in human life, the ultimate foundation is God. There are two further statements to add.

God the creator makes the human person capable of living, capable of understanding life, capable of organizing his/her life and therefore his/her social life. As creator, he is the ultimate foundation of authority and obedience; he makes them active and positively effective through the responsibility of those creatures to whom he has given the capacity to organize their own lives in a reasonable and full way (according to *recta ratio*).

God the redeemer of humanity reminds us not to forget the need for an outlook in which the concrete appears to us not only in its guises, but also in its foundation of hope. If God is the redeemer of humanity, he is therefore, in addition to being creator, also redeemer of *human meaning* and the *human possibility of living the meaning* of authority and obedience themselves. In this sense, also, the relationship of authority and obedience must be experienced in terms of faith, without separating the human from the «Christian», but rather by succeeding in recognizing a human that can become so *human* as to have the capacity of signifying *beyond* the human (that is, beyond what is immediately visible and quantifiable as immediate outcomes here and now), so as to testify by it to God's saving presence.

Recognizing in God their ultimate foundation, we must remember that the direct foundation of authority and obedience is their *relationship to the common good.* One can speak about the «direct foundation», because it can be identified, just as one can verify the connection, functionality, and appropriateness of the ways assumed and instruments used. Every claim, right, and affirmation of validity about human authority and obedience to it must be indicated in its visible and explicit relationship with the common good, just as the morality of any behavior must be able to be indicated and manifested on the basis of the worth of the values one chooses and their relationship to the worth of the values of others (those that are omitted or those that one accepts as contradictory). When there is not this capacity *to indicate the meaning* (on the basis of the relationship with the direct foundation), or when one does not wish to recognize the need to do it (both from the point of view of authority and that of obedience), obviously there is a pretense of justifying behavior on the basis of an arbitrary and not objective preference, as, for example, by virtue of the fact that «I affirm» what is just. The content of the value affirmed could be materially just or false, but the conduct would be morally bad in each case.

In every society it is necessary to know *who is* the person who exercises authority. It is a question of the cognitive foundation or «legitimizing» of the person in authority. This will not happen unless it involves something like *designation* or *recognition,* which as far as it regards the *manner* of its future, will be different, but which, however, must be an objective, certain indication, recognized as such, as legitimate and valid, by the society within which authority and obedience live. This process of validation is an element that belongs to the *necessary public-social visibility* of social functions. It is an element that will be determined by society itself, in regard to the way of expressing and safeguarding it. It will be the church itself that determines what is the way in which we can come to know that the Pope is that specific person and not another. Internally, the social organization of the church, as a function of its social being and being church, must indicate recognized criteria suitable for identifying who is, at various levels, the person who cares for the community, whose function is the exercise of authority. Similarly, a specific civil society itself will determine and establish on the basis of what rules and criteria the forms of government and the people designated to govern will be decided.

Thus, in the same way we can ensure that the legitimate authority of a king or president of the republic, president of a council of ministers or a mayor, is linked back to God's authority, not, however in the sense that this specific person receives authority over the community personally from God; that is, this person is not God's personally designated representative before the community. But this person, as socially indicated as the one who must care for the community and recognized as being able to do it, nevertheless will be God's representative, by virtue of his/her function and as far as this person can correctly exercise that function. In fact, if a legitimate authority (therefore recognized as such and representing God, in the civil or ecclesiastical sphere) orders that something be done that is contrary to morality, one could not recognize the will of God in that concrete exercise of authority. Instead, the will of God and authority would have to be recognized in the *voice of conscience.* This possibility of an extreme case (which does not mean a being free from obedience, but rather a *having to «disobey»* the letter of the voice of authority in order to obey God as recognized in the voice of conscience) is only explicable insofar as the ultimate foundation is understood as the foundation that is explained through human nature, in its historic and social context, and through the human and socially perceivable indication of a function (within a society, in regard to a goal to be reached); the function of authority also indicates the criteria and limitations of its exercise, as does its authoritativeness. With regard to the foundation, therefore, its levels, too, should not be confused in connection with the similar character of the concepts of authority and obedience.

6
Authority and obedience in the church

All that belongs to the significance and human possibilities of obedience and authority (that is, all that has been said up to now) is considered as directly relevant to the being and exercise of authority and obedience within the church. The fact of living these realities as virtuous human and Christian conduct, in the sphere of the common ecclesial life, will have as specificity what defines a community *inasmuch as it lives and recognizes itself in faith in Jesus Christ.* The specific common good that directs the society-church is not identical to that by which the society-family or society-state is ordered. This does not mean that it must necessarily distinguish itself in different or even opposing realities. It means that the aim of the common witness is not identical. When we speak of church we define the field by indicating this *societas* in its specificity, so that, even if it were in fact (a local church, for example) completely co-extensive with a civil society (geographically and numerically), as church we could never define it with the same «boundaries».

Authority will be at the service of that *bonum commune* which is the aim of such a *societas* as a *community of believers*. Today this is fairly obvious with regard to certain themes and roles, for example, the fact that in dealing with earthly questions and issues (social organization, politics, «investment», and so on.), no specific authority, as representing God, derives from being authority in the church community.

From the point of view of authority and obedience, the pursuit of the proper and specific aims of a specific civil society is accomplished through the authoritative competence of people who in that society, and not in another, are invested with authority (or rather have the precise task of ordering things to those ends). The co-presence of an ecclesial authority, in a framework of problems and decisions that belong to the purposes of a civil society, does not entail any *competence of authority* that can be attributed to ecclesial authority in civil society. This does not mean that ecclesial authority «cannot have anything to say» to believers about non-ecclesial problems. It means that it will no longer be a question of authority, but can only be (and this is not insignificant, however, but it is another level of relationship) a question of *authoritativeness*. The church's authority will also be able to point out conduct as the most suitable, in the civil environment, at a specific moment, but this is not *ratione auctoritatis*. It is possible that such indication may be exacting and also binding in a strict sense for conscience, but by virtue of the value that it suggests, which will have the rationale of proper evidence of the value itself. It is important not to confuse the fields in order not to confuse the nature of the duties, and in that case the duties themselves. Since the meaning of authority and obedience depend on their function in regard to the common good, the diversity and specificity of the common good will involve also diversity in the identification of the relationship that entails obedience. In the case in which the same people have a relationship of obedience to two (or more) different legitimate authorities, this will be from different points of view, in regard to aims defined by different areas of social interaction.

The competence of authority (and the relative competence of obedience) is, therefore, restricted to the area of aims proper to the relative *societas*. The fact of living and recognizing itself—as community— in faith, speaks also of a call to a greater transparency in living and realizing the meaning of the relationship of authority and obedience. If it is true that we live as a community of believers and that as such we recognize the roles to which are connected the virtues of the correct exercise of authority and obedience, the fact of our being rooted in faith in Christ, and the attribution to this of our common life as church, raises a precise question-task, which is to ensure as well that the diversity of roles and attributions be experienced in a transparent manner. If that does not happen, while together we say we want to witness to our *common* belonging to Christ, in the manner of living *together*, we demonstrate instead the fact of letting ourselves be guided by rationales different from communion, which will in some way be searching for one's own good. Instead, the practice of authority and obedience within the church must be capable of expressing as much as possible, through the transparency of relationships, how this process of order-obey may be at the service of the church's specific common good, which is communion in Christ, without mingling with other rationales or purposes.

Thus, the church community of believers shows a visible face; its internal relationships can be seen. Therefore the relationships of authority and obedience, as experienced concretely and visibly in the church, are one of the public places for Christian witness, as *witness to the human values assumed and interpreted in a Christian manner*. This is one of the places in which we publicly show what it means for us to live honestly, as people, on this earth, in a structured society, in the light of the Gospel. That is, it is one of those places in which what is authentically human (such as relationships, criteria and rationale of relationships) needs to be sincerely experienced and truly suggested, not just through words, but through the forms, even institutional, of the *common ordered way of relating*, within a *societas* that shows its capacity to order itself toward a true sharing of life.

It is a matter of witnessing to and suggesting in a significant way the human values assumed in a Christian fashion, with a view to the common good and purpose, and with the reciprocity that links between them the two figures of relationships and therefore the subjects that exercise authority and obedience.

7

Free and responsible communion-edification

In this societas that is the church, by virtue of the specificity that constitutes it as community founded on faith in Jesus Christ, its task is to indicate and emphasize *free and responsible communion-edification.* This will be the criterion, that is,the interpretive term of reference, which helps to assess, understand and resolve eventual conflicts —criterion therefore of unique obedience to Christ in obedience to human authority.

We clarify the meaning of this phrase by stating that, for Christians obviously, it is a matter of any human authority, both church and civil, as long as it is truly authority and in the specific sphere of its being authority. It means that the very reasons for authority (and obedience) as such must be understood and experienced in a Christian manner; therefore there will be no room for an interpretation of the civil arrangements that understands them differently from ecclesiastical arrangements in terms of the distinction between *sacred and profane.*

We say once again that on the ethical level, responsible communion-edification must become a *sanctioning and demarcating criterion* for authority itself and the way it is exercised in the ecclesiastical and civil spheres. In speaking of «free and responsible communion-edification», one can only translate into significantly Christian terms what was said previously about the *meaning of authority*, in its being a function of the life of a *societas*, in its being an element of the *ordinatio ad bonum commune.* Therefore one cannot interpret the meaning of authority in the church in one way and the meaning of authority in civil society in another.

To illustrate the consequences of this, one thinks of the so-called *mere poenales* laws. One has to say that either they are not so or they are not just laws, that is, morally they do not have the value of laws. In the face of a civil law, in ethical terms, one cannot be released from it for reasons that in fact signify self-privilege; before the civil authority, I am responsible for respecting and promoting it as an authority. Participation in social life, even from the political-administrative view point, will also be a question of the correct exercise of obedience, since that requires making oneself responsible, insofar as it depends on us, for the existence of the authority and its correct exercise as service to the common good. Of course one can say that sometimes it is difficult to work out obedience to

Christ in obedience to a civil authority (for example, the one which legislates or governs in a democratic-parliamentary regime). But, as believers, we must work it out if we want to correctly interpret and assume on an ethical level our relationship to the civil laws.

Let us take the phrase «God's authority in human authority» to understand the corresponding meaning of obedience. One perspective of interpretation has been (and still is for some) the idea that a person constituted in authority may be him/herself, as person, the one representing God on earth and so one obeys that person «as [one obeys] God». If at this point one imagines parliament as a legislative body, some problem will arise. At first glance in a monarchical structure it would be easier to grasp, however at the risk of sacralizing authority. We require criteria to see if the exercise of authority can also be incorrect, to see if authority has a limited field and on what basis. Can a nation's president or the mayor of a city rule legitimately, and therefore make it important for conscience that all citizens dress in yellow? The example is deliberately banal because one sees immediately that a similar decree would be meaningless. But why would it not be a correct exercise of authority, if posted by the legitimate authority?

If my duty of obedience is tied to that person because he/she is a representative of God, one cannot see why one should not obey his/her command, even of this type. Moreover, the command does not require anything immoral in itself. If, on the other hand, «representing God», and therefore recognizing God's authority in human authority, binds him to the discourse of *recta ratio,* which, in terms of the social-human phenomenon, recognizes within itself, historically, the need for a specific task of caring for communion as caring for the common good, as organization-direction to the common good, then it matters little whether one is thinking about a monarchy or an oligarchy or democracy. The one or those who undertake this role, by virtue of this role, and insofar as it is the exercise of this role, have authority; toward them obedience has ethical meaning and value; their function and what objectively determines the field of their function, will be defining the field of authority and obedience. Therefore, at different levels in the various fields of social interaction, always and in whatever way, this representing God —and the corresponding recognition of God in human authority— will be connected with responsibility for the common good, that is, the exercise of responsible obedience and not just the simple execution of an order; the exercise of responsible authority and not the exercise of authoritative representation. This implies decisions, words, and conduct that express, in a mutual and complementary way, the assumption of a common task, in a dynamic of relationships suitable for pursuing the realization of the common good. Thus, one will have an exercise of authority that does not spill over from its own field, but that is a necessary and valuable service within the respective *societas*, and that does not confuse its own right to speak (even an «authoritative» right due to ones recognized competence and wisdom) with the pretense of obedience in areas and levels different from its own.

There is a New Testament theme, linked to Paul, in this idea of obedience «as [if obeying] God». The general meaning provides us with an ethical indication, that «as [if obeying] God» (in the same way as the motivation «every authority comes from God») can be correctly understood in all its strength in a perspective of *lex naturae* interpreted in a Christian manner. Every authority comes from God just as every social organization comes from God, inasmuch as he is creator of a humanity capable of organizing itself socially. But that does not mean that, if there is a tyrant and if we let him remain a tyrant, it is God's fault, as if he desired that tyranny. It does not mean that, if there is a democracy that functions in a malicious way, that it is God who wants it to function thus. That is, we cannot infer from these situations, through some form of sacralization of authority, a legitimization of the power situation whatever it is; we cannot deduce from it the divine legitimization of the *status quo*.

At least in passing we must say that the reflections carried out to this point are also valid in reference to the church in a similar way. Obviously there are differences, but the basic references remain. When we wish to obey the ecclesiastical authority (or teach to do so) it is always a matter of carrying out a gesture that is morally positive. If, faced with normative guidelines (of great or small importance), the criterion were simply that of obeying «because it is ordered», one would have an attitude of an irresponsible person. Another case is when one has «good motives» for entrusting oneself to authority without being able to verify the correctness of its directions. The fact remains that the attitude with which one usually lives out the relationship to ecclesiastical authority must be *responsible*. In the face of conscience the criterion is *the good*, not what is already *ordered*; in fact it could happen that what is ordered of me is not good. It is not that the attitude must be guided by a *praesumptio* of doubt; in simple terms it is a matter of living obedience *in conscience* as well, if one wants that to be a *virtue*. Therefore we have indicated *free and responsible communion-edification* as criterion not just for authority, but also for obedience.

When we speak of authority and obedience, we use terms very close to the terms *law and conscience, norm and conscience.* It is a matter of assuming responsibly a life of moral conscience that knows how to integrate the various elements of which life is comprised, in order to lead to an understood and authentic ethical experience. In the context of the themes we are examining, in order for there to be a moral authenticity of the common life, it is a matter of an authority that makes itself responsible for obedience, and a disobedience that makes itself responsible for authority, each one mutually looking after the necessary conditions for the authenticity of the other.

8
Temptations

The possible temptations regarding the exercise of authority and obedience work basically in two directions.

The first is that of a positive *privileging one's own good or of the group to which one belongs* at various levels. The group to which one belongs can be large, and it can also be a structured, in itself legitimate *societas.* It can be the parish community, or an association in the town in which one belongs, a religious institute, a party, a trade union or company, a regional structure within a state, or a state in a confederation of states—all those realities of associated life that can represent a particular group affiliation with reference to a broader society. For us there can be (perhaps it is not just mere possibility) the temptation to privilege one's own good (or of one's own group) both in the exercise of authority (which would become power), and in the exercise of obedience. Similarly, the manner of exercising obedience, too, (or non-obedience) can be guided by privilege for one's own good, as for example, by the refusal to speak a word of disapproval, or by saying something misleading, and likewise, just as for words, the same is true for gestures and concrete behavior.

The other line of temptation is the *resigning, passive or resigned* attitude, the refusal to exercise responsible obedience and to exercise authority. The attitude of resignation in obedience is also in some way a privileging for a self-(even supposed) good, seen as the *quiet life.* In this case one wants to connote the privilege of a presumed good that is actually motivated and justified by the prior assessment that the common good is not feasible from the point of view of social relations, or that «it is not worth the bother». In the practice of authority, the attitude of resignation is that which, by a presumed advantage of authority (authoritativeness, prestige), or in order *not to take risks*, and using similar justifications as those mentioned previously, renounces a true exercise of authority. When the role is to care for the common good, that role is entrusted as a task, not as a personal thing to dispose of at one's own pleasure, and therefore at issue is the free responsibility of conscience in renouncing the correct exercise of authority. In the terminology «correct exercise», *correct* evokes the possibility of inappropriate use, and *exercise* evokes an active role and not a show of appearance.

In the correctness of their respective exercise, authority and obedience will find their reciprocity in the common service of the common good. While still in progress, they will be a realization of communion in historically possible feasibility.

Chapter 16

Freedom and responsibility in the ecclesial community

We must look briefly and directly at this level and manner of ecclesial social interaction, considering the life of the church as one of the expressions of living together. It will therefore be a partial and limited reflection, concerning an aspect of our being church: the dimension of *societas* as it involves the elements that engage subjects' free responsibility and their ethical life in the relations that make *society* what it is.

1
Unity and growth in the church

The term *unity* is sufficiently clear: we are referring to *koinonia.* The term *growth* here refers both to individuals and to the community as such. We are speaking, therefore, of the growth (process of maturing, of journey) of the individual within the ecclesial community and the growth of the church itself in its capacity to manifest and live in a more suitable manner its being church.

Let us call to mind two New Testament images: *the building* and *the body.* The image of the building conveys something systematic, something in which the individual element belongs to a unity of meaning, in which the individual element needs others and the others need it. It speaks, especially when the verb is used, of a reality that needs to be built.

In particular it speaks of the need of *construction* on that foundation which is Christ himself. With that, the individual believer's responsibility is directly classified as responsibility in relations, as a need to participate in collaboration for the common end, which is to build this edifice on this cornerstone. To understand the reality *church* through the image of the edifice, it is not possible to think of a loose stone, an individual Christian *complete* as such in his/her individual relationship with the cornerstone, so as to consider then the rest as accidental. If this were the case, there would be no edifice, but rather an accumulation of stones. The reality signified asks of us free responsibility as co-existing believers within the believing community, free responsibility toward others and toward a common purpose.

The common good is not simply the sum of the elements that structure this edifice and from which every one can draw benefit; the common good is the edifice itself, its being well-made, and its being solid and founded through cohesion.

The image of the *body* speaks further about this reality, indicating even more strongly the close connection and interdependence between the members, the mutual affiliation of the members of a *societas* that is a *living body*. Thus, the free responsibility is the growth of the individual and of the body, for the life of the body from which the individual lives; not that the individual uses the body, but lives from the life of the body to which he/she belongs and cooperates to make it be.

From the body that is the church, as experience of it, we receive all that we have as believers: the experience of faith, contact with the head, the foundational relationship with Jesus Christ, spiritual experience. This reality indicates the free responsibility of individuals (and therefore of the community), because the life of a member in a living body is not the same, does not have the same possibilities, in a body that may be alive and lively as in a body that might be tired and weak. Personal freedom is risked in the responsibility of testifying in a true, effective, lively manner the common belonging to Christ, the being founded in him, the spiritual experience. The idea of believers who as passive subjects draw on sacramental praxis, the structuring of the communities, parish life, and so on, therefore finds no justification.

It is not certain, however, that the idea of a similar *making use* as passive subjects has been completely overcome; it could still be present, from the point of view of an individual's perception, from that internal understanding that perhaps is not explicit, but that prompts you to make choices, directs, and gives immediate operative assessments. Perhaps we must pay attention to this, because it is not a question of claiming rights, but a question of acting in such a way that the building remains standing, that the body functions, because a member of the body being ill makes the whole body ill. That also means that if I make someone ill I make the whole body ill. Everyone must have his/her space, role, awareness, capacity for speaking and listening; if this is not mutually recognized and experienced with all the possibilities and tasks that derive from it, the problem is not only that someone is excluded, but also in such a way it is the *body* that is not well; that is, neither are the others in a position to carry out their role and function, to exercise their charisms for the common good.

This reciprocity of roles expresses a de facto solidarity and suggests *solidarity-communion as a task*. Here could be considered the way in which the themes *freedom and charity* are articulated in the New Testament. The relationship between these two aspects of Christian conscience is particularly suitable for indicating how to live out free responsibility in that society which is the church of Christ.

It is a matter of living as *co-responsible* in the communion that is given to us, the common being rooted in Christ, the being together liberated in Christ (cfr.. *Gal* 5). *Co-responsibility* here seeks to underline the dimension of responsibility as an element of the ethical attitude, its being constituted in a community and constituting the community.

The *indicative-imperative dynamic*, in regard to the establishment of the church and its life as believing community, speaks directly about what we have seen to be the meaning of social life as the fundamental significance of being together, of co-existence. This is said in faith, indicating that it is a genuine possibility, here and now already present, not by virtue of our weak good will, but by virtue of a foundational salvific intervention by God, by virtue of being rooted in Christ. It speaks of this possibility and therefore the task that stems from it; that is, the free assumption of this co-responsibility belongs internally to the adherence of faith. My adherence of faith is not true without this assumption of co-responsibility.

2
Christ, foundation and hope

Foundation and hope are correlative terms: as much hope as foundation. For the believer, recognizing this means to live one's own life in the possibility-necessity of making significant gestures. The believer is called to give *signs*, that is, gestures that signify the reality, and in this way to live out his/her usual relationship with others. The relationship between believers is called to have meaning in such a way that visible gesture-means become something that is greater than what is done and is visibly describable and understood. Their mutual relationship (*charity*) intends to be a sign of salvation: by this others will recognize that the Father sent «me» as the witness of *Christus praesens.*

Charity is a term fairly close to *solidarity*, *social interaction*; if it is true that fraternal love is the life of charity of the Christian, then it is the foundational attitude that leads him/her to a manifold string of gestures that testify to the salvific reality in and of Christ. Thus, we have here a *medium*, that is, the witness of human fraternity that is expressed in a particular Christian quality (charity). It is an indication on the part of believers of the truer and more sensible reality of human life. The way of life within the church is called to be an indication of the authenticity of living social interaction. It could be said that the Christian is called to be, in this sense, as well, a collaborator in God's plan. Obviously, *collaborator* will not mean that, equal to and alongside God, there is a human person to give him a hand; there is, however, some significance in using the term «collaborator». It is more precise than the term «instrument», because it is God who works all in all, but it is God who works *through* and not through an instrument in which the *ratio instrumenti* (that is, his being instrument) says everything about his reality, but rather through subjects who are themselves the terminus of the relationship that God establishes. They are subjects called to be instruments according to their nature, that is, with their capacity to understand and desire, with their free responsibility, with their capacity for obedience and creativity in life from person to person.

It is in this sense that the human person is a collaborator with God. Being in the church (for the church and the world) as witnesses of *hope* is particular to the life and witness of believers, always in reference to that foundation and hope that is Christ. If I live and express a resigning attitude of renunciation in regard to the possibilities of genuine *koinonia* within the church, if I resign myself to division, opposition, and so forth, by this I testify to the non-meaning of hope, the non-presence of Christ; in fact I state that there is no reason to believe and hope, that in fact the human reality, verifiable in its way of expressing itself, is the victorious reality, not the reality of Jesus Christ present and salvific.

There is an internal link between the capacity to live the concrete reality, without illusions but without resignation, and the truth and credibility of the explicit testimony of faith, within the church as mutual testimony and in the world as presence of a church capable of being a meaningful way of authentic human life.

3 *Unity-communion as criterion for discerning charisms and tasks: why a criterion for discerning good*

From what has been said it emerges that the criterion for discerning charisms and tasks within the church is the criterion of unity-communion. It is not just a criterion of effectiveness, however much it has a certain sense from the point of view of succeeding in obtaining results. Here the unity is not indicated as an instrumental value in regard to another aim, but it is indicated as reality-value within the significance, the meaning, the purpose. This *telos* of unity-communion, then, becomes the criterion for discerning charisms, functions and roles within the community. It says that this goal or purpose, proposed to us and assumed by us as a task to aspire to a full and genuine communion, is capable of speaking about the meaning and non-meaning, the measure of the value of those concrete or daily realities we are living; it is capable of indicating the concreteness of what I call the *response of vocation.*

Here at heart we have the possibility of expressing clearly in terms of faith what was before indicated as *reality-criterion that discerns what is good and what is evil.* Unity-communion is the social expression in the community-church of the reaching out to *give oneself over*, that is, of *morality:* morality not of the individual as individual, but of individuals as together they constitute the believing community. Along with this consideration we can make a further clarification. The attention to the good of one's brother/sister is not something that imposes itself as a duty through a rationale external to it, in the sense of an external norm, or in the sense that, all things considered, *it would be better* if I were not constrained to be attentive to the good of my brother/sister (I am alluding to the presence of the other person as *limiting* one's own freedom).

In the Hellenist believing communities of early days, in addition to the *strong* (the *free* people, who knew that flesh sacrificed to idols was flesh the same as any other, due to the fact that there weren't any idols), there were people *weak in faith.* One could be tempted to think: *how unfortunate*!, imagining an ideal of community in which there would be no such weak people. On the contrary, the ideal in the church is not that there are only strong people. The presence of those who are weak makes them strong at the moment when they are capable of taking on the good of their brother/sister as a guide for their own conduct. Specifically, this presence makes them capable of living their faith in the morality of daily life. Attention to the good of the brother/sister is a constitutive factor of true freedom and true personal responsibility; therefore it is also its criterion. This gratuitousness in surrendering to the other person through concrete gestures is not simply doing beneficence to the other person; it is being truly a believer, incarnating a morality and mature faith, living one's own morality as a believer. The perception of my *giving* as distinct from *receiving* my gift, on the model of the distinction between benefitting-beneficiary, distorts at its very roots the meaning of charity and the meaning of morality.

Ecclesial life as social life of a believing community

I would like to draw attention to the fact that there is an inevitable human dimension in the development of intra-ecclesial relationships. The dimension of the church's social interaction is such that, if we want to contribute to the establishment of a church that may be *church*, we must pay attention to all those elements that make it humanly *society*. That is, all those elements that we have considered as important for the building up of a correct social interaction necessarily must be the object of attention and care for the establishing of church as church. The structuring of interpersonal relationships, the constitution of roles, functions and attributions, respect for these roles and their promotion, all those things that belong to the *visibility* of the church as *societas*, while still not being everything (or, if you will, the specific quality) that comprises the church as church, are those things without which one could not make the church as church on the earth.

In the «family» *societas* it is important that the father be truly father, that the brother be truly brother and the sister, sister; the son's being-son is important for the father's being-father (and so on for the reciprocity of all the other relationships). The same can be said, in a similar way, for the reciprocity of relationships in the church. One cannot make a leap into the supernatural sphere, because being a *societas* of believers, being a community of visible fraternal love, is something that is done according to the human rationale of interpersonal relationships. It is clear that the structure of the church does not coincide with the church, but it is also clear that what is negative that we bring into the structuring of the church will be something negative, an impediment and hindrance or burden, which will have its influence on the church's being-church. Again, by analogy, it is true that a person's corporeality does not coincide with the person, but it is true as well that if I receive a physical wound, this can come to impede (not to annul, but certainly to impede) the expressive opportunities of my person, of my spirit. So a church, which from the point of view of *transparency of relationships*, of mutual respect and promotion in the exercise of roles is imperfect, is by the same token inadequate in expressing what it is called to express *specifically as church*. A banal example: I can give a homily stating correctly the meaning of a Gospel passage, therefore explaining the gospel message in a correct way, but nevertheless I do it in a context of relationships (with those people of my parish, those of my true community), in which I have no respect for the roles of each, in which, for example, I tend to constrain, perhaps even sharply, the other members of my believing community to follow not simply the passage of the Gospel, but my way of understanding, of seeing, of guiding, of probing the reality. In such a case that homily, even though correct in itself, will have an impact on church life, an opportunity to be understood and experienced, necessarily limited by what I am as a vehicle for the message. This is in direct relationship with the one who preaches the homily, his role as presbyter, and the other members of the community; but it is also valid from the point of view of a community's visibility, with its relationships, in regard to the visibility of a broader society. The correct word of the Gospel that I pronounce needs not only to be correct as word, but also as a gesture corresponding to life.

Let us add that the Christian dimension of the church's life, therefore its *being church as such, is not reducible to its visibility*, to the form in which it expresses itself. There is *something more*, the *working presence of the Spirit*, and this is a reality, not just spoken as a word. That is, we are not waiting for a result of the church's presence in terms of specifically measurable effectiveness about the visibility of the manner of being-church. Even the first Christian community and subsequent communities, as well, were church in a limited way, not in a perfect manner. We know from within the texts themselves that they had their internal problems from the point of view of the visibility of relationships and transparency of gospel meaning. However, this church of the early days succeeded in passing on the message. But it remains true that there is a relationship of effect between the measure of non-transparency and the capacity for meaningful words, insofar as it depends on us. If that is not the case, we will be forcing the Holy Spirit to *carry out a salvage operation*; *despite our testimony of the gospel*, we cannot escape our responsibility for transparency in life.

Our theme here is *freedom and responsibility in the ecclesial community*. We are responsible for the building up of a church community that, from the point of view of the visibility of relationships, also, may be meaningful and witnessing. For this we must take into account *two dimensions*: the human dimension of constructing these relationships in the believing community and the spiritual dimension (in the sense of *life in the Spirit*) of these same relationships.

Let us consider their *distinctiveness*, because they are not interchangeable; they cannot be substituted one for the other; and we are called to live them as *correlative.*

Accepting the fact that we are called to witness in a visible corporeity that is not perfection is part of Christian responsibility. Here, too, witnessing is about *testifying to a hope*, which means not deferring elsewhere what is our task, but also not using the pretense of substituting ourselves for the work of the Spirit. It is important to pay attention to living correctly the limitation and possibilities that derive from this dimension of the visibility of a church that is not only visible. To live this limitation responsibly means impinging upon the concrete possibilities of the church's being-church; it means creating historical conditions and opportunities for the capacity of free responsibility of other believers in the church. That is, we must see how the dynamic of the social interaction of human life, which is realized at any level and situation of human co-existence, is articulated within the life itself of the church. And we must see how this belongs to the outward appearance of an interiority that is animated by the Spirit; how it belongs to the visibility of a non-visibility that is the reality of grace, to a historicity of expression of that absolute which is the salvation given to us; and to see how it belongs to the sacramentality of the church's existence. It is to be a sign of something *greater* (because it depends on God) than what it is. The sign is not the reality, but must be such as to signify the reality.

The term *sacramentality* of the church's existence also calls to mind the aspect of the sign's efficacy. It is not tied just to God's will and action, but rather, by virtue of God's will and action, also to the free collaboration of the Christian who witnesses; our participation in God's plan as the believing community must necessarily take on the responsibility for this meaning, in visibility and historicity, that it may be the most transparent possible as a lived reality —and therefore capable of being a sign— of the gratuitous salvation that is given to us.

Here I wish to draw attention to the fact that sometimes we can be tempted to consider the mysterious reality of the church as important, and its concrete, visible reality as secondary. To evoke an image: be careful not to consider a person's corporeity as secondary; otherwise the spirit will not be given the chance to be spirit.

Assuming the responsibility for being instruments-collaborators, being signifiers, as individuals and as a believing community, is part of the truth of our saying yes to Jesus Christ, and therefore part of the truth of faith. In other words, if the *correctness of relationships* between one person and another is fundamental to moral life, and if it is fundamental for the social interaction of life, it will be even more so when it is a matter of relationships *between believers*, for the truth of the existence of individual believers, and for the truth and credibility of the existence of believers as a believing community. It is like a passage emphasizing from one moment to the next (considering the various levels) the importance and urgency of that simplest element, which is the witness of *morality* in making oneself responsible for the other person freely and in making him/her free and responsible. A motive for this insistence is the fear that this dimension of life in the church is not sufficiently taken seriously, when in fact in no way is it secondary or of little importance, from the point of view of personal honesty (because if there is no personal honesty there is no honesty of faith, that is, there is no truth of faith) and from the point of view of the church as such, in its possibilities and in its task of being a witness in the world. It is not a question of being scandalized if there are irresponsible people, from one point of view or another, within the church, or if there are visible structures that are hardly transparent; whoever is scandalized should see if they are in a position to throw the first stone. But it is a question of having eyes open to these realities, because either we agree (and we make ourselves co-responsible for the negative) or we support a greater transparency by our way of being present.

Here too without the pretense that we can resolve the truth of the church, we will continue to need, every time the Eucharist is celebrated, to begin by asking forgiveness, and yet with the positivity of a presence conscious of the horizon toward which we journey.

Bibliography

1

As believers in social life

ABIGNENTE D., *Decisione morale del credente. Il pensiero di Josef Fuchs*, Piemme, Casale Monferrato 1987.

_______, *Conversione morale nella fede. Una riflessione etico-teologica a partire da figure di conversione del vangelo di Luca*, Gregorian University Press-Morcelliana, Roma-Brescia 2000.

AUER A., *Morale autonoma e fede cristiana*, Edizioni Paoline, Cinisello Balsamo 1991 (orig.: Düsseldorf 1971).

BASTIANEL S., *Autonomia morale del credente. Senso e motivazioni di un'attuale tendenza teologica*, Morcelliana, Brescia 1980.

_______, «Il rapporto a Gesù Cristo nella decisione morale» in *Did (L)* XXXI (2001) 13-25.

_______, *Teologia morale fondamentale. Moralità personale, ethos, etica cristiana*, (for students' use), PUG, Rome 2005.

_______, *Vita morale nella fede in Gesù Cristo*, San Paolo, Cinisello Balsamo 2005.
BÖCKLE F., «Fede e azione» in *Conc (I)* 10 (1976) 1673-1690.

_______, *Morale fondamentale*, Brescia 1979.

CARLOTTI P., *Le opere della fede.* Spunti di etica cristiana, Roma 2002.

DEMMER K., *Interpretare e agire.* Fondamenti della morale cristiana, Cinisello Balsamo 1989.

_______, *Fondamenti di etica teologica*, Assisi 2004.

DEMMER K., SCHÜLLER B., (ED.), *Fede cristiana e agire morale*, Cittadella, Assisi 1980.

FUCHS J., *Etica cristiana in una società secolarizzata*, Casale Monferrato 1984.

_______, *Il Verbo si fa carne. Teologia morale*, Casale Monferrato 1989.

_______, *Essere del Signore. Corso di teologia morale fondamentale*, Roma 1996.

_______, *Ricercando la verità morale. Teologia morale*, San Paolo, Cinisello Balsamo 1996.

GINTERS R., *Valori, norme e fede cristiana. Introduzione all'etica filosofica e teologica*, Marietti, Casale Monferrato 1982.

GOFFI T., PIANA G., (ED.), *Corso di Morale, 1, Vita nuova in Cristo. Morale fondamentale e generale*, Queriniana, Brescia 1983.

PINTO DE OLIVEIRA C.-J., *La crisi della scelta morale nella civiltà tecnica*, Borla, Rome 1978.

RIZZI A., *Crisi e ricostruzione della morale*, SEI, Torino 1992.

SCHÜLLER B., *La fondazione dei giudizi morali. Tipi di argomentazione etica in teologia morale*, San Paolo, Cinisello Balsamo 1997.

WEBER H., *Teologia morale generale. L'appello di Dio, la risposta dell'uomo*, Cinisello Balsamo 1996.

WILS J.-P., MIETH D., EDD., *Concetti fondamentali dell'etica cristiana*, Queriniana, Brescia 1994.

2 *Morality and politics*

ANTONCICH R., MUNÁRRIZ J.M., *La dottrina sociale della Chiesa*, Assisi 1991.

CARRIER H., *Dottrina sociale. Nuovo approccio all'insegnamento sociale della Chiesa*, Cinisello Balsamo 1996.

COZZOLI M., *Chiesa, Vangelo e società.* Natura e metodo della dottrina sociale della Chiesa, Cinisello Balsamo 1995.

DONATI P., *Pensiero sociale cristiano e società postmoderna*, Roma 1997.

FREEDEN M., *Ideologie e teoria politica*, Bologna 2000.

GOFFI T., PIANA G., EDD., *Corso di morale, IV*, Koinonia (Etica della vita sociale), Brescia 1994.

KERBER W., *Etica sociale.* Verso una morale rinnovata dei comportamenti sociali, Cinisello Balsamo 2002.

KRIPPENDORFF H., *L'arte di non essere governati.* Politica etica da Socrate a Mozart, Roma 2003.

MEHL R., «La politica», in LAURET B., REFOULÉ F., EDD., *Iniziazione alla pratica della teologia. 4. Morale*, Brescia 1986, 585-608.

MOSSO S., *Il problema della giustizia e il messaggio cristiano. Elementi di teologia morale sociale*, Piemme, Casale Monferrato 1982.

PIANA G., *Nel segno della giustizia.* Questioni di etica politica, Bologna 2005.

PRINI P., *Il cristiano e il potere.* Essere per il futuro, Roma 1993.

VIDAL M., *Manuale di etica teologica/3.* Morale sociale, Assisi 1997.

______, *Etica civile e società democratica*, Torino 1992.

ZABREBELSKY G., *Il crucifige e la democrazia*, Torino 1995.

3 *Morality and the economy*

CAPRIGLIONE F., *Etica della finanza e finanza etica*, Bari 1997.

CARLOTTI P., *Etica cristiana, società ed economia*, Roma 2000.

CHAFUEN A., *Cristiani per la libertà.* Radici cattoliche dell'economia di mercato, Macerata 1999.

CHIAVACCI E., *Teologia morale. 3/1.* Teologia morale e vita economica, Assisi 1988.

———, *Teologia morale. 3/2.* Morale della vita economica, politica, di comunicazione, Assisi 1990.

CIPRIANI S., ED., *Nuove frontiere dell'etica economica*, AVE, Roma 1990.

FALISE M., REGNIER J., *Economia e fede*, Brescia 1994.

GUZZETTI G.B., *Cristianesimo ed economia. Disegno teoretico*, Milano 1987.

LOMBARDINI S., *La morale, l'economia, la politica*, Torino 1993.

LORENZETTI L., MARZANO F., QUAGLIO A., *Economia/finanza.* Per un'etica degli affari, Assisi 2000.

MANZONE G., *Il mercato.* Teorie economiche e dottrina sociale della Chiesa, Brescia 2001.

MARZANO F., *Economia ed etica: due mondi a confronto.* Saggi di economia ed etica dei sistemi sociali, Roma 1998.

MATHON G., «L'economia», in LAURET B., REFOULÉ F., (ED.), *Iniziazione alla pratica della teologia. 4. Morale*, Brescia 1986, 505-577.

PITTAU M., *Economie senza denaro. Sistemi di scambio non monetari nelle economie di mercato*, Bologna 2003.

RICH A., *Etica economica*, Brescia 1993.

SACCONI L., *Economia, etica, organizzazione. Il contratto sociale dell'impresa*, Bari 1997.

SPIRITO P., *Etica ed economia. Verso nuovi paradigmi nella ristrutturazione delle imprese*, Cinisello Balsamo 1999.

UTZ A.F., *Etica economica. Filosofia, teologia, sociologia*, Cinisello Balsamo 1999.

VELASQUEZ M.G., *Etica economica*, Venezia 1993.

ZAMAGNI S., *Economia ed etica. Saggi sul fondamento etico del discorso economico*, Roma 1994.

4
Morality and development

BASSI A., *Dono e fiducia: le forme della solidarietà nelle società complesse*, Roma 2000.

BERTHOUZOZ R., PAPINI R., SUGRANYES DE FRANCH R., EDD., *Etica, economia e sviluppo. L'insegnamento dei vescovi dei cinque continenti*, Bologna 1994.

BUONOMO V., PAPINI R., *Etica ed economia. Religioni, sviluppo e liberazione in Asia*, Bologna 1998.

CALVEZ J.-Y., *Etica per una società in trasformazione. La Chiesa di fronte alle emergenze mondiali*, Roma 1992.

CESAREO V., (ED.), *L'altro. Identità, dialogo e conflitto nella società plurale*, Milano 2004.

CHIAVACCI E., «Un futuro per l'etica: il coraggio di andare oltre» in *Progetti di etica. Dieci anni di attività della Fondazione Lanza*, Padova 2002, 79-122.

COCCOLINI G., «Multiculturalismo» in *RTM* 29 (1997) 281-296.

KUSCHEL K.-J., MIETH D., (ED.), «Alla ricerca di valori universali» in *Conc (1)* 4 (2001).

MANCINI R., *Comunicazione come ecumene. Il significato antropologico e teologico dell'etica comunicativa*, Brescia 1991.

PAPINI R., (ED.), *Globalizzazione: solidarietà o esclusione?*, Napoli 2001.

PESCH R.C., *Il miracolo della moltiplicazione dei pani. C'è una soluzione per la fame nel mondo?*, Brescia 1997.

PINTO DE OLIVEIRA C.-J., *La dimensione mondiale dell'etica, Situazione e futuro del mondo umano*, Edizioni Dehoniane, Bologna 1986.

QUARTA C., (ED.), *Globalizzazione, giustizia, solidarietà*, Bari 2004.

SOBRINO J., WILFRED F., EDD., «La globalizzazione e le sue vittime» in *Conc (1)* 5 (2001).

SUNDERMEIER TH., *Comprendere lo straniero. Una ermeneutica interculturale*, Brescia 1999.

5
The story of evil, the story of good

ARENDT H., *La banalità del male. Eichmann a Gerusalemme*, Milano 2000.

BACCARINI E., THORSON L., EDD., *Il bene e il male dopo Auschwitz: implicazioni etico-teologiche per l'oggi*, Milano 1998.

BASTIANEL S., ED., *Strutture di peccato. Una sfida teologica e pastorale*, (Moralia Christiana 3), Piemme, Casale Monferrato 1989.

BRENA G.L., ED., *Mysterium iniquitatis. Il problema del male*, Gregoriana Libreria Editrice, Padova 2000.

BUBER M., *L'uomo tra il bene e il male.* Formare la propria vita secondo la dottrina del Chassidismo, Milano 2003.

CANOBBIO G., DALLA VECCHIA F., *Il male, la sofferenza, il peccato*, Brescia 2004.

COMPAGNONI F., PRIVITERA S., EDD., *Vita morale e beatitudini. Sacra Scrittura, storia, teoretica, esperienza*, San Paolo, Cinisello Balsamo 2000.

COZZOLI M., *Etica teologale. Fede, carità, speranza,* Cinisello Balsamo 1991.

EICHRODT W., *Teologia dell'Antico Testamento, I. Dio e popolo,* Brescia 1979.

LOSS N., «La dottrina antropologica di Gn 1-11» in G. DE GENNARO, ED., *L'antropologia biblica,* Napoli 1981, 141-206.

MATEOS J., CAMACHO F., *L'alternativa Gesù e la sua proposta per l'uomo,* Assisi 1989.

MOSER A., LEERS B., *Teologia morale: conflitti e alternative,* Assisi 1988.

PIANA G., *L'agire morale tra ricerca di senso e definizione normativa,* Assisi 2001.

RAVASI G., «Genesi», in ROSSANO P., RAVASI G., GIRLANDA A., (ED.), *Nuovo Dizionario di Teologia Biblica,* Edizioni Paoline, Cinisello Balsamo 1988, 565-573.

SCHNACKENBURG R., *Il messaggio morale del Nuovo Testamento. 1. Da Gesù alla Chiesa primitiva,* Brescia 1989.

———, *Il messaggio morale del Nuovo Testamento. 2. I primi predicatori cristiani,* Brescia 1990.

VIDAL M., *L'etica cristiana,* Roma 1992.

WÉNIN A., *Non di solo pane... Violenza e alleanza nella Bibbia,* Bologna 2004.

6
Morality and the sturcturing of relations

COSI G., «Ordine e dissenso. La disobbedienza civile nella società liberale» in *Jus* 31 (1984) 93-155.

DUQUOC C., «Obbedienza e libertà nella chiesa» in *Conc (I)* 16 (1980) 114-128.

FUCHS J., «L'autorità di Dio nell'autorità civile», in ID., *Sussidi 1980,* Roma 1980, 45-57.

GOFFI T., «Obbedienza», in FIORES S. DE, GOFFI T., (ED.), *Nuovo Dizionario di Spiritualità,* Roma 1982, 1074-1091.

HÄRING B., «Norma e libertà», in DEMMER K., SCHÜLLER B., (ED.), *Fede cristiana e agire morale,* Cittadella, Assisi 1980, 201-230.

MAJORANO S., *La coscienza.* Per una lettura cristiana, Cinisello Balsamo 1994.

SCHILLEBEECKX E., «Critica laica all'obbedienza cristiana e reazioni cristiane» in *Conc (I)* 16 (1980) 35-55.

VALADIER P., *Elogio della coscienza,* Torino 1995.

VAN IERSEL B., «La via dell'obbedienza. La vita di Gesù nel vangelo secondo Marco» in *Conc (I)* 16 (1980) 56-71.

YANNARAS CH., *La libertà dell'ethos. Alle radici della crisi morale dell'Occidente,* Bologna 1984.

Morality in social life

This book was printed on *thin opaque smooth white Bible paper,* using the *Minion* and *Type Embellishments One* font families.
This edition was printed in D'VINNI, S.A., in Bogotá, Colombia, during the last weeks of the fourth month of year two thousand ten.

Ad publicam lucem datus mensis aprilis, festivitatem Divina Misericordia